UNDERSTANDING YOUR BIBLE!

Getting the Best out of the Greatest Book!

observations on biblical hermeneutics

by Ken Chant

COPYRIGHT © 1997 BY KEN CHANT. ALL RIGHTS RESERVED WORLDWIDE.
KEN CHANT MINISTRIES
P.O. BOX 79, WERRINGTON NSW 2747, AUSTRALIA
ISBN 1 875577 35 1

TABLE OF CONTENTS

STATEMENT OF FAITH 9

PART ONE
SWORDS AND SERMONS

CHAPTER ONE
EAVESDROPPERS 17

CHAPTER TWO
HOW NECESSARY? 23

CHAPTER THREE
DAUGHTERS FOR SALE 29

CHAPTER FOUR
SAVAGE SERMONS 41

CHAPTER FIVE
THE RENAISSANCE 51

PART TWO
REALISED AND REVEALED

CHAPTER SIX
THE FIVE KEYS 61

CHAPTER SEVEN
MYSTICS AND OTHERS 69

CHAPTER EIGHT
PRAYING THE BIBLE 83

PART THREE
SIX DIMENSIONS

CHAPTER NINE
"COMB" THE BIBLE 93

CHAPTER TEN
WHAT DOES IT MEAN? 105

CHAPTER ELEVEN
WORD FOR WORD 111

CHAPTER TWELVE
MIXED UP METAPHORS **121**

CHAPTER THIRTEEN
MANY TREASURES **129**

PART FOUR
LONG, LONG AGO!

CHAPTER FOURTEEN
THE PROTESTANT PRINCIPLE **143**

CHAPTER FIFTEEN
FARM BOYS AND SCRIPTURE **149**

CHAPTER SIXTEEN
AN OBSOLETE BOOK? **155**

CHAPTER SEVENTEEN
DANGEROUS SECRETS? **159**

CHAPTER EIGHTEEN
SPARE THE ROD! **169**

CHAPTER NINETEEN
WHIP YOUR SLAVE **181**

PART FIVE
CROSSING THE GAPS

CHAPTER TWENTY
THE MISTS OF TIME **191**

CHAPTER TWENTY-ONE
THEY TALK STRANGELY **195**

CHAPTER TWENTY-TWO
IRONIC – ISN'T IT? **203**

CHAPTER TWENTY-THREE
BURN THE WITCH! **211**

CHAPTER TWENTY-FOUR
BRIBES AND LOTTERIES **221**

CHAPTER TWENTY-FIVE
HOW BIZARRE! **227**

CHAPTER TWENTY-SIX
GOD AND A STORM **239**

CHAPTER TWENTY-SEVEN
READING THE PROPHETS **251**

CHAPTER TWENTY-EIGHT
ARE WE ANY BETTER? **261**

A NOTE ON GENDER

It is unfortunate that the English language does not contain an adequate generic pronoun (especially in the singular number) that includes without bias both male and female. So *"he, him, his, man, mankind,"* with their plurals, must do the work for both sexes. Accordingly, wherever it is appropriate to do so in the following pages, please include the feminine gender in the masculine, and vice versa.

FOOTNOTES

A work once fully referenced will thereafter be noted either by "ibid" or "op. cit."

ABBREVIATIONS

Abbreviations commonly used for the books of the Bible are

Genesis	Ge	Micah	Mi
Exodus	Ex	Nahum	Na
Leviticus	Le	Habakkuk	Hb
Numbers	Nu	Zephaniah	Zp
Deuteronomy	De	Haggai	Hg
Joshua	Js	Zechariah	Zc
Judges	Jg	Malachi	Mal
Ruth	Ru		
1 Samuel	1 Sa	Matthew	Mt
2 Samuel	2 Sa	Mark	Mk
1 Kings	1 Kg	Luke	Lu
2 Kings	2 Kg	John	Jn
1 Chronicles	1 Ch	Acts	Ac
2 Chronicles	2 Ch	Romans	Ro
Ezra	Ezr	1 Corinthians	1 Co
Nehemiah	Ne	2 Corinthians	2 Co
Esther	Es	Galatians	Ga
Job	Jb	Ephesians	Ep
Psalm	Ps	Philippians	Ph
Proverbs	Pr	Colossians	Cl
Ecclesiastes	Ec	1 Thessalonians	1 Th
Song of Songs	Ca *	2 Thessalonians	2 Th
Isaiah	Is	1 Timothy	1 Ti
Jeremiah	Je	2 Timothy	2 Ti
Lamentations	La	Titus	Tit
Ezekiel	Ez	Philemon	Phm
Daniel	Da	Hebrews	He
Hosea	Ho	James	Ja
Joel	Jl	1 Peter	1 Pe
Amos	Am		
Obadiah	Ob	2 Peter	2 Pe
Jonah	Jo		

1 John	1 Jn	Jude	Ju
2 John	2 Jn	Revelation	Re
3 John	3 Jn		

- *Ca* is an abbreviation of *Canticles*, a derivative of the Latin name of the *Song of Solomon*, which is sometimes also called the *Song of Songs*.

- *Note*: scripture translations are my own, unless otherwise noted.

STATEMENT OF FAITH

> Now, who shall arbitrate?
> Ten men love what I hate,
> Shun what I follow,
> slight what I receive;
> Ten, who in ears and eyes
> Match me: we all surmise,
> They this thing, and I, that:
> whom shall my soul believe? [1]

You have probably echoed the poet's cry: "Whom *shall* I believe?" We open the Bible and at once voices on every side cry at us to follow their way of reading it! But which pathway to understanding is the true one? How can I know which teacher to follow, or what commentary to believe? Or should I simply follow my conscience? The best help in this dilemma is a good understanding of an art called **hermeneutics.** That is what this book is about.

"Hermeneutics" comes from the name of the god *Hermes,* which the Greeks borrowed and used to describe any act of "explaining" something. They did this because *Hermes,* among other things, was the chief messenger of heaven and the guardian of speech and writing. He carried a magical golden staff, a gift from his older brother Apollo, which enabled him to convey the will of Zeus to humans, and to supervise every kind of communication. Upon him rested the burden of bridging the gaps that often prevent a message from passing correctly between sender and receiver.

Nowadays we use *hermeneutics* to describe the art of correctly interpreting a piece of literature, especially the Bible. To this modern science the ancient "golden staff" now belongs, and if it is used properly it will lead the reader toward the truth. Sometimes, sadly, the "staff" loses its magical sheen, becomes tarnished, and may do people more harm than good. That is to say, a corrupt hermeneutic may be worse than none at all! I hope to avoid that fault and to put into my readers' hands a brightly shining wand that will truly help them to discover the mind of God.

But first, I should say something about the Bible itself, and the foundations upon which the following pages are built. Where one *begins* a journey often

---

[1] Robert Browning, <u>Rabbi Ben Ezra</u>, st. 22.

determines where it will *end*. I think you have a right to know your starting point, so that you may have some idea of where you will finish! Here then is my *Statement of Faith* about the Bible –

(1) The Christian church possesses a collection of books that are reckoned by all denominations to be normative for faith and practice –

- this collection bears the title *"Holy Bible"* and is also variously known as *"scripture"*, *"the scriptures"*, *"holy scripture"*, and the like

- the collection consists (for Protestants) of 66 books, which together are called the *"canon"* of scripture, a word that means the supreme guide or rule (*canon*) that God has given to bring us safely into his eternal kingdom [2]

- of this canon we may say that it is

  - ***complete*** – nothing can be either taken from it or added to it; and that it is
  - ***sufficient*** – we need no other guide, nor can there be a better one.

(2) Among Christians there are five different views of scripture [3]

(a) <u>**The Roman Catholic View**</u> – which holds that God has revealed himself truly in the written revelation of scripture, and that the scriptures must be obeyed as the sure Word of God. Nonetheless, the church, exercising its *magisterium*, has a teaching authority that is ultimately superior to the sole rule of scripture. That superiority has two major aspects –

- *first*, while the church cannot *change* the scriptures, nor enlarge the canon, it may *add* to the Bible a body of teaching drawn from its own traditions and based on its own authority

---

[2] Roman Catholics, Orthodox, and some others, add a further group of writings, varying in number, which Protestants collectively call the *Apocrypha* – that is, "hidden" books, from the idea that they are not part of the "canon" and therefore should only be used privately and not in public worship.

[3] Parts of the following summary are drawn (with much alteration) from <u>Let The Earth Hear His Voice</u>; Worldwide Publications, Minneapolis, 1975; Section VII (A), "The Authority of the Bible," by John Eui Whan Kim; pg. 985-987.

- *second*, the church alone has the right to fix the meaning of the Bible and to determine valid doctrine. [4]

(b) **_The Liberal View_** – which denies to the Bible any full measure of divine origin or authority, rejects its supernatural content, and credits its composition almost entirely to human thought and initiative. The Bible, since it is a human book, must be supposed to contain many errors, not just of inconsequential detail, but also in matters of belief, perception of reality, historical records, concepts of God, and the like.

(c) **_The Neo-Orthodox View_** – which agrees with liberals that the Bible is primarily a natural (not supernatural) record of various human religious experiences, but adds that it does also contain a revelation of and from God. That revelation, however, does not consist of an objective statement of truth, but rather is subjective, coming to each reader in a different form, in response to individual faith, personal need, and singular perception. Thus the Bible cannot do more than *contain* the Word of God, and that Word means something different to each person who encounters it.

(d) **_The Fundamentalist-Evangelical View_** – which holds that the Bible is entirely the Word of God, infallible in all that it affirms, inerrant in all that it contains, verbally inspired by the Holy Spirit, so that no single word contains any fault. However, since the manuscript copies of the ancient texts at present available to us do contain a host of errors, and since no translation of even a faultless text can avoid being at least partially faulty, the claim of inerrancy must be restricted to the original documents. That is, when the various books of the Bible first emerged from the pens of either their authors or final editors they were completely free from any error of fact or revelation.

(e) **_The Conservative-Evangelical View_** – which is the stance of this book. *Conservative evangelicals* agree with a large portion of the fundamentalist viewpoint, but modify it in various ways, as the following chapters will show. Fundamentalists, of course, will still find here much to please them, but many would demur from the more open position on

---

[4] Thus the Roman Catholic Jerome Biblical Commentary, commenting on the *Vatican II* document *De Revelatione*, says – "It stresses (2:9) that Tradition and Scripture 'in a certain way merge into a unity and tend toward the same end,' but 'it is not from Sacred Scripture alone that the Church draws her certainty about everything that has been revealed.' On the relation between the Church and Scripture, the Council (2:10) insists that the teaching office of the Church authentically interprets the word of God, and yet this teaching office is not above the word of God but serves it." (72:13). Geoffrey Chapman, London,1978.

infallibility and inerrancy that I have taken. The *conservative-evangelical* view could be summarised as follows –[5]

(3) A Description of the Bible

(a) God is transcendent so that it is impossible for fallen humans to think about him properly or to conceive by ourselves all that he is. Thus we urgently need that God should reveal himself to us in terms that we can comprehend. The Father has done this in the pages of scripture, and the Bible is the only wholly reliable revelation of himself that he has given us.

(b) The only trustworthy *opinion* about the Bible is what the Bible affirms about itself. If the Bible cannot be trusted to speak truly about itself, then no other statement it makes can be relied upon. The Bible declares itself to be the *Word of God*, which is a claim that the reader must either accept or reject. I accept it unequivocally.

(c) If the Bible is the Word of God, then no higher authority can be appealed to. Therefore sound doctrine can arise only out of submission to the divine inspiration, the authenticity, the authority, the trustworthiness of scripture. What the Bible says, God says. Christians surely ought to agree with Jesus' testimony to the divine inspiration of the Bible (cp. Mt 5:17-19; 10:19-20; Mk 12:26, where he bases an argument upon the verbal form of a single word; 12:36; 14:27; Lu 16:17; Jn 10:35; 14:26; 16:13-15).

(d) God chose to speak through human channels without suppressing the individuality, writing style, and freedom of each writer; yet he did so in such a way that their writings, when properly understood within the context of the entire Bible, affirm only what is true. Thus the Bible has a *divine-human* character which, on the one hand, makes it appear like any other book, yet on the other makes it wholly the Word of God. As St Thomas Aquinas said: "All is from God; all is from man."

(e) The Bible does not merely *contain* the Word of God, it *is* the Word of God, wrought by the Holy Spirit (2 Ti 3:16), who so moved upon the writers of scripture that they wrote nothing contrary to the purpose of God. Thus the ultimate origin of the Bible is not human but divine (1

---

[5] The summary is my own; however I think it fairly states the *conservative* opinion on the Bible, as distinct from the strictly *fundamentalist* view – although, as I have said, there is much more agreement between the two views than there is disagreement. Indeed, many who call themselves *fundamentalist* are conservative in some things, and many who call themselves *conservative* are in some things fundamentalist.

Th 2:13; He 1:1; 1 Pe 1:11-12; 2 Pe 1:3-4, 16-21). We might call this the ***doctrine of the plenary inspiration of scripture***, which holds that the Bible is inerrant in all that it actually affirms or teaches. That is, whatever the Holy Spirit intended to say in scripture has been spoken truly and reliably. The Bible is therefore the only fully God-given source for Christian doctrine, faith, principles, and practice.

(f) Final authority concerning Christian belief and duty rests only in the Bible itself, not in the various dogmas, concepts, and structures that the church has drawn out of the Bible. That is, while the Bible may be infallible in all that it truly affirms, that infallibility does not pass to any church nor to any person. All other books, writings, teachings, creeds, or philosophies must be measured against the Bible, and reckoned true only insofar as they agree, or at least do not disagree, with the things scripture truly affirms.

(g) This however does not mean that the Bible is equally a source of truth in matters of history, geography, astronomy, biology, medicine, diet, and the like. It is not a text book on the various sciences, but a revelation of the way to salvation. As the Vatican II document *De Revelatione* put it: "The Books of Scripture must be acknowledged as teaching firmly, faithfully, and without error that truth which God wanted put into the sacred writings for the sake of our salvation." [6] Readers should look elsewhere for instruction in other matters.

(h) The highest testimony of scripture relates to Christ, so that all true exposition of the Bible will give Christ pre-eminence and point people to Christ. Scripture, rightly understood, will draw men and women to repentance and to faith in Christ as the only Saviour. Through him alone can sins be forgiven and entrance gained into the kingdom of God.

(i) The Bible we now have, with all its difficulties, is the Bible God intended us to have, and it is fully adequate to bring men and women into union with Christ through faith, and to enable them to discover and to fulfil the purpose of God for their lives.

(4) Those propositions are all easy to state. Finding out what they mean in practice, and applying them to life, is not so easy. That is what the remainder of this book is about. I should perhaps add, however, that you will find little or no discussion here on the nature of biblical *inspiration*,

---

[6] 3.11. Cited in the Jerome Biblical Commentary, 72:14.

nor on the formation of the *canon*. Those are matters for separate study. This book begins with the premise that **the Bible as we now have it both contains and is the divinely inspired canon**, and from there concentrates on how to read, understand, believe, and obey that Word so as to fulfil the highest purpose of God.

> Heroism is indeed the beautiful in the soul. It is the old image of God coming to the surface again, as when, in scraping off a dingy wall in Florence, the workmen came upon the portrait of Dante. Often there come men who throw aside the rags of self, the tattered vestments of beggars, and let out the image of God within. Into no institution of man, into no philosophy, into no school of art, has there entered such a band of heroes as is seen filing down into this book of God. It seems perfectly wonderful that each page of the Christian's book should have been composed by one of these children of heroism. The Bible is a Westminster Abbey, where none but the great sleep.
> – David Swing [7]

---

[7] I have scattered throughout this book several quotes in boxes about the Bible.

PART ONE

SWORDS AND SERMONS

I have undertaken, you see, to write . . . my opinions . . . As you proceed further with me, the slight acquaintance which is now beginning betwixt us, will grow into familiarity; and that, unless one of us is in fault, will terminate in friendship. •• *O diem praeclarum!* [8] •• then nothing which has touched me will be thought trifling in its nature, or tedious in its telling. Therefore, my dear friend and companion, if you should think me somewhat sparing of my narrative on my first setting out, • bear with me, • and let me go on, and tell my story my own way: •• or, if I should seem now and then to trifle upon the road, •• or should sometimes put on a fool's cap with a bell to it, for a moment or two as we pass along, –- don't fly off, • but rather, courteously give me credit for a little more wisdom than appears on my outside; • and as we jog on, either laugh with, or at me, or in short do any thing, •• **only keep your temper!** [9]

---

[8] "O splendid day!"

[9] Laurence Sterne (1713-1768), The Life and Opinions of Tristram Shandy (first published in 1759); Oxford University Press, Oxford, 1991 edition; Volume I, Chapter VI.

CHAPTER ONE

EAVESDROPPERS

The problem is, many people, failing to linger in contemplation of the great men and women who speak through the pages of scripture, commit the fault complained about by Walter Weir –

> Clumsy eavesdropping must be worse than the blind spying on the blind. You've not only got to know what is said, but what is meant. There's a lot of difference between listening and hearing. [10]

Yet how many there are who never get past "eavesdropping" on scripture! They "listen" to a verse here, a dogma there, a paragraph somewhere else, but never truly "hear" the message of the Bible. They know it in bits and pieces, but not in its whole. They understand *doctrine*, but not the *Word of God*. We can avoid this problem by observing two necessities: *first*, read the Bible, **thoroughly**, over and over again; and *second*, read it **intelligently**, following sound rules of interpretation. The latter is the main object of this book, which explores the art of **hermeneutics** [11] – how to catch the message of God that lies embedded in the Spirit-breathed pages of scripture. That art means different things to different people, so before we go any further you had better work out what kind of Bible reader you are.

The first NCLS [12] assessment of church-goers in Australia uncovered three basic attitudes –

---

[10] G. K. Chesterton, The Thirteen Detectives; Dodd, Mead & Company, New York, 1987; "The White Pillars Murder" (a detective story, in which Walter Weir is one of the heroes); pg. 16.

[11] In case you missed it, "hermeneutics" is defined at the beginning of the previous chapter.

[12] The National Church Life Survey, involving some 20 Protestant and Pentecostal denominations, was begun in Australia in 1991, by the Uniting Church Board of Missions (NSW), and by the Anglican Diocese of Sydney.

- ***Literalists***, who take the Bible in its entirety as the infallible Word of God and insist that it must (as nearly as possible) always be read and acted upon literally.

- ***Contextualists***, who agree that the Bible is the Word of God, yet say that it must be read in the *context* of the times before we can understand its implications for us today.

- ***Valuists***, who treat the Bible simply as a valuable book, parts of which may reveal God's Word to us, or at least teach us useful things. [13]

About one third of church-goers fell into the latter category, about one fifth were *literalists*, but the greater number were happy to call themselves *contextualists*, which is where this book stands. So if you are a *literalist* or a *valuist* some of the following pages may not bring you much joy. But as Sancho said, "Forewarned, forearmed." [14] You could therefore abandon this book right now, or prepare to defend your position to the last drop of blood – or, less nobly, of sweat. Or perhaps instead, you could read with a searching eye, willing to allow that there may be something here for you to learn. At the end, even if you prefer to stick to your original view, I hope you will at least be better informed.

If you are a *contextualist*, then these pages will guide you, I trust, into a wiser use of the Bible and a richer appropriation of its treasures. But what does it mean to call someone a ***contextualist***?

DIVINELY INSPIRED

Let me say at once that there is nothing in the *contextualist* position that denies, or could deny, the biblical claim that *"all scripture is inspired by God, for its words did not arise from some human whim, but men and women spoke as they were moved upon by the Holy Spirit"* (2 Ti 3:16). I am therefore committed to the authenticity and authority of the Bible. I accept heartily that the collection of writings we call scripture comprises a divinely given canon, [15] and that the

---

[13] Winds of Change, various editors, pub. by NCLS, 1994; Chapter Four, "A Map For the Journey – Attender Attitudes to the Bible," pg. 45, 47.

[14] The Adventures of Don Quixote, by Miguel Cervantes; Book II, Chapter Ten.

[15] "Canon" comes from a Greek word that means a "rule", or a "measure"; it is used to describe any collection of authentic writings, such as "the Shakespearean canon". In Protestant circles

Footnotes continued on the next page

Bible is the only infallible revelation we have about God and his purpose for men and women. However, the Bible must remain ineffective until it is both ***intelligently read*** and ***wisely understood***, which is the task of good ***hermeneutics***.

My concern in these pages is to develop a hermeneutic (a method of interpretation) that will enable each Bible reader to hear well, believe well, and gain full access to what God has actually commanded or truly promised. How necessary this is! Over the years I have seen too many shattered Christians, improperly informed, who have tried to claim what God has not promised to do. Their pain could have been prevented if they had been wiser in their handling of scripture and careful to draw from it no more than it actually says.

So then, nothing in these pages will call into question the reliability of the *Bible*; but I *will* raise questions about various common ways of reading (or should I say misreading?) it. Yet still I will do little more than put into a consistent form what even the most fervent literalists [16] do in practice: that is, they adjust scripture to suit the 20th century. No reader of an ancient book, not even the Bible, can avoid this practice. Whether consciously or not, every Bible reader must to some degree observe the following rules –

- some parts of scripture can be embraced and applied just as they stand, without any modification

- some parts are useful only after they are much modified, usually by reference to other scriptures (e.g. Mk 9:43-47); [17]

- some parts not even the most fervent literalists attempt to activate in modern life (e.g. Nu 5:11-31; [18] Le 14:33-53 [19]).

(as you will find in the *Statement of Faith*, above) it usually means the collection of 66 books that comprise our present Bible. A canonical book is one that belongs in the Bible; a non-canonical book is one that does not.

[16] I have used this word three or four times already, and will use it again, but with some diffidence. Someone could easily misconstrue my meaning. In many respects I am myself a *literalist*, and also a *fundamentalist* – that is, I agree that a great part of the Bible should be read literally and accepted without reservation. But in the more technical meaning of those two terms – someone who accepts *every* word of the Bible unequivocally, who believes in the strict verbal inspiration of scripture, who insists that the Bible is wholly inerrant – I would shun both titles. See again the *Statement of Faith*, above.

[17] *"If your hand causes you to sin, cut it off ... If your foot makes you stumble, cut it off ... And if your eye leads you astray, pluck it out!"*

What alarms me is the inconsistency and arbitrariness that frequently lies behind those choices. It seems to me that people often commit two faults –

- they actually follow the contextual rules, yet refuse to admit that they observe them, and are offended if their (probably unconscious) practice is pointed out to them; or
- they consciously follow the rules, but without full rigour – that is, they take the process only so far, and then stop, because to go further would bring their dogma of absolute biblical inerrancy under attack.

This book is an attempt to avoid those faults by suggesting a consistent and coherent rule of interpretation. I am looking for a hermeneutic that can be applied anywhere in the Bible, one that will remove from the way scripture is read any suggestion of mere caprice. My aim is to establish a godly basis upon which any intelligent reader of the Bible can understand scripture correctly and employ it sensibly in daily life. After all, how shall I bring my life into harmony with the Bible until I know what it teaches? And how shall I know what it teaches without a sound rule of interpretation?

THE FOUNDATION

A correct understanding of scripture begins with four things –

- a reliable text of the Bible
  - *that is, a good modern translation that will bring me as close as possible to what the original authors wrote*

- a well-informed intelligence
  - *the Bible was written on a pre-supposition of substantial literacy, along with a capacity to handle different kinds of writing; it yields its treasures only to careful meditation* (Ps 1:1-3)

- an understanding of Christian tradition

---

[18] Moses enjoined trial by ordeal as a test of marital fidelity – but only when it was a woman (not a man) who had fallen under suspicion.

[19] The peculiar ritual for curing a house after God was reckoned to have afflicted it with leprosy.

- we cannot reasonably dismiss twenty centuries of biblical study and formulation of doctrine, for we must generally allow that the Holy Spirit has led the church into the truth

- some personal experience of God
- one must be a genuine friend of the Author before his words can become truly meaningful.

BRIDGING THE GAP

I expect dissent (even from contextualists) against some of the details in this book, but hardly opposition to its general thrust: namely, that **readers of the Bible must recognise the antiquity of scripture, and adjust their reading accordingly.** Here is an ancient Book, composed within a long series of cultures, all of whose worldviews and literary milieus differed (sometimes radically) from ours. As nearly as possible, that historical and cultural gap must be bridged before the Bible can be accurately interpreted.

There is nothing new in that idea, of course, for it is one of the most basic rules of hermeneutics ("find out what scripture meant to its first readers before you ask what it means today"). What will perhaps be new in these pages (to some readers) will be the way in which I address and attempt to solve that problem. But do remember that you are holding in your hand only an *attempt*, which must have the tentative quality that belongs to all interpretations of scripture. Belief in an inerrant [20] *Bible* is one thing, but inerrant *teachers* are another! There never has been such a creature except Jesus, and there will not be another this side of the resurrection!

To put it differently, if we are talking about the Bible itself, then I will fight for, and I hope die for the Book as readily as any lover of God's Word. But if we

---

[20] This is perhaps a dangerous word to use, because it means different things to different people. To fundamentalists *inerrancy* means that every word of the Bible is without fault, that scripture contains no error in history, geography, philology, botany, biology, astronomy, or any other field of learning. For me, *inerrancy* means only that the Bible is true in all that it affirms, and that it speaks infallibly only on matters of faith and Christian practice. This is the position taken by most conservative evangelicals. It was also, interestingly, the position originally taken by the *Assemblies of God* in the USA. In their first *Statement of Faith*, adopted in April 1914, they refrained from using either "inerrant" or "infallible", but under the heading "Scripture" said, "The holy inspired Scriptures are the all-sufficient rule for faith and practice, and we shall not add to or take from them." (Anointed to Serve: The Story of the Assemblies of God; Gospel Publishing House, Springfield, Missouri; 1971; pg. 99-100.) Since I belong to the pentecostal movement, the position of the A/G is interesting to me.

are talking about very fallible readers of the Bible, then there is much room for tolerance and for respect of different opinions. We are all struggling toward the truth. None of us has yet found it fully, except in Jesus himself. Just look at the sometimes astonishing theological disagreements and diverse practices that exist among Bible-believing Christians. Those quarrels show plainly that none of us has arrived yet at the perfect way of reading, interpreting, and applying scripture.

THE TWO KINDS

It is commonly said that there are two kinds of hermeneutics –

- ***general hermeneutics***: which look at the whole Bible, its background and origins, the formation and collecting of the canon, the authenticity of each book, their dates of composition, authorship, editing, inspiration, and everything to do with the Bible as a piece of writing.

- ***particular hermeneutics***: which provide rules for understanding the contents of the Bible, paying special attention to the various literary styles employed, the intention of each writer, and the like.

I have made no attempt to separate those two kinds of hermeneutics, or even to deal with each aspect of what they cover. My major focus is on *particular* rather than *general* hermeneutics, but you will find elements of both of them scattered across these pages. The structure of the book is my own; I have made no attempt to follow any classical model of hermeneutical studies.

I am not content with this book – it has many deficiencies, it leaves many questions unanswered; but then, so does every other discussion I have ever read on the subject. I make no claim to infallibility. I am, like all others, a person *"looking through a dark glass"*, who at best can *"see only in part and know only in part"*. So I try to remember, with a little humility, that the glass I am looking through is just as dark as anyone else's! I cannot forget Sirach's warning that no-one can hope to comprehend fully the Word of God –

> Consider the Book of the Covenant of the Most High God . . . It overflows with wisdom, and like the River Pishon in full flood it surges with understanding. It is like the running of the Tigris at the time of firstfruits, and like the Euphrates spilling over its banks, or the swelling of Jordan at the time of harvest. Like the inundation of the Nile, so it pours out instruction, and flows like the flooding Gihon at vintage time. The first man never knew wisdom fully, nor will the last encompass her. The span of her thoughts is wider than the vast ocean, and as the abyss is fathomless so is her purpose! (24:23-29)

CHAPTER TWO

HOW NECESSARY?

Do we really need a set of rules for understanding the Bible?

If there were nothing in scripture, or in our culture, to hinder or mislead Bible readers, then the simplest of rules would be sufficient. But that is not the case. God has seen fit to present us with a book that taxes the skills of the loftiest scholars. When not even the experts can agree about its meaning, it is no wonder that ordinary readers have trouble!

There are many reasons for these difficulties (which are taken up here and there throughout this book), but one of them is the very way in which the Lord has chosen to communicate his message. Scripture seldom speaks in plain language without any kind of literary adornment! Rather, the Holy Spirit has sent the Word of God to us through dreams, visions, metaphors, similes, types, shadows, signs, allegories, riddles, historical examples, proverbs, songs, poetry, oracles, miracles, polemics, parables, biographies, debates, and in other ways.

So the texture of scripture is marvellously diverse. It is splendid with all the colour, drama, excitement, love, and life that make it a magnificent weaving of the entire range of human experience. This both enhances and hinders its meaning. The different ways in which the Bible speaks means that there is something in it that touches the heart of every reader. But those diverse methods of communication also make the work of interpretation harder. People often misunderstand the message; they hear it, but fail to catch its proper sense. Into that confusion steps *hermeneutics*, providing reliable rules that help to bridge the communication gap.

But now someone may ask: "Surely those rules were developed long ago. Why then has the church not reached agreement on what the Bible means?" I cannot fully answer that question, but here are some suggestions –

RULES MUST BE APPLIED

Not all Bible readers, or even preachers and teachers, use the rules – many don't even know them. How can any rule do any good until it is understood and used?

Then there are few people (if any) who lack a "blind spot" – most of us allow some kind of cultural pre-conditioning, or prejudice, or dogma, occasionally to over-ride a responsible approach to the things we read. Not even the best of scholars, the most neutral of commentators, are wholly immune from this fault. [21]

Then every Bible reader is also inescapably shaped by

ENVIRONMENTAL INFLUENCE

For better or worse, we are each of us a product of the environment in which we were raised and in which we live. We cannot avoid bringing to the reading of any book, including the Bible, a set of pre-determined ideas, our own particular way of looking at things and of relating to them. This inevitable colouring of our world not only differs a little for each of us, but can change dramatically from generation to generation. It is nearly impossible for anyone today to read the Bible in the same way that our forefathers did. They looked at the Book through different eyes; they saw different things, they experienced a different response to its words. [22] That is one reason why scripture has to be newly interpreted for each new generation, and the work of theology done over and over again.

---

[21] "All critics, however dispassionate, bring to their subject thick encrustations of personal prejudice and, which they are probably even less well equipped to notice, assumptions which are attributable to the spirit of the age." A. N. Wilson, C.S Lewis: A Biography, William Collins Sons & Co. Ltd., London, 1990; pg. 173.

[22] For example, across more than a thousand years the church (quoting Moses and the Greek philosophers) forbade anyone either to exact or to pay interest on money. The rule was finally demolished (except for "usury", defined as exorbitant interest) some 400 years ago. The cause was the rise of capitalism and the development of an extensive mercantile class who demanded freedom in their financial transactions. Under great social pressure, and despite what scripture was once thought to teach, the church was obliged to modify its doctrines, or at least its practice. So too, the once near-universal keeping of the Sabbath laws on Sunday has been thoroughly jettisoned by most of the church. Christian people nowadays, after fulfilling their Sunday church duties, seldom scruple to engage in any outing or activity they please.

SPIRITUAL QUALITIES

People, including scholars and commentators, vary enormously in their spiritual gifts and abilities – just as they differ in all other skills –

- Sometimes those differences are *innate* – that is, some are born with a *spiritual* genius just as others are born with a genius for music, or art, or some other attainment. Such people will inevitably see more things in scripture than a less gifted eye can discover.

- Sometimes the differences reflect various levels of *maturity* – whether intellectual, emotional, spiritual, or some other expression. A person whose spirituality is shallow cannot hope to gain from scripture as much as someone who is far advanced in faith.

- Sometimes people differ in how much they apply themselves to the task before them. A person who works with persevering *discipline* will find more and better treasures than those who are casual and haphazard in study.

- Sometimes the difference is simply one of the *"measure of faith"* God has given (Ro 12:3,6). Like trees and bushes, shrubs and flowers in a garden, none of us can grow beyond the limits that are already built into our nature.

Whatever the differences may be, they certainly affect each person's capacity to read scripture and to interpret it wisely. Those restraints are just as influential on scholars as on ordinary readers. None of us are immune from them. Nor can we escape the woes caused by

LANGUAGE PROBLEMS

>Yet all world languages die at last:
>Greek of grammar and factions; Latin
>Of clotted syntax and Renaissance purism;
>French of bad admirals and over-subtle vowels;
>English and Chinese of their written forms;

Russian of subject people's hate. [23]

Language is one of the great mysteries of human life. What are these sounds we make that enable us to communicate with one another? Why are they so different from nation to nation? How precise are they? Do they have any meaning in themselves, or only such meaning as each person allows them? Is there somewhere a perfect language, from which all other tongues are derived, and of which they are but imperfect copies? Is our capacity for speech an acquired skill, fully dependent upon environment and imitation, or is it innate, deeply embedded in each new-born baby?

Linguists have been arguing about such questions for generations, and still have no certain answers. Lewis Carroll, for example, who was himself a mathematician and linguist of genius, humorously raised this mystery several times in the charming stories he told his little friend Alice about her namesake. In one of them Humpty Dumpty debates with Alice –

> "When *I* use a word," Humpty Dumpty said, in a rather scornful tone, "it means just what I choose it to mean – neither more nor less."
>
> "The question is," said Alice, "whether you *can* make words mean so many different things."
>
> "The question is," said Humpty Dumpty, "which is to be the master – that's all." [24]

The problem is that words seldom have the same meaning among those who use them, not even for people who share a similar culture, education, and social background. Think how within our own English-speaking society words may carry quite different nuances. As George Bernard Shaw once said,

> England and America are two countries separated by the same language. [25]

How often have your own words been misunderstood? We all suffer from the pain of innocent statements being given sinister meanings! Few words have a fixed definition; they tend to be fuzzy around the edges and to carry a quantity of baggage that is unique to each user. Language holds hidden eddies of meaning for each speaker, and it is easy for hearers to be caught in an undertow of misconstrual and carried away into a blunder. Then again, because of their

---

[23] Mark O'Connor, Australian poet, dramatist, and short-story writer; Lingua Romana.
[24] Charles L. Dodgson (1832-1898), Through the Looking Glass, Chapter Six.
[25] Reader's Digest, 1942.

differing background and knowledge, hearers draw unlike layers of understanding from what they hear. This lack of clearly defined boundaries explains why no one ever fully knows what another person is saying, nor how their own speech is understood by those who hear it. [26]

Think how even a simple word like "rose" may conjure up an array of images. For one person it produces a picture of a cemetery; for another a splash of colour, or a garden, or the face of a sweetheart, or any of a hundred other associations. No collection of formal rules can hope to detail the vivid cluster of associations, memories, emotions, moods, that words differently carry for all who use them. And those problems, of course, all increase immensely when one is dealing with a foreign language and a long-dead culture.

Shall we then scornfully reject as worthless the rules of hermeneutics? Shall we say that the barrier of language is impossible to cross?

That would indeed be foolish! Our rules are not infallible, and they may be used differently by different people and bring different results, yet for those very reasons we need them all the more! They do provide *some* guidelines, they prevent egregious errors, and in much of the Bible they do cause scholars to arrive at similar conclusions.

> Do you know a book that you are willing to put under your head for a pillow when you lie dying? Very well; that is the book you want to study while you are living. There is but one such book in the world. (Joseph Cook)

---

[26] As a preacher, I am often astonished at what people say they heard in one of my sermons, and just as often astonished at what they failed to hear! What they claim I said frequently bears scant resemblance to what *I* thought I had said!

CHAPTER THREE

DAUGHTERS FOR SALE

Don't go out into the desert, for it is haunted by **Satyrs**, those dreadful demons that look like goats. **Lilith**, the *Night Hag*, bewitches the dark hours; she likes to capture and enslave wandering children, and she fills the minds of careless men with lust. **Rahab**, the female denizen of the deep, is the chief terror of sailors; and who but a fool would anger great **Beelzebub**, the all-devouring *Lord of the Flies*? Travellers in the wilderness are driven mad when they hear the awful howlings of **Azazel**, the *Desert Haunt*; and would you dare to challenge the **Basilisk**, whose burning eye can kill the unwary with a glance?

Those demons, along with some others, are all mentioned in the Old Testament. [27] Did the writers who referred to them actually believe in their existence? The matter is unsure. Perhaps the Bible does no more than reflect popular superstitions; or the authors may have been using the demons simply as a poetic device. [28]

But whether or not the prophets believed in phantoms, those grotesque spirits do stand on the pages of scripture, and they reveal a culture far removed from ours. Undoubtedly, large numbers of the common people *were* thoroughly convinced of the scary reality of such fiends, and of other creatures like them, and they lived in dread of them. If that were not so, why would the prophets have bothered to employ the demons as symbols of God's wrath? If few people had known about them, or believed in them, the oracles would been stripped of

---

[27] See my book <u>Demonology</u> for a fuller discussion of the Hebrew views on Satan and demons. Note also that Jesus referred to *Beelzebub* (Mt 12:27; etc), although he apparently used this name, not to refer to some distinct demon, but as a synonym for Satan.

[28] For example, did Isaiah (34:14) actually believe in the existence of *Lilith*, the Babylonian Night Hag, and in the *Satyrs* (goat-demons), or did he simply engage a widespread fallacy to provide colour and effect for his oracles?

their force. In any case, the Hebrews were surrounded by nations that held widespread fears of a large number of vividly depicted and individually named spectres.

Today the existence of such mythical horrors would hardly be credited by anyone. What do you suppose would happen to a modern preacher who tried to threaten his people with the terror of *Rahab*? He might think himself fortunate if he provoked nothing more than a vigorous protest! Or if a modern parent used the name of *Lilith* (as the ancient Hebrews did) to frighten a child out of wandering away from home, what would the neighbours think? At best such a superstitious parent would be dubbed foolish, and more likely deemed crazy. So too, any Sunday School teacher who warned children against the pitiless eye of the *Basilisk* could expect a severe rebuke and instant dismissal. Yet the Hebrews belonged to a society where such terrors were part of everyday life.

Can you imagine what it was like to live in a world that was haunted by *Azazel* and his companions? Life had a different aspect for those people. Their culture took on a different shape. Their environment held a different cluster of potential perils, and different possibilities of pleasure. Inevitably, they approached each new day with an attitude far removed from ours.

Therefore, when we try to understand what the words of the Old Testament meant to their first readers, and how those words should be applied to life today, we must take that altered perspective into account. Unless we learn how to bridge the cultural hiatus that lies between the past and the present we cannot hope to understand the Bible properly. So I am returning here to an idea raised in the last chapter – the environmental gulf that exists between us and the ancient Hebrews. It is a principle important enough to deserve special emphasis [29]

GOTHIC HORRORS

J. A. Froude, a famous British historian of the past century, once said, "It is not possible for us to grasp the medieval mind." In fact, I will update the scholar and say that for us it is hardly possible to grasp even the *19th-century* mind! Think about the theatre productions that we today call *melodramas*, and treat as absurd comedies – yet in their own time they were viewed seriously, and audiences were swept with grief at the sufferings of the sweet heroine, or

---

[29] We will come back to it again in *Part Five*.

stormed with rage against the cruelties of the villain. We cannot understand how they could have been so moved by scenes that to us seem merely ludicrous.

Indeed there are many things about the culture of our forefathers that remain incomprehensible to us. Think how females of the last century were prone to faint upon the slightest pretext; but if any woman were to behave like that today she would be viewed, if not with scorn, at least with astonishment.

Consider too the newspaper cartoons that so amused our great-great-grandparents, yet leave us puzzled, searching in bewilderment for the joke. [30]

Nowadays it is considered unmanly for a gentleman to weep without great provocation. Two hundred years ago, the opposite was true! Marion Chesney is a Scottish writer and the author of a series of Regency romances, which contain many well-researched descriptions of life in England during the early 19th century. In one of them she describes a duke who had been absent from England for several years. When he returned

> he had forgotten many things about the conduct of society, including the fashion for weeping copiously on all occasions. A gentleman was expected to have "bottom" – meaning courage, coolness, solidity. But a gentleman was also expected to have sensibility. It was an age in which the diarist Thomas Creevey coined the phrase "not a dry eye in the house," by which he meant the House of Commons, where politicians would vie with each other to see who could cry the most. . . . An elderly lord had dropped dead in White's a bare half hour before the duke's arrival there earlier in the day, and all the members were roaring and bawling and crying as if he had been their dearest, closest relative, instead of a crusty old gentleman of loose morals who had risen to meet his Maker in a cloud of brandy fumes. [31]

---

[30] The *Bulletin* magazine regularly publishes a cartoon from 100 years ago, but without the original punch-line, and then invites its readers to submit a new caption. The original "joke", along with the best of the readers' suggestions, is published in the next issue. The results are often hilarious. But our forefathers would have been as much puzzled to discover why we find the modern caption amusing as we are to find what made them laugh at the original one.

[31] *Rainbird's Revenge*, Chapter Three. In another novel she mentions the same idea, and links it also with the brutal discipline children endured in the schools: "Bottom was one of the most prized virtues in the Regency. It meant having coolness, courage, and solidity. It was a necessary quality in this age where epidemics such as typhoid, cholera, or small pox could wipe out whole families. Even the most effete fop learned at an early age to endure pain, as flogging was so prevalent in public schools that there were several rebellions, one in Harrow lasting over three weeks. The strange thing about the men of the Regency was that their pistolling, boxing, flogging, gaming, boozing, and enduring were combined with sensitivity.

Footnotes continued on the next page

Or consider two of the most famous novelists of an earlier generation, whose names will be unknown to most readers, and whose books we would all find nearly impossible to read. The first is Samuel Richardson (1689-1761), who is remembered today by scholars only because he was one of the chief founders of the modern novel. He wrote many books, of which the most celebrated was *Pamela*, a work that received an amazing measure of universal acclaim. Its contemporary renown has probably not been equalled and certainly never surpassed by any other piece of fiction. During the author's lifetime it was reprinted many times, translated into several languages, and inspired paintings, poetry, sculpture, and a host of imitations. Yet modern readers find *Pamela* intolerable. It is drearily prolix, full of maudlin sentiment and tedious moralism, and contains an impossible plot featuring an unbelievably virtuous heroine. It is amazing that anyone ever managed to read it once, let alone several times! A best-seller? The idea seems laughable to us. But that just shows how much we have changed since the 18th century!

Then there is the celebrated Gothic novel by Ann Radcliff (1764-1823), *The Mysteries of Udolpho*. Mrs Radcliff's horror stories were already so famous that her publishers in 1794 gave her what was then an unheard of advance of £500 [32] to write *Udolpho*. They were not disappointed. The public clamoured for copies of the dark mysteries, [33] and Mrs Radcliff quickly became by far the most

---

They were not bruisers, cried easily, had a real enjoyment of literature, wit, culture, delicacy, and eccentricity." (Perfecting Fiona, Chapter Eight.) How different is our own age from that one, less than 200 years ago!

[32] An enormous sum of money in those days. In the mid-18th century a house-maid was paid only a shilling a week, plus keep (there were 20 shillings in a pound), so a girl would have to work 200 years to earn Mrs Radcliff's advance payment! Even a century later, in the mid-1800s, Charles Dickens was able to present this scene in his novel The Old Curiosity Shop (1841; Chapter Twenty-One) –

> (Kit) was formally hired at an annual income of Six Pounds over and above his board and lodging, by Mr and Mrs Garland, of Abel Cottage, Finchley.
>
> It would be difficult to say which party appeared most pleased with this arrangement, the conclusion of which was hailed with nothing but pleasant looks and cheerful smiles on both sides. . . .
>
> "Well Mother," said Kit, hurrying back into the house, "I think my fortune's about made now."
>
> "I should think it was indeed, Kit," rejoined his mother. "Six pound a year! Only think!"
>
> "Ah!" said Kit, trying to maintain the gravity which the consideration of such a sum demanded, but grinning with delight in spite of himself, "There's a property!"

[33] The title page of the book carries the motto: "Fate sits on these dark battlements and frowns, / And as the portal opens to receive me, / A voice in hollow murmurs through the courts / Tells of a nameless deed."

famous novelist in England. Yet her turgid prose, her absurd perils and rescues, her sentimentality, make her books virtually unreadable today. [34] Modern readers cannot understand how their ancestors ever enjoyed such stuff. But enjoy it they did, and immensely, and devoured every word over and over again. Their tastes were certainly unlike ours!

If we cannot comprehend the 19th-century mind, or the medieval mind, how shall we cope with a culture more than twenty centuries in the past? Sabine MacCormack confronted this problem when he tried to grasp the worldview of people in the days of the Caesars –

> What is most difficult to understand about the past is what at that time people took for granted. Many aspects of the past look deceptively similar to what we know ourselves until we look more closely and find that we have stumbled upon an entirely different method of looking at life and the universe. [35]

Readers of ancient literature ignore this subtle yet vast cultural gap at peril of thoroughly misunderstanding what they read. The Bible is not exempt from this danger. We have to recognise that the Hebrews had a lifestyle and culture far removed from ours, which the following pages will try to reveal.

NOT TRANSFERABLE

Anthropologists have discovered two significant things about cultural practices:

(1) Everything done in a given culture has a meaning, and the practice has no value apart from that meaning. That is, nothing significant is ever done just for the sake of doing it. People do things, or adopt customs, because they gain some benefit from them, whether personal or corporate. If for some cause a custom or practice loses its reason for being, then it will either vanish or be adapted to a different purpose.

(2) There are no practices that automatically carry the same meaning in all cultures. [36] Even when a practice is carried from one culture to another it undergoes at least some change of meaning. More surprising still, a

---

[34] Jane Austen parodied Ann Radcliff in her novel, "Northanger Abbey".

[35] From The Twelve Caesars, by Gaius Suetonius Tranquilius; tr. by Robert Graves; Penguin Books, Middlesex, 1986; pg. 56.

[36] Think, for example, about the different ways the simple act of kissing has been practised, and the different meanings it has had at different times and in different cultures.

practice passed from one generation to the next within the same culture seldom remains intact! That is because customs are not important in themselves but rather in the meaning they hold for those who use them, and inescapably that meaning keeps changing with the times.

Those two discoveries about culture are important for hermeneutics, for this process can be observed happening in the Bible. For example, sacrifices and temple rituals that were apparently endorsed by God for one generation are later startlingly reproved (see Ps 40:6; 50:7-9; 51:16; Is 66:3; Am 5:21-24). Why? Simply because their meaning had changed in the minds of the users, so that the sacrifices no longer fulfilled the intention of God. The Lord wanted the people to continue serving him; but to do so they either had to recapture the original meaning of what they were doing, or find a new practice that would achieve his purpose. In their case, the final solution was a combination of both ideas – the old custom melded to a new meaning. At least that is how it worked for a time; but they soon drifted away again from God's design.

A similar situation exists in relation to women exercising leadership or ministry within the church. What is more important: the unchanging *principle* that underlies the apostolic teaching; or the changeable cultural *practice* through which that teaching is expressed? The *principle* is twofold –

- the need to maintain divine order in the church; and
- the need to avoid giving unnecessary offence to people outside the church.

Paul upheld that twofold principle by making several rules that were appropriate for his time; but in our time those same rules create an unacceptable oppression. They are used to deny women a cluster of gospel liberties and full opportunity to express their God-given gifts in the service of Christ and the church. We must keep Paul's *principle*, but find a different *practice* through which to express it – one that is conformable to the demands of our modern culture. One writer put it this way –

> This being the case, the primary question ceases to be, "How can we maintain the *forms* that are commanded in the New testament?" We recognise, rather, that these commands, as all commands in scripture, are couched in culture-specific forms and that these forms (like all forms in culture) are designed to convey meanings. It is these *meanings*, then, not (as the Pharisees believed) the *forms* of scripture that are normative for today. The questions we are to ask, therefore, are, *first,* "What are the meanings that the scriptural authors intended to get across," and *second*, "What cultural forms in our culture will adequately express those meanings?" Such a principle provides an antidote to Pharisaism. It can also enable those theologians who seek to retain a belief in the authority and applicability of biblical teachings in contemporary contexts to embrace many of

the insights of modern scholarship without abandoning a high view of scripture.[37]

Unhappily the "pharisee syndrome" is still common, and Christian people are often burdened with *forms* that in the end deny the far more important *principles* of the Word of God. My hope in this book is to explain how we can look past the contemporary *practices* of the Hebrews to the unchanging *truth* that lies embedded in them. Nonetheless, we do need *first* to understand those practices in their original settings; so let us now return to an examination of that long-vanished culture, beginning with their

FAMILY LIFE

The different social relationships that existed between men and women, adults and children, rulers and subjects in Bible days are sometimes incomprehensible to modern readers. Some of the things we most treasure in family life were unknown to them. For example, there is no word in Hebrew that has the warm feel of our word "family". They spoke instead of a "household", which (in wealthier homes) included the patriarch, his wives, concubines, children, retainers, servants, and slaves. The emotions and images conjured up by our word "family" lay outside both their vocabulary and their experience.[38] Neither is there in Hebrew a word identical with "marriage". They viewed a wedding mainly as a contract arranged between two fathers or guardians. The girl in particular usually had little or no say in the matter; she could be betrothed by her parents in infancy and married as soon as she was pubescent.[39] Women could be, and were, treated as little more than chattels, owned by their husbands in much the same way as they owned a horse or a dog. The *Tenth Commandment* encouraged this view, with its admonition, *"You must not covet your neighbour's wife, nor his ox, nor his ass, . . . nor anything else that belongs to him."* A man's wife had a status only slightly above an ox! Centuries later, an old rabbi echoed the same idea of possession, as if a wife were not a

---

[37] Theology Today journal, January 1985; article "Cultural Anthropology: Meaning for Theology"; author unknown to me; pg. 397, 398. Slightly modified.

[38] Harper's Encyclopedia of Bible Life, ed. Madeleine S. and J. Lane Miller; Harper & Row, New York, 1978; pg. 89; plus several other passages on the family in OT times scattered throughout the book.

[39] That is, as young as 12 years of age. Mary, the mother of Jesus, was probably at the most in her early teens (perhaps only 13 or 14) when the Holy Spirit overshadowed her and she became pregnant with the Messiah.

living person, but a mere object. He also puts children and slaves on the same low level, and treats them as his personal property, to do with as he pleases –

> There are some things you should never be ashamed to do: ... Discipline your children often; draw blood from the back of a rebellious slave; bolt the door against a wife you no longer trust; and put things under lock and key when many people are around. [40]

Still more centuries later, and still citing the same Old Testament authority, Christian men joined the rabbi, arguing that their wives were their own holding, to dispose of as they chose. Thus Petruchio, in Shakespeare's *Taming of the Shrew* (III.ii), says of his wife –

> I will be master of what is mine own –
> She is my goods, my chattels, she is my house,
> My household stuff, my field, my barn,
> My horse, my ox, my ass, my any thing ... [41]

Later, after taming his termagant wife, Petruchio demands that she tell "what duty (wives) do owe their lords and husbands". Katherina, now thoroughly subdued, at once declaims –

> Thy husband is thy lord, thy life, thy keeper,
> Thy head, thy sovereign. ...
> Such duty as the subject owes the prince,
> Even such a woman oweth to her husband;
> And when she is froward, peevish, sullen, sour,
> And not obedient to his honest will,
> What is she but a foul contending rebel
> And graceless traitor to her loving lord? [42]

If Shakespeare could safely end his play by putting such abject words into the mouth of his heroine, [43] we cannot wonder that in Christian England in the 17th

---

[40] Sirach 42:2, 5-6. Mark too how women are excluded from the Commandment, for nothing is said about *them* coveting their neighbour's husband! They were thought too lowly to warrant such notice.

[41] There is of course a "tongue-in-cheek" aspect to the scene, being part of an exaggerated comedy. Nonetheless, if there is no fire there can be no smoke. The sarcasm of Petrucchio reflected a real state of affairs in the world of that time.

[42] Act V, Scene 2.

[43] However, Shakespeare does put a barb in it, in the very last words, which are spoken by Lucentio: "'Tis a wonder, by your leave, she will be tam'd so." The suggestion is, that had Katherina been a woman of real spirit, she would not have been so easily tamed! But when the surrounding culture gave all its support to male dominance, resistance was hard.

century (at least among the lower classes) women had a base position. The approved manner for a man to divorce his wife was to lead her to market wearing a halter and there offer her to the highest bidder. Although the buyer may have been arranged in advance, perhaps with the wife's approval, it remained a humiliating practice built upon a wrongful use of scripture – that is, the practice of taking a passage that might have been appropriate for ancient Israel, and improperly applying it to Christian behaviour. [44]

Let us again return to life in Israel.

Within the confines of that largely rural society, many couples had no doubt grown up together and were already mutually affectionate. Parents, too, wanting happiness for their children, probably tried to unite young people who were known to be fond of each other. Nor was romantic love absent from the culture. One has only to read the *Song of Solomon* to learn how passionately a young man could court the maiden of his dreams. Nonetheless, in most cases marriages were arranged by parents or guardians, whether or not the young people were in love. The presumption of the culture was contrary to ours. They expected people to fall in love (if at all), not *before* marriage, but rather *after* it.

Even then, whether love came before or after marriage, few if any Hebrew men would have loved their wives as, for example, I have loved my wife Alison for more than forty years. One of the most charming stories in the Bible is the romance of Boaz and Ruth. Yet the patriarch loved his lady, not as a woman who was his equal partner, holding an equal dignity and worth, but as a precious possession. Hence Ruth placed herself at his feet, acknowledging him as her lord. There was no place in the culture for the kind of connubial fellowship and mutual bonding that is our ideal. [45] Hebrew spousal relationships were very different from ours; hence it is extraordinarily difficult for us to capture the "feel" of an Israelite home. Yet we must try to do so before we may reasonably commend or criticise their behaviour, and especially before we try to impose upon a modern family the example of a biblical household.

---

[44] The English Bible and the Seventeenth-Century Revolution, by Christopher Hill; Penguin Books, London, 1993; pg. 403.

[45] That is, an ideal of shared love, equality, and partnership (reflecting *Ephesians 5:21-33*), rather than a relationship of ownership and subjugation.

KEEP THE VIRGINS

Nothing more reveals the alien structure of Hebrew family life than their seemingly callous attitude toward their children and servants –

- A man facing financial ruin could lawfully sell his daughters into concubinage or his sons into slavery, or worse, as shown in the ghastly story of Lot (Ge 19:6-8; and see also Ex 21:7-11; Ne 5:5).

- Can anyone today read without horror the macabre fate of the concubine at Gibeah? (Jg 19:23,24).

- Notice how Isaac accepted without question his father's right to kill him (Ge 22:9). Likewise, Jephthah's daughter acknowledged his right to immolate her, and, apart from begging two months' grace, she embraced her futile and untimely death without protest (Jg 11:36-37).

- The scant concern shown in the ancient world for women and children is visible in Moses. He calmly told his troops to kill them all except virgin girls, whom they might keep for their own pleasure (Nu 31:14-18; and cp. also De 20:13-14).

Fervent Christians during the 16th and 17th centuries saw no reason why they should not follow such admirable examples, and did so, with enthusiasm. Records show, for example, that many of the early Protestant preachers heartily approved the sentence of burning to death that Judah wished to impose upon Tamar (Ge 38:24). [46] Citing those passages as their authority, they delivered their own "fallen" women to the torturer and the flames. Yet how impossible such barbarity would have been if they had recognised the invalidity of those old statutes for this Christian era.

Nowadays, of course, we cannot hmagine how godfearing people could behave so savagely, nor how the ancient Israelites could treat their children so cruelly. But that just shows how wide is the gap between their culture and ours, and how careful we need to be about transporting biblical notions into our society. [47] I do not mean, of course, that those ideas cannot be transported at all.

---

[46] Christopher Hill, op. cit. pg. 403-404.

[47] Even today, of course, there remains a huge diversity in various cultures. For example, Mr Lee Kuan Yew was Prime Minister of Singapore for 30 years, until he resigned in 1990. Under his leadership Singapore enjoyed extraordinary economic and social development,

Footnotes continued on the next page

They all have *something* to teach us. But as we saw a couple of pages back, we must learn to distinguish between *form* and *meaning*. Thus the *details* of scripture frequently belong only to the past while the *principles* it enshrines are applicable in every generation. We must search for those unchanging values, for they alone retain validity, not only for our time but for all time.

> So great is my veneration for the Bible that the earlier my children begin to read it the more confident will be my hope that they will prove useful citizens of their country and respectable members of society. . . . I have for many years made it a practice to read through the Bible once every year.
> – John Quincy Adams, sixth president of the USA

which made it Asia's most prosperous city. When he was asked if, in retrospect, he would have done anything different, Mr Lee replied that his greatest mistake was to legislate for equality between the sexes. He said that his government had been "idealistic and ignorant" when it passed that legislation. The end result was that large numbers of now highly educated and professionally qualified women would never be able to marry. As Mr Lee said, "Asian men don't like a wife who is seen to be his equal. Not wearing the pants is an enormous loss of face!" I will come back to this idea of *modern* cultural gaps (as an illustration of those of the past), in Chapter Twenty-Five.

CHAPTER FOUR

SAVAGE SERMONS

> England has two books: the Bible and Shakespeare. England made Shakespeare but the Bible made England. [48]

The tempestuous history of the English Bible shows how much the church needs a good hermeneutic, For while the Bible may be said to have "made England", it may also be said to have **destroyed** England. Indeed, the saying became tragically true: "*Scrutamini scripturas.* These two words have undone the world." [49]

How did this happen?

The art of printing from movable type was invented in Germany in the 15th century. For the first time in history it became possible to put a copy of the Bible into every hand. English translations, despite bursts of opposition and persecution, soon began to appear and were eagerly read by princes and peasants alike. By the end of the 16th century the Bible had gained an amazing dominance over every aspect of Britain's life. Everybody acknowledged its authority. All new laws had to be founded either on biblical principles, or better, on Bible verses. Kitchen maids eagerly learnt to read so that they could search the scriptures. Farm labourers saved their pennies to buy a Bible, and they gave the Book pride of place in their homes. Monarchs and merchants, philosophers and priests, shepherds and scholars revered scripture as the infallible Word of God. The Bible became the fountainhead of all learning and knowledge, the base of all rule and authority. Probably no other period in history has seen an entire nation so thoroughly permeated with scripture as

---

[48] Victor Hugo (1802-1885), French poet, novelist, and dramatist.
[49] "Let us examine the scriptures." John Seldon (1584-1654), <u>Table Talk</u>: *Bible, Scripture.*

Britain was at that time. When the *King James Version* was published in 1611, and began the ascendancy it would hold for 300 years, the Bible was already acknowledged as the one foundation upon which the English nation would surely flourish.

But many of its devout adherents understood scripture poorly. They gave enormous and nearly equal weight to every pronouncement, from *Genesis* to *Revelation*. The Bible took on a mystic aura, which created among the people superstition rather than genuine faith. Biblical statements that should never have been linked with contemporary events were used to justify practices that mocked the gospel. The nation became harsher and more intolerant than it had been for centuries. Obedience was demanded to biblical precept, and warring sectarianism flourished.

Nonetheless, England was named by many preachers a latter-day revival of ancient Israel, a nation in covenant with God; therefore the statutes hewn by the finger of God at Sinai had to be kept. So the stern laws of Moses, along with the angry fulminations of the prophets and all the most violent aspects of the Old Testament, were deemed to be still in force. Prudent and humane voices were frequently raised in protest against such follies, but a fierce biblicism had gripped the nation and wiser insights were brushed aside.

CIVIL WAR

As the status of the Bible rose ever higher it gained irresistible force at every level of government. Biblical literalists insisted with increasing vehemence upon surrender to every scriptural decree. They opposed with growing violence anyone who dared to read the sacred page differently. Partisan groups arose, fiercely condemning anyone who stood outside their ranks. Each sect furiously insisted that it alone held the true doctrine. Bitter conflicts broke out between Anglicans, Baptists, Presbyterians, Independents, and others – while Roman Catholics and Jews were loathed by them all.

For a time the Anglican bishops prevailed and cruelly persecuted the various groups of Dissenters. But then the Puritans clawed their way to power, banished the episcopacy, arrested and executed the archbishop, and began to impose their own joyless strictures upon the entire population. But the Puritans were themselves divided. So the nation had to endure the scandalous spectacle of the dominant Independents and Presbyterians angrily describing each other's doctrines as stinking piles of blasphemous heresy. Apart from the exalted authority they gave to the Bible, the squabbling factions were unanimous only in one thing: they were all eager to defend their dogmas with blood – especially the blood of their enemies!

The brawl eventually narrowed into a struggle between Parliament and the King. The Parliament, stacked with Presbyterians and Independents (who had temporarily formed an uneasy alliance), demanded on the authority of the Bible the right to hold free elections, to make laws, to raise money, and to resist the rule of any monarch. Charles I, equally fervent in quoting scripture, insisted on his divine right to rule, pronounced himself above any human law, and avowed that he was answerable to God alone.

ROUNDHEADS AND CAVALIERS

War became inevitable. The belligerents converged into two armies: the *Roundheads* for Parliament; and the *Cavaliers* for the King.[50] Both sides maintained the divine rectitude of their cause, and waged a malicious war of words. Not content with bullets, bayonets, and bombs, they threw an incessant barrage of biblical slogans at each other. Royalists and Puritans alike were sure they had God's support. How could they doubt it? Were they not in possession of dozens of texts that supported their goals? By reading the entire Bible literally, and by giving equal force to every passage from both Testaments, the feuding parties were easily able to find scriptural warrant for the merciless slaughter of all who opposed them.

"A curse upon the man who holds back his sword from shedding blood!" cried the stern Roundhead (quoting Jeremiah) as he hacked, hewed, and killed the loyal supporters of King Charles.[51] *"Butcher them all without mercy or pity!"* roared the zealous Cavaliers (quoting Moses) as they blasted away with cannon and muskets. *"Happy is the man who takes your babies and smashes them on a*

---

[50] I do not mean that the Bible was the sole, or even major cause of the English Civil War; nonetheless, the literal view of scripture held by all sides was beyond denial a substantial contributing factor. The "Roundheads", by the way, were so called because of a temporary fashion among the working class for short hair. The style was never adopted by the gentry or the noblemen (not even those who were Puritans), so the royalists were able to use it as a term of derision. They applied it mockingly to the parliamentary party, because it enjoyed much support among the common people. "Cavalier" was likewise an insult, hurled by the supporters of parliament against the soldiers of the king. Derived from a low Spanish word for "cowboy", it did not have the romantic and dashing sense that we now attach to it. "Cavalier" in those days was used in much the same jeering way as people now sometimes use "cowboy" as an epithet against a person they want to insult.

[51] *Jeremiah 48:10* was of course cited just as enthusiastically and bloodthirstily by the Cavaliers, as was also the next scripture (De 7:2) by the Roundheads. Indeed, any biblical reference that could be taken to authorise pillage and death against anyone who was reckoned an enemy of God, was eagerly used to justify the most appalling crimes.

rock!" [52] both armies cried (citing the sweet psalmist) as they razed cities and castles, putting to death not only those who carried arms, but also unarmed men, women, and even children.

Nor were such feral calls heard only on the battlefield. From a multitude of pulpits across the land preachers vied with each other in choosing the most bloodcurdling Old Testament texts to apply to the conflict. [53] How sure they were, preachers and warriors together, as they carved a swathe of terror across England, that they were doing the will of God! Indeed, both sides piously argued that they were driven to such extremities solely out of love for God and in obedience to scripture, and the more blood upon their hands the more certainly they expected to merit Paradise.

A LOST DREAM

So the terrible Civil War raged on, bringing appalling misery in its wake. And this horror was fermented in the name of the Bible, quoted in a way that foully distorted its true meaning. The warring parties, of course, did not think so. The captains and troops in both armies mightily revered scripture, and joined with their preachers in giving indiscriminate authority to its every edict. They found no difficulty in persuading themselves that their killings, rapine, and havoc were all in harmony with the purpose of God. Did they not have before them the example of ancient Israel? The Bible was held aloft on both sides as a God-given banner of battle. Its words were used to justify hideous crimes. [54] Sane men and women (who seemed sadly few in number) protested against this vile abuse of scripture, but the literalists prevailed and barbarity engulfed the nation.

Parliament eventually won the war and executed the king. A cry of triumph rang across Britain. How the exultant Puritans rejoiced! The bloody tyrant was dead! Surely the great Millennium was about to begin! Had they not prepared the way for Christ to come again? What could now hinder the King of kings

---

[52] *Deuteronomy 7:2,* and *Psalm 137:9.*

[53] One visitor to a church in Blackfriars in 1653, voiced his reaction to the sermon: "Good God! what cruel, and abominable, and most horrid trumpets of fire, murther, and flame!" (From Cromwell, Our Chief of Men, by Antonia Fraser, Methuen Paperbacks, 1985; pg. 440. Numerous other examples of this kind of savage preaching, and of the extraordinary place the Bible held in the nation's affairs, are given in the book.)

[54] Rather like the Inquisition of the Roman Catholic Church, which solemnly talked about the "infinite compassion and mercy of the Church" while it applied rope, water, and fire to the shrieking victims of its torture chambers.

from mounting the throne of God's New Israel and reigning from it as true Sovereign? See how abundantly Bible prophecy had been fulfilled! Who could doubt that the everlasting Kingdom of God was about to appear on earth? From England, Christ (whose coming must now be imminent) would spread his dominion across the whole earth. After centuries of darkness God's new age had dawned at last!

But their delighted expectations were short-lived. Oliver Cromwell (whose letters, despatches, and speeches were richly laced with Bible verses, prayers, and pious sayings), held supreme power as Lord Protector for only five years, then took ill and died. Yet how hard he had laboured to create a political system absolutely grounded upon scripture! To the end of his life he never stopped insisting that all his actions had been determined by Divine Providence. Among ambassadors and kings, as well as the common people, he never wearied of expressing his gratitude to God, nor of stating his conviction that under the hand of God a splendid and holy era had arrived. England, he said, was assuredly favoured by God above all nations, and the British Commonwealth would usher in the Millennium and the reign of Christ on earth.

How cruelly Cromwell's death, at the height of his power, seemed to mock all those pretensions! How could Fate so callously shatter the noble dreams of the Puritans? They watched in dismay as the new Commonwealth, which had hardly emerged from infancy, began to collapse into ruin. Faced with chaos, the nation turned back to the monarchy. Parliament invited the profligate Charles II [55] to come, in place of Christ, and resume his father's throne. Those of the former regicides who were still living were put to death, and the victorious royalists enthusiastically set about damning Oliver Cromwell and his Bible-quoting followers as the blackest villains who had ever lived. [56]

Everywhere in England there was relief and joy; yet the Restoration was also darkened by despair. Vast numbers of men and women had been sure that *"the*

---

[55] For whom John Wilmot, the Second Earl of Rochester (1647-1680), later wrote an epitaph –
    Here lies our sovereign lord the King
    Whose word no man relies on,
    Who never said a foolish thing,
    Nor ever did a wise one.

[56] In Cromwell's case, the reputation is ill-deserved. He has with some justification been called "the greatest of all Englishmen". However, he *was* a fervent citer of scripture (particularly from the Old Testament), in which (as he thought) he found full justification for rebelling against the king and for supporting and then leading the English Civil War, including the later invasion of Ireland with its associated savagery and dreadful loss of life (in which barbarity, by the way, the Irish defenders were hardly less innocent than the English invaders).

last days" were upon them. They had felt that the horrors of the Civil War were excusable because they were paving the way for the kingdom of God. On countless occasions they had heard the once-victorious Puritans claiming that God was on their side, and that he had shown approval of their cause by granting them such great triumphs. But now the crusade was lost and the old and decadent monarchy restored. Rivers of blood had been shed in vain. Where was the promised Paradise? Where was the coming of Christ? Where was the beckoning Millennium?

The people were bewildered; their confidence was shaken; they could not understand why God had abandoned his Word. Had they not suffered and died for his kingdom? Where then were the spoils of victory? How was it possible that a dissolute *man*, and not *Christ*, was again installed upon England's ancient throne? How could God permit all the advances gained by the War to be so quickly and totally reversed? Perhaps their preachers had misled them? Perhaps the whole matter had been a lie? Perhaps the victories gained earlier by the Roundhead armies had not after all been wrought by God? Perhaps God was not so involved in human affairs as they had so much believed? Perhaps the Bible could not be trusted?

So across the land the embittered people rejected not just the misuse of scripture but *scripture itself*, and the Bible was pulled down from the lofty eminence it had gained. The tragic results of Puritan zeal, so distant from the dream, caused a massive discrediting of biblical authority, and a surge within the people of disgust for the very idea of creating a New Israel.

A DECLINING IMPORTANCE

So the Civil War had a profound effect upon the place of the Bible in the life of Britain. From a position of unquestioned supremacy over every part of society, the Bible now began to diminish in stature. Utterly weary of fanatics who cited scripture to excuse atrocity, deeply sick of religious partisans with their wild enthusiasms, exasperated by sectarian quarrels, the people turned their backs on the Bible. The new king himself (Charles II), while declaring his personal devotion to scripture, nonetheless preferred to appoint to high ecclesiastical office men who believed almost anything *except* the Bible! He knew that the nation was glutted by biblicism, had vomited out the excess, and now yearned for a moderate and practical approach to religion. The ardent quoters of scripture had in the end made themselves its worst enemies.

A sensible hermeneutic, if it had not been able to stop the war, might at least have prevented each side from wickedly claiming God's allegiance, and would have removed from the struggle its self-righteous frenzy. Without the biblicism that made both armies so sure they were guiltless, they would have lacked an excuse for their ever-greater barbarities. The measureless odium aroused by the awful struggle would not have fallen so heavily upon the Bible.

But since they lacked a sensible hermeneutic, the abused and angry people cast aside not only the wild quoters of scripture but also the sacred text that had been so horribly misused. It has ever since been impossible for any political party to build a platform of government by quoting biblical principles. The very sight of a Bible-quoting politician is enough to throw the media and the populace (including most church-goers) into a fever of derision. Knowing the behaviour of such zealots in the past, who can blame them?

The period of the English Civil War, of course, is only one example. Many other stories could be told of men and women who had the highest possible view of the Bible, yet used it to justify bestial behaviour. Our society still has horrific memories of the havoc wrought by biblical literalists, who in the name of God sold men and women into slavery, tortured, burnt, robbed, and raped them, committed genocide, invaded foreign lands, and did more wickedness than a thousand volumes could record. Yet they called themselves servants of God, and never lacked a Bible verse to support their actions. The consequences of such villainy were inevitable. Despite occasional surges of revival, the influence of the Bible in English-speaking countries has steadily declined. Year by year, with accelerating persistence, the Bible has been driven ever further away from any central role in the government and life of the nation.

Yet there has been one compensation. Out of the debacle there has emerged

A COSTLY BENEFIT

The Bible, properly understood, allows none of the crimes that have been committed in its name. Instead it urges an ethic of love, gentleness, goodness, justice, and tolerance. But everything hinges upon a wise hermeneutic. Lacking that, the wildest things can be pulled off the sacred page; with it, good sense and moderation will prevail. This wiser hermeneutic is one of the benefits that began to emerge from the carnage wrought by the old rabid biblicism. Scholars and people alike began to search earnestly for a wiser, safer, sweeter way to read, understand, and apply the Bible. Everybody knew that some parts of the Bible are easy to understand – even a child can grasp and use them. But other parts are obviously fraught with difficulties. How should *they* be read? What is the correct way to use scripture? How can we avoid the insanities of the past? Out of those questions arose the study of hermeneutics as we presently understand it. Society became more gentle, the church more kindly. Why?

Because scholars began to focus most of their attention upon the New Testament and largely abandoned the literal use of the Old Testament.

Both Testaments, of course, were, are, and will remain equal partners together in creating the canon of scripture. Nonetheless, the New Testament itself insists that the old covenant, in its entirety, must now be interpreted in the light of the new. Christ is the measure of truth. We may do and be only what is possible for men and women who are in sweet union with Christ through faith.

CULTURE OR SCRIPTURE?

What has all this ancient history got to do with me, you may ask? Simply this: the manner in which those preachers in the past quoted scripture, while it has now been rejected by the *nation*, is unhappily still common in parts of the *church*. There is, however, *one* difference: today the law of the land prevents even the most ardent fundamentalists from practising literally more than a fragment of the Old Testament. Nonetheless, many people remain in our churches who gladly quote whatever they can get away with! Consider, for example, the people who use scripture to justify flogging *children* while ignoring similar verses that enjoin flogging *adults*. Their only reason for doing so is cultural pressure. They certainly have no biblical reason for such discrimination. Any hermeneutic that allows the *first* whipping must equally command the *second*. [57]

Further, any Christian who cites *Proverbs* (say) to warrant beating a child inescapably creates a mandate to quote literally any part of the Old Testament – which is why, across the centuries, the church has been able to find biblical support for burning to death adulterous daughters, executing rebellious sons, flogging lazy servants, selling people into slavery, and the like. Yet no literalist today would dare to advocate such cruelties. But why not? Certainly not because their hermeneutic denies them a biblical mandate, but simply because they cannot flaunt the culture. But is that a proper stance? Hardly! Christian choices should be determined by scripture, not by society. That is why a good hermeneutic is so necessary. When scripture is read in the right way people can make right choices wholly on biblical grounds, without having to engage in some kind of culturally-forced compromise.

---

[57] See below, my chapter headed "Spare the Rod!"

Notice too, if it is absurd to bring *some* of Israel's ancient laws into our society, then it is just as absurd, except for one modifier, to carry *any* Old Testament passage *unchanged* into our modern world. What is that modifier? Any Old Testament teaching that is either repeated in or endorsed by the New Testament must of course be obeyed by the church. Indeed, we Christians must always keep the Old Testament submissive to the higher revelation now given to us in the New Testament. For us, nothing is true save what is true in Christ. [58]

What then shall we do with the remainder of the Old Testament? Does it have no use? Of course it does! It is immensely valuable; but those riches are not found by insisting upon a literal application of every passage, and even less by using only those passages that are socially permissible. Rather, the treasures of both Testaments are located in the eternal and undeviating spiritual and ethical principles that underlie the entire Bible. God does not change. His ways are unalterable. But the manner in which the eternal law of heaven is worked out on earth *does* change radically from age to age.

TWO OR THREE

Another principle that should be utilised is the rule of *"two or three witnesses"* (De 19:15; Mt 18:16; 1 Ti 5:19). That is, do not place too much weight on any idea that lacks substantial biblical support. One verse is not enough to make a dogma. Especially, an Old Testament *concept* needs the support of a New Testament *doctrine* before it can be made mandatory for the church. Or, to express it differently, before Christians give allegiance to Old Testament ideas they must be filtered through the New Testament and take on a Christian shape. Instructions that were appropriate for a small *nation* long ago are not applicable without change to the universal *church* today.

So let scripture explain scripture. We should build up a body of evidence before setting up a way of life. Follow the rule: later and higher revelation countermands, or at least modifies, earlier and lower concepts. The greater must surmount the lesser. Two scriptures outweigh one, and three outweigh two. All who interpret scripture should tread cautiously and act responsibly, emulating Paul, who stressed his own anxiety about building a shaky house (1 Co 3:10-15). Those who create, or adhere to, poor doctrine, said the apostle, will have much to fear on the day of judgment. They themselves may be saved, but their false dogmas will be consumed, they will *"suffer loss"*, and may be scorched,

---

[58] The closing paragraphs of this book will bring us back to Christ as the measure of all truth.

like someone who barely escapes a burning building. I tremble myself when I contemplate these things.

But now, back to our major point. I am hoping to convince you (if you need convincing) that our use of scripture should be determined, not by some *cultural demand*, but by *the Bible itself*. And the way we interpret scripture should be consistent. We cannot approve a method that obliges us to pick out what bits we can safely use in the modern world while ignoring the remainder. Our hermeneutic should allow us, without doing violence either to law or culture, to treat the whole Bible seriously, and wisely learn the message for today that lies in every part of it.

CHAPTER FIVE

THE RENAISSANCE

Jesus said that *"the scriptures cannot be called untrue"* (Jn 10:35). With joy I assent to that proposition. Truly the Bible is the Word of God, given into our hands for our salvation. But possessing a true Bible and arriving at a true understanding are not the same thing. The truth of scripture will bring no benefit if it is falsely read – which was the very point Jesus was making in his quarrel with the Jewish leaders (see vs. 31-36). That, of course, is also what our present enterprise is all about: finding the right way to read the Bible.

The task has not been made any easier by another great event that has profoundly influenced our culture: the ***Renaissance***, [59]. which six centuries ago caused an astonishing flowering of knowledge. This "new birth" of learning caused a renovation of art and architecture, the growth of technology, the expansion of communications, the beginnings of the "scientific method" of research, the development of multiculturalism (along with other social experiments), and diverse innovations that have changed our society dramatically. The full ramifications of the Renaissance are still working themselves out all around us. Its humanistic focus created a sceptical approach to claims of absolute authority, exalted the importance of individual responsibility, emphasised freedom of choice, and, ironically, helped to pave the way for the ***Reformation***. [60] Why "ironically"? Because the Reformation itself, which put the Bible into the hands of every citizen, and insisted upon the

---

[59] "The great revival of art, literature, and learning in Europe in the 14th, 15th, and 16th centuries, which began in Italy and spread gradually to other countries: it marked the transition from the medieval world to the modern." (Websters New Twentieth Century Dictionary.)

[60] "In church history, the movement started by Martin Luther in the 16th century that aimed at reforming the Roman Catholic church and resulted in the establishment of Protestantism." (Ibid.)

individual's right of freedom of conscience, opened the way for a multitude of sects to develop. The chaos caused by hundreds of emerging cults has still further undermined the public's confidence in scripture. If so many people can read it in so many different ways, and draw from it so many different doctrines, how can it be depended upon to guide the affairs of a nation?

Those developments have all contributed to thrusting the Bible away from the centre of national life, and to confining it within a religious ghetto. The supposed friends of the Book must accept much of the blame for this sad condition. If they had been saner in their use of scripture, better in their understanding of it, then the English Bible, instead of gaining and then losing supremacy so rapidly, might today be waxing ever mightier in the government of our land.

What is the answer? Certainly not a return to the follies of the past. But a wise people handling the Wisdom of God wisely might begin to reverse the centuries of decline, and gradually carry the Bible back to its rightful and central place in our society. [61]

MANY VERSIONS

Another problem in grasping the message of the Bible arises from the thousands of differences in the texts that are available to us. You may have wondered why our various English translations sound so unlike each other in some places? Mostly those changes arise from the first necessity in translation, which is to create a *standard text* out of the multitude of ancient Hebrew and Greek manuscripts that have survived the decay of centuries. Scholars compare all these texts and from the host of variant readings try to reconstruct the wording

---

[61] I should perhaps say again that such moderate and wise voices were not lacking in the 16th & 17th centuries, nor have they been lacking since. There were always in the past (as there are today) a number of thinkers and writers who abhorred what the fanatics were doing. Unhappily, during the time of the Civil War they were few, and their counsels remained unheeded by the fierce fundamentalists. Indeed, some of the "dissenters", damned as heretics because they dared to question fundamentalist assumptions, suffered terrible tortures and hideous deaths. Some were "hung, drawn (disembowelled while still alive), and quartered"; others had to endure prolonged agonies, mutilations, imprisonment, confiscation of their goods, and countless other miseries. All done, of course, for the glory of God, while their tormentors piously quoted scripture! (See Antonia Fraser, op. cit.; Christopher Hill, op. cit.; The Grand Quarrel, ed. Roger Hudson, Folio Society, London, 1992; The History of England From 1485-1685, Thomas Babington Macauley, Folio Society, London, 1985; ditto The Eighteenth Century; and almost any secular or sacred history of the period.

of the original documents. That edited text becomes the source upon which their translation is based. However, no standard master-text has yet been accepted by all churches, or all publishing houses. So the various translations are based upon different sources, which inevitably leads to different results. No major doctrine is affected; but readers will certainly discover some startling changes in wording from version to version.

Translators actually depend upon six sources to build up the master-text that will become the foundation for their work –

- ancient manuscript copies (of which some hundreds are extant) in the original Hebrew, Chaldee, Aramaic, and Greek tongues

- ancient versions; that is, early translations of the scriptures into other languages, such as Latin, Syriac, Coptic, and the like

- scriptural quotations found in the works of ancient authors, especially that group of men from the first two or three hundred years known as the Church Fathers, but also Jewish rabbis, and even enemies of the church

- clues gleaned from other contemporary literature to suggest the meaning of obscure, missing, or obviously incorrect words

- comparisons of all the available old manuscripts in an effort to arrive at the most probable original reading of each passage

- the traditions of the particular segment of the church within which they are doing their work, or toward which they will direct their marketing. [62]

The aim, of course, is to arrive at a final text that will be as close as possible to what the original authors wrote, while remaining acceptable to the desired market. But in the end, differences of opinion will remain, and many matters cannot be decided at all. Nonetheless, despite the variations, virtually all modern translations, especially those produced by reputable publishers, can be trusted to bring the reader very near to the Word of God as it was first written.

---

[62] For example, Evangelical Protestants, Liberal Protestants, Roman Catholics, Orthodox, all have their own translation preferences. No one version has yet managed to achieve equal and universal acceptance among all the churches.

DR JOHNSON'S WISDOM

Now as this part of my book draws to a close, may I call your attention to a piece of wisdom from the pen of the great Dr Samuel Johnson. In 1756 he published a *Life of Sir Thomas Browne*, in which he rebuked the hardness of certain critics. They had fastened upon a few statements in Browne's writings and then pronounced him a heretic, a fault for which Dr Johnson rightly admonishes them – [63]

> (Consider these) men of rigid orthodoxy, cautious conversation, and religious asperity. . . . A sally of levity (by an author), an idle paradox, an indecent jest, an unseasonable objection, are sufficient, in the opinion of these men, to efface a name from the lists of Christianity, to exclude a person from eternal life. Such men are so watchful to censure, that they have seldom much care to look for favourable interpretations of ambiguities, to set the general tenor of life against single failures, or to know how soon any slip of inadvertency has been expiated by sorrow and retraction; but let fly their fulminations, without mercy or prudence, against slight offences of casual temerities, against crimes never committed, or immediately repented. . . . Men may differ from each other in many religious opinions, and yet may all retain the essentials of Christianity; men may sometimes eagerly dispute, and yet not differ much from one another: the rigorous persecutors of error, should, therefore, enlighten their zeal with knowledge, and temper their orthodoxy with Charity.
>
> . . . (Sir Thomas Browne) may, perhaps, in the ardour of his imagination, have hazarded an expression, which a mind intent upon faults may interpret into heresy, if considered apart from the rest of his discourse; but a phrase is not to be opposed to volumes . . . (And) he cannot surely be charged with a defect of faith, who "believes that our Saviour was dead, and buried, and rose again, and desires to see him in his glory" . . .
>
> The opinions of every man must be learned from himself: concerning his practice, it is safest to trust the evidence of others. Where these testimonies concur, no higher degree of historical certainty can be obtained; and they apparently concur to prove that Browne was a zealous adherent to the faith of

---

[63] The essay appears as an *Appendix* in Sir Thomas Browne: the Major Works; ed. C. A. Patrides; Penguin Classics, London, 1977.; pg 509-511. Sir Thomas Browne, physician, philosopher, Christian, is most renowned for Religio Medici ("The Faith of a Physician"), which is a gracious, brilliant, eccentric, and noble exposition of Christian life, published in 1642, and never since out of print. He was greatly admired by Dr Johnson. Notice also, barely a century after the English Civil War, how Dr Johnson's attitude reflected a firm rejection of any kind of fiery biblical literalism. His temperate approach, in contrast with the earlier crazed intemperance, had by then become dominant in England.

Christ, that he lived in obedience to his laws, and died in confidence of his mercy.

At once I can hear someone say: "But you're a fine pot to be calling a kettle black! What about your own invectives against certain literalists and fundamentalists? How are *your* diatribes to be excused?" The criticism is fair. My defence is twofold –

- it is hard not to speak firmly against a hermeneutic that has (and in some parts of the world still does) encourage Christians to behave violently, cruelly, and (in the end) ungodly against other people; and

- I have not the slightest desire to hang, draw, and quarter any man, or even to rap his knuckles, merely because of his opinion.

Even if I think a particular viewpoint is a damnable heresy, I never do no more than say so. My protest is not so much against a particular way of looking at scripture as an alarm about two things that seem to me to be grave faults –

- *first*, the inescapable inconsistency that must enmesh any literalistic approach to the whole Bible; and

- *second*, the fearsome consequences that have historically followed a literalistic approach and would still follow it were it not for the restraints imposed by law and custom.

Perhaps I should add, no one questions the genuine Christian faith of even the most furious biblicist. No doubt avid advocates of *literalism* are just as much children of the kingdom of God as are avid advocates of *contextualism*! I am not talking about *faith* but about *interpretation*, and about the consequences of reading the Bible either this way or that. I am no burner of heretics nor smiter of those who may disagree with me. But I will certainly defend vigorously the truth as I see it. So whether or not my readers agree with all that they find in these pages, I hope they will heed Dr Johnson's advice, and accord me the grace of calling me "Christian". For my part, I gladly offer the same grace to other believers, no matter how wrong I think their views are! So long as we together hold to Christ as our only Lord and Saviour, believing that he died for our sins and rose again for our justification (Ro 10:9-10), then we are members of the family of God. How can we do other than love each other in Christ?

"Never forget, gentlemen," he said to his astonished hearers, as he held up a copy of the 'Authorised Version' of the Bible, "never forget that this is *not* the Bible." Then, after a moment's pause, he continued, "This gentlemen, is only a *translation* of the Bible."

– Archbishop Richard Whately (1787-1863), addressing a meeting of his diocesan clergy.

PART TWO

REALISED AND REVEALED

At any street corner we may meet a man who utters the frantic and blasphemous statement that he may be wrong. Every day one comes across somebody who says that of course his view may not be the right one. Of course his view must be the right one, or it is not his view. We are on the road to producing a race of men too mentally modest to believe in the multiplication table. We are in danger of seeing philosophers who doubt the law of gravity as being a mere fancy of their own. Scoffers of old time were too proud to be convinced; but these are too humble to be convinced. The meek do inherit the earth; but the modern sceptics are too meek even to claim their inheritance. It is exactly this intellectual helplessness which is our (modern) problem. [64]

---

[64] G. K. Chesterton (1874-1936), Orthodoxy, Chapter Three.

THE SIX WISE MEN OF INDOSTAN

It was six men of Indostan
To learning much inclined,
Who went to see the elephant
(Though all of them were
    blind),
That each by observation
Might satisfy his mind.

The *First* approached the
    elephant,
And, happening to fall
Against his broad and sturdy
    side,
At once began to bawl:
"God bless me! but the
    elephant
Is nothing but a wall!"

The *Second* feeling of the tusk,
Cried: "Ho! what have we here
So very round and smooth and
    sharp?
To me 'tis mighty clear
This wonder of an elephant
Is very like a spear!"

The *Third* approached the
    animal,
And, happening to take
The squirming trunk within his
    hands,
Thus boldly up and spake:
"I see," quoth he, "the elephant
Is very like a snake!"

The *Fourth* reached out his
    eager hand,
And felt about the knee:
"What most this wondrous
    beast is like
Is mighty plain," quoth he;
"'Tis clear enough the elephant
Is very like a tree!"

The *Fifth*, who chanced to
    touch the ear,
Said: "E'en the blindest man
Can tell what this resembles
    most;
Deny the fact who can,
This marvel of an elephant
Is very like a fan!"

The *Sixth* no sooner had begun
About the beast to grope,
Than, seizing on the swinging
    tail
That fell within his scope,
"I see," quoth he, "the elephant
Is very like a rope!"

And so these men of Indostan
Disputed loud and long,
Each in his own opinion
Exceeding stiff and strong,
Though each was partly in the
    right,
And all were in the wrong!

So, oft in theologic wars
The disputants, I ween,
Rail on in utter ignorance
Of what each other mean,
And prate about an elephant
Not one of them has seen!"

    – John Godfrey Saxe (1816-87);
    American humorous and satirical poet.

CHAPTER SIX

THE FIVE KEYS

"Do not go beyond what is written," says Paul, [65] thus providing a rule that must control our approach to reading and interpreting the Bible. Instead, too many have aped the follies of those "six wise men", arguing with vast confidence about things they have at best seen only through *"a dark glass"*. [66] We need to be sure that we deal with scripture honestly, and not jump to false conclusions based upon inadequate understanding.

In the study of *hermeneutics*, then, we are looking for a set of rules that will help us to interpret correctly, or explain properly, any and every portion of scripture. But since our *hermeneutic* can only be as good as the rules that undergird it, we must make sure to adopt proper rules that enable us to read scripture responsibly, and to apply it wisely and well. Even so, the best hermeneutic in the world is worthless until there is something to study. So before God's people long ago could begin the joyful task of encountering scripture they had to get the Book into their hands. All Bible knowledge begins here, with the simple fact that before anyone can read it, scripture must be **written,** then **recognised** as the Word of God, then **read** by the people of God, then **understood** as the divine Author intended. We can unlock this process with *five keys* –

---

[65] *1 Corinthians 4:6.*

[66] *"Our knowledge is piecemeal and our prophesying is fragmentary ... We are like people trying to look through a cracked mirror – everything is distorted and turned into a riddle!"* (1 Co 13:9,12. The Greek word sometimes translated as "dim" or "dark" means a "mystery", or "puzzle".)

(I) SCRIPTURE MUST BE RECOGNISED

The process by which the Bible came into being across many centuries is called "the formation of the *canon* of scripture". This is not the place for a study on the canon; I am happy here simply to endorse the present canon, and to affirm that the Bible we have is the one God intended we should have. Indeed, we must accept the Bible with a sure belief that it is the Word of God given to us by the Holy Spirit; there is no room for an attitude of so-called "neutrality". It is impossible to establish a relationship with anyone by doubting his honesty; people who are suspicious of everyone they meet are paranoiac and cut off from others; society could not function if we did not generally trust people until they prove untrustworthy. If I insist upon viewing each new acquaintance with suspicion, refusing to accept either him or his word at face value, then I must expect to find myself angrily shunned! In just the same way, the Bible discloses its finest treasures only to those who approach it with confidence, accepting its own claim that it has come to us as a gift from God.[67] Should the Book prove false, then of course I may scorn it. But how could that be? *"Not a single word has ever failed of all his good promise that he has spoken!"* (1 Kg 8:56)

But suppose you misconstrue what someone says to you, and expect him to do what was not promised? You may well go away feeling disappointed, cheated, and muttering to yourself that you should never have trusted a stranger. Yet the fault was not in the words the stranger spoke, but only in your understanding of them. So too, the Bible has shown countless times that it can be trusted absolutely, so long as one does not read into it either more nor less than it actually says. A good hermeneutic prevents that fault and helps us to grasp the precise meaning of scripture.

ATHEISTS AND OTHERS

But what about atheists[68] who have been converted while trying to mock scripture? They are exceptions of grace. Most unbelievers are confirmed by the Bible in their unbelief, just as most persecutors (unlike the early Paul) are

---

[67] *2 Timothy 3:16*.

[68] For example Lew Wallace, who intended to write a book on atheism until his researches led to his conversion. So instead of producing an anti-Christ diatribe he turned his research into that novel much-loved by Hollywood, Ben Hur, which in its original version had the sub-title: "A Story of the Christ."

confirmed in their violence by persecution. While some torturers have been won to Christ by the unshakeable courage and love of their victims, most were provoked to wilder fury. They construed the heroism of the martyrs as wilful intransigence and stubborn fanaticism. [69] Similarly, someone who approaches the Bible with scepticism will see little reason to believe it, but will readily find a hundred things to confirm unbelief.

ORDINARY PEOPLE

A necessary corollary to our trust in the divine origin of scripture is confidence that the Bible was written to be understood by ordinary people; it generally uses everyday words with common meanings; it is not written in some kind of esoteric religious jargon; its message is not hidden behind a morass of secret devices or mystical ciphers. Mostly, it can be plainly read and understood. But that does not mean it is always easy to understand. Things that were self-evident to the people, two, three, or four thousand years ago, who first opened the various books of the Bible, may be obscure to us. Some of the ideas contained in scripture are also among the most profound ever expressed in human language, and cannot be fully grasped by casual or careless readers. So there remains a necessity for hard work and diligence. More than twenty centuries ago an old rabbi put it like this –

> A cheerful face is the sign of a happy heart; but creating proverbs demands painful thought. [70]

---

[69] Eusebius has stories of both reactions, but especially the latter. Here is one example, paraphrased a little: "A young man by the name of Sanctus, who was a deacon in the church at Vienne, also endured marvellously and superhumanly all the outrages that he suffered. The wicked men hoped, by the continuance and severity of his tortures, to wring from him something that he ought not to say. But Sanctus girded himself against them with such firmness that they could not force him to tell them even his name, nor what nation or city he came from, nor whether he was a slave or a free man. To all their questions he answered in the Roman tongue only with the words: 'I am a Christian.' ... <u>There arose therefore on the part of the governor and the torturers a great desire to conquer Sanctus</u>; but having exhausted all their tortures, and finding nothing more they could do to him, they finally fastened red hot brass plates to his body. Then his body became a plain witness to his sufferings, being turned into one complete wound and bruise, drawn out of shape, and altogether unlike a human form." (<u>Ecclesiastical History</u> 5.1.20; emphasis mine). See also Foxe's <u>Book of Martyrs</u>.

[70] Sirach 13:26. In a later passage Sirach enthusiastically commends people who devote themselves to study of the entire word of God, which he describes as "the Law, Wisdom, and Prophecies" (the familiar Hebrew threefold division of the ancient scriptures, more commonly called "the Law, the Writings, and the Prophets). They must work hard, says the rabbi, but the rewards are great (38:34b-39:11).

It takes just as much "painful thought" to grasp deeply the *meaning* of the proverb!

NO EASY ANSWERS

Sadly, many people refuse to apply themselves vigorously to scripture; they prefer an imaginary Bible, simple, void of complexity, free from difficulty, lacking obscurity. They want a Bible that contains no ambiguities, no apparent contradictions, no dark places or dead ends, a plain, easy, practical, and artless Bible. They certainly don't want a Bible that demands from them hard work – a Bible provocative, uncomfortable, sometimes simple but sometimes tangled, sometimes sweet but sometimes bitter, sometimes bringing joy but sometimes sorrow.

Yet that other Bible would not reflect real life, which itself is full of paradox – indeed, apart from the knowledge of Christ, our entire human experience must be called either a cosmic farce or an infinite tragedy. Who is not aware of the injustice, the mystery, the raw unfairness of life – how a few have so much, and most have so little. Yet withal, there remains much love and laughter, many happy things mixed in with shadows. So also is the Bible. Surging with the naked energy of human experience – in parts brutal and savage, in parts gentle and kind; now weeping, now merry, now soaring the noblest heights, now wallowing in sordid shame; a parade of poetry and fiction, fact and drama, history and prophecy, song and lamentation, the Bible is a magnificent reflection of all that it means to be human – a creature both of earth and of heaven. So it shares the complexity and absurdity of life, its drollness and darkness, its certainties mixed with vagueness, its joys mixed with sorrows, its divine vision mixed with earthiness, its beauty mixed with ugliness, and its finally indestructible love and unquenchable hope. None of that makes the Bible easy. But it does make it like us: wrought by the hand of God, and reflecting both a human and a divine image.

THROUGH A DARK GLASS

We all know that *life* is "fuzzy", fraught with ambiguity, chilled by wintry winds, often racked by inexplicable pain and exhilarated by equally undeserved joy. [71]

---

[71] Note that happiness is no less a mystery than suffering. If someone demands from you an answer to the riddle of pain, ask him first to solve the riddle of joy. There is no more cause for the one than there is for the other; they are both of them inexplicable within a framework of human logic or natural reasoning.

But *scripture*? How can it be said that the Bible is "fuzzy"? Surely that is wrong? But think about the *Sermon on the Mount*, where Jesus said that we should

- *"turn the other cheek"* to anyone who wants to hit us;
- allow a thief to steal not only our coat but *"also your shirt"*; and
- *"give to everyone who asks for money, and never refuse anyone who wants to borrow from you"* (Mt 5:39-42).

Suppose we take those sayings literally and actually start behaving like that? Word would quickly spread that any rogue could take anything he wanted from Christians without fear of retaliation or retribution. What a recipe for social chaos that would be! Did Jesus really mean it? Is it *desirable*, is it even *possible*, to obey his instructions fully? How *should* we understand his words? Or look at his *Olivet Discourse* (Mt 24:3-44). Commentators have been searching out the meaning of those oracles for nearly twenty centuries and are no closer to consensus now than they were at the beginning! [72] Apart from a general doctrine about his eventual return to this earth, and the certainty of the coming judgment, no one really knows how to interpret Christ's prophecies about Jerusalem, the Temple, the Jews, and the end of the age.

Then consider the controversies that continue to convulse the church on such basic matters as

- *water baptism* (by immersion or sprinkling; for believers only, or infants; essential for salvation, or a public sign of it; only a ceremony, or a vehicle of grace?);
- the *eucharist* (a means of conveying grace, or simply a memorial, and to what extent is Christ present in the bread and the cup?);
- *salvation* (once saved always saved, or can a Christian lose salvation?)
- *Holy Spirit baptism* (conterminous with the new birth or discrete from the new birth; given to all Christians or requiring a prayer of faith; with or without glossolalia?) – and many others.

We may turn to various commentaries for diverse solutions to all those puzzles, but in the end will still find people of good will arguing fervently for opposing views. Even Peter had to admit that in Paul's writings there were things he could barely understand (2 Pe 3:16); and Paul himself acknowledged that he was like a

---

[72] I will come back to this discourse later.

man peering through a piece of clouded glass (1 Co 13:12). In fact, as I have already mentioned in a footnote, in the Greek text he uses the word "riddle" – which provokes in me a paraphrase of Sir Winston Churchill. We might say of the Bible (or at least of some parts of it) what he said about Russia: "Here is a riddle wrapped in a mystery inside an enigma." But then, do I really want an easy Bible, as superficial as an infant's primer? What if scripture *were* like a nursery picture book, all soft pastel colours, gentle landscapes, pretty butterflies, and dainty fairies, charming but unreal? If its entire meaning could be gained at first glance, like a grade-one reader, how long would the Bible stay interesting? The very power of scripture, its magnificence, its fascination and vitality are a product of its ruthlessly honest picture of the pulsating confusion of real life.

THE BEST BOOK OF ALL

Oscar Wilde once wrote, "Truth is rarely pure, and never simple." [73] By "pure" he meant unshadowed by any ambiguity, and by "simple", lacking any contrary notion. How pleasant it would be if truth *were* straightforward, always "pure", invariably "simple"! Instead, it is mostly complex, with different shades of meaning, offering diverse applications, suggesting variable possibilities. The same contrasts are vividly displayed in scripture. Alert readers will therefore be wary of glib interpretations; they will turn away from any usage of the Bible that is too facile. They will see instead that scripture reflects life as it really is, and speaks to us as we really are – that is, we must all live like the man for whom

> there was much to be endured: the individual's isolation from other men, his inability to communicate, his sense that his fate is beyond his own control, that he is hopelessly subject to petty chance. [74]

To such people, living in such a world, the Bible speaks. There has never been a better mirror of heaven and earth than the Bible, nor of all the lightness and darkness of human life. In its pages we each see reflected our own face and also the face of God.

---

[73] The Importance of Being Earnest, Act One.

[74] Ian Campbell Ross. From his *Introduction* to Laurence Sterne's 18th-century work, the bawdy but deeply humane and ultimately moral, The Life and Opinions of Tristram Shandy, pg. xxiii.. The observation is true to life: each one of us is ultimately an island, isolated from our fellows, unable to communicate with full honesty, substantially governed by factors we can seldom even influence, let alone control – such as, where we were born, when, to whom, at what level of society, whether we escape harm on the freeway, whether thieves attack us, whether we escape serious illness, the economic conditions around us, what opportunities come our way, etc, etc. (You will find another quote from *Tristram Shandy* on the title page of Part One, above.)

A favourite way to study the Bible with me is, first, to take up one expression, and run through the different places where they are found. Take the *"I ams"* of John: *"I am the bread of life"*; *"I am the water of life"*; *"I am the way, the truth and the life"*; *"I am the resurrection"*; *"I am all, and in all."* God gives to His children a blank, and on it they can write whatever they most want, and He will fill the bill. And then the promises. A Scotchman found out thirty-one thousand distinct promises in the Word of God. There is not a despondent soul but God has a promise just to suit him. (D. L. Moody)

CHAPTER SEVEN

MYSTICS AND OTHERS

Tristram Shandy introduces one of the chapters of his fictional biography with the observation –

> What a jovial and a merry world would this be, may it please your worships, but for that inextricable labyrinth of debts, cares, woes, want, grief, discontent, melancholy, large jointures, impositions, and lies! [75]

In the midst of all this confusion, one Book speaks with clarion truth. Yet that truth comes to us in many guises, and we must learn to unravel them. So this chapter continues the last one, and brings us to the second Key to unlocking scripture –

(II) SCRIPTURE MUST BE EXPLAINED

What has been written and recognised as the canon of scripture must now be read and *historically* understood; that is, understood the same way it would have been by its first readers. We should look, not so much for the "literal" meaning of a passage, as for its "natural" sense. Which brings us to the question –

(A) WHAT DOES IT *MEAN*?

For example, what did the psalmist mean when he sang, *"The trees clap their hands"*? [76] The Bible contains scores of such expressions, whose true import has

---

[75] Ibid. Volume VI, Chapter XIV, opening lines.

little to do with their literal sense. So the first thing to look for when you open your Bible is an answer to the question: what was the author of this passage intending to say? No interpretation that is altogether disconnected from that original intention can ever be valid.

Whatever literary form the writers used – whether metaphor, allegory, symbolism, fiction, history, poetry, debate, and so on – they all set out to say *something*, and the most vital part of understanding scripture is to begin with discovering what that was. The text is falsified when the reader imposes upon it a meaning that is not natural.

Bible readers need to remember also that God had to speak in terms that were meaningful to the ancient Hebrews, just as he must when he speaks to us in our own time. Suppose he were to try to address us in the cultural idioms and expressions that will be prevalent, say, four thousand years from now – a date that is as far distant from us in the future as Abraham is in the past? Or suppose he had tried to talk to the patriarchs using the imagery of radio, television, atomic energy, rockets, space capsules, computers, and the like? Of course they lacked even the words to describe such things, let alone any ability to visualise them. So when God spoke to Abraham, he had to do so in terms that were meaningful, not to the 20th century *after* Christ, but to the 20th century *before* Christ.[77] Bible readers forget that gap at their own peril.

(B) SCIENCE FICTION

Have you ever watched a "science fiction" film that was made, say, in the 1920s? It pretends to be set in the distant future, yet unmistakably (and to our eyes quaintly) reflects the culture of 70 years ago. Likewise our grandchildren may watch, say, the *Star Wars* films of the 1970s and find them just as curious as we find those earlier films. Yet primitive films may still retain a powerful ethical message, which can be well understood, even though viewers chuckle at their archaic imagery and obsolete techniques. So too the Bible. It may in places employ antique symbols and concepts, yet beneath every passage there lies a message as modern as tomorrow.

---

[76] In its context (Is 55:12), the expression is a poetic way of saying that all of nature will be filled with gladness when the redeemed of the Lord enter their inheritance.

[77] I do not mean, of course, that his words have no meaning for us, only that we must first try to discover how the patriarch understood God's words before we can search out how they might speak to our generation.

The task of discovering what the words of the Bible meant to its writers, editors, and first readers is called *exegesis* = "to ascertain the sense" of something (from a Greek word, "to guide someone out of a complexity"). As much as possible, all *exegesis* should be done free from the influence of present pressures, needs, or prejudices – otherwise what will result will not be exegesis so much as *eisegesis* = "to introduce one's own (mistaken) ideas", a fault that has been often committed. Here for example are some of the peculiar ways in which the Bible has been interpreted over the centuries: [78]

(1) ALLEGORIES

(a) Some have depended upon allegorical [79] interpretations, where meanings have been found that have no connection with what the text actually says; thus denying any plain correspondence between words and their message. The Bible, of course, uses allegory as a literary device; [80] but I am referring here to the practice of "allegorising", where the reader looks for some hidden meaning that is not obvious from the passage itself. In this method a deeper significance is seen in the most commonplace things and events – a man walking down a street, the wind blowing, a cloudy sky, a hill, a river, and indeed, anything and everything that is mentioned or described in the Bible takes on a mystic sense. The chaos that must emerge from such a method, with every allegoriser discovering something different, is obvious.

(b) Others have taught that the *entire Bible* is an unbroken allegory (like John Bunyan's *Pilgrim's Progress*), and they assume that on every page the real message lies hidden beneath the surface. What each passage actually says is thought to have little or no value, except as camouflage to hide the truth from unworthy eyes. Although this was a popular method for many centuries, the dominance of the *grammatical-historical* [81] approach in our time has limited the use of allegory to those parts of the Bible that plainly require

---

[78] I have included here only examples of methods that at least begin with the pre-supposition that the Bible is the Word of God, inspired by the Holy Spirit. I have ignored liberal approaches that strip the Bible of all supernaturalism and reduce it to a wholly natural or man-made book.

[79] An allegory is usually defined as "an extended metaphor". For example, in *Luke 22:31;* the word "sift" is a *metaphor* meaning "put under critical examination"; while *John 6:35-38* is an *allegory* in which Jesus describes the spiritual nourishment he offers by likening himself to "bread".

[80] Another example: *John 10:1-16*, where Jesus likens himself to a shepherd.

[81] That is, the first meaning to search for is the sense the words had in their historical context, and in the way they were used in the contemporary society.

it – such as *Ezekiel 16:1-22*, where Israel is likened to a young and faithless bride.

(2) MYSTICISM

(a) Some have clothed scripture with a mystical aura, ascribing profound and secret meanings to every line of the text. Clement of Alexandria (circa 200), for example, saw five levels of meaning in every biblical statement –

- *Natural*: the surface meaning, that is, the one intended by the writer.
- *Theological*: the doctrine that arises out of the text.
- *Prophetic*: the manner in which the text reveals something about the future.
- *Philosophical*: the moral and ethical values taught by the text.
- *Mystical*: the meaning most sought for, which rests upon allegory and metaphor.

Clement's method allowed one to make the Bible say almost anything, to teach almost any dogma. There could hardly be a more unreliable way to approach the sacred text.

(b) Origen (185-254) argued similarly that just as we humans possess *body, soul, and spirit*, so every statement in the Bible possesses three meanings –

- *Natural* – such as we would ourselves look for, using the *grammatical-historical* method
- *Moral* – that is, the ethical, moral, and religious ideas embodied in the text
- *Spiritual* – by which he meant the secret, hidden, meaning of the text, which only those who are properly initiated into the faith can hope to discover.

(c) But such arbitrary methods, depending so heavily upon the bias of the interpreter, must and did lead to wild and speculative ideas. Why then were the Fathers so enamoured with allegorical and mystical interpretations? Part of the reason lay in the difficulties they saw in the Hebrew scriptures. They read things there that seemed to be either intellectually incredible, [82] or morally indefensible, [83] especially when those passages are read literally. The only way to make such stories acceptable was either to allegorise or spiritualise them. The *grammatical-historical* method of study that we now use has enabled us to arrive at far better solutions for such problems.

(3) SUBJECTIVISM

Many readers have treated the Bible as a wholly private domain, claiming that the Book has no meaning apart from the message it conveys to each searcher personally, through the whisper of the Holy Spirit. These people talk much about an "inner light", and the "ray of truth" that must come uniquely to each humble searcher. They look for an "illumination" to shine into the human heart and convey from the pages of scripture some private or secret revelation. The dangers are obvious. Where is there any objective test against which to measure these singular communiqués? What accountability do the recipients yield for their ideas?

(4) LETTER-PERFECT

A common folly has been the assumption that every word, even every letter, of scripture has equal value; nothing is superfluous, so that major doctrine can be built upon just one word. Even the great Martin Luther was not immune from this fault. In his magnificent passion for the supremacy of the Word of God he sometimes allowed his zeal to carry him too far –

> He who carefully reads and studies the Scriptures will consider nothing so trifling that it does not at least contribute to the improvement of his life and morals . . . Not one letter in Scripture is purposeless . . . If they believed them to be God's words, they would . . . consider even one tittle and letter greater than the whole

---

[82] Such as the Six Days of creation, the sun and the moon standing still, the story of Jonah, and various seeming discrepancies (e.g. did the Flood last 40 days or 150? [Ge 7:17,24]; etc.) I have compiled a longish list of such apparent contradictions and/or errors. Many ingenious explanations are offered for them by various commentaries, which simply confirms the fact that they do exist. Similar faults found in other writings, say, the Qur'an, or the Hindu scriptures, or other sacred writings such as the Hebrew Apocrypha, would be enough to brand them as erroneous, or at least as lacking literary perfection. Why should the Bible be treated differently? There is no need to do so when biblical infallibility is confined to its salvific function, and when a proper hermeneutic is adopted.

[83] Such as the genocide commanded by Moses and Joshua (11:14-15) against the Canaanites. See below (Part Five) for a further discussion of several of these problems.

world and would fear and tremble before them as before God himself . . . They would know that one article is all and that all is one. [84]

No doubt Luther's claim is sometimes true, [85] but those instances are rare. There are several reasons why care should be taken before putting too much weight on a single word or even phrase in scripture –

- Notice how repeated accounts of various incidents often differ strikingly from each other. [86] This suggests that in many places the exact wording of a story was not so important to the biblical writers as telling it in a way that was consistent with their purpose.

- The apostles quote the Hebrew scriptures freely in their writings, seldom taking any care to get the wording exactly right. They mostly prefer a paraphrase that conveys to the reader the Christian sense of the original passage. When it suits them too, they frequently quote from the Greek rather than the Hebrew version of the Old Testament.

- The thousands of variations among the ancient manuscripts that are available to us preclude any possibility of leaning heavily on every letter or word in the master-texts that we develop.

- Since most of us have to rely upon the scriptures in translation, and since the translations are all at least slightly different, we cannot place too much dependence upon a single word or phrase. That is, a teaching drawn from one word, phrase, or sentence in the Bible should be accepted as true only if it conforms to the larger testimony of scripture.

---

[84] What Luther Says, compiled by Ewald M. Plass; Vol. I-III; Concordia Pub. House, St Louis; 1959; selections #180, 188, 193, 4783.

[85] See, for example, the emphasis on a single mark, letter, or word, that is made in such places as Mt 5:18; 22:31-32; Mk 13:31; Jn 10:34-35 with Ps 82:6; Lu 16:17; Ga 3:16.

[86] For example, the variations in the several stories about David, both as youth and king; the marked differences between the histories of the same events in *Kings* and *Chronicles*; the discrepancies in the Pentateuch about the events of the Exodus and the 40 years Israel spent in the desert; the changes made from gospel to gospel in telling the story of Jesus; the very different manner in which Christ speaks in *John* contrasted with the way he is reported as speaking in the other three gospels; and so on.

(5) CIPHERS

Some have seen a hidden code, or secret cipher, in scripture, and by using it have given exotic and disconnected meanings to its words and phrases. Such people are prone to argue that the surface meaning of scripture is just a "dead letter", which must be unlocked by the Holy Spirit. The Bible to them is like a spurious message that a spy might write. The open message may read sensibly enough, but what lies on the surface is largely fiction; to find its real meaning one must employ the proper code. But to treat the Bible in that way is to reach for delusion; it creates wild suppositions that lack any responsible foundation.

(6) UNIFORMITY

Others have insisted that once the meaning of a word is found it must have exactly that same meaning no matter where it occurs in scripture. They also add the idea that the context of a word must always be carried along with it. Thus, for example, each verse containing the word "mighty" must be talking in some way about the ideas contained in every other verse that uses "mighty". By the end of the Bible each word is carrying such a massive load of dogma that all valid sense is crushed to death.

(7) SILENCE

Great weight has often been placed upon "the argument from silence". For example, many people have argued that since the NT letters do not mention the use in church of musical instruments, all such tools must be banned from Christian worship. The Puritans of the 17th and 18th centuries were prone to that sort of argument –

> Here were, in compliance with the temper of that dispensation, a great variety of musical instruments used, *"harps, psalteries, cymbals"* (1 Ch 25:1,6), and here was one that *"lifted up the horn"* (vs. 5), that is, used wind-music. <u>The bringing of such concerts of music into the worship of God now is what none pretend to.</u> But those who use such concerts for their own entertainment should feel themselves obliged to preserve them always free from anything that savours of immorality or profaneness, by this consideration, that time was when they were sacred; and then those were justly condemned who brought them into common use (Am 6:5), *"They invented to themselves instruments of music like David."* [87]

---

[87] The 18th century Puritan commentator, Matthew Henry, on 1 Chronicles 25:1-6. The emphasis is mine. Elsewhere in his commentaries Matthew Henry draws a similar disparaging contrast

Footnotes continued on the next page

There are still hundreds of churches that insist upon musically unaccompanied worship, and think it a mark of spiritual decadence to use an organ, or orchestra, or anything beyond perhaps a simple pitch pipe. Similarly, the silence of scripture has led various groups to develop other dogmas about Christian life and behaviour – such as forbidding the use of a wide array of modern inventions, or commanding a primitive life-style. Yet those same people inescapably employ things, both in public and private life, that find no mention in scripture. It is impossible not to do so. Thus they make themselves in the end slaves to mere caprice.

(8) TYPOLOGY

Some have put excessive weight upon biblical *typology*, out of which they develop irresponsible, and sometimes wild, interpretations. It is a mistake to read too much meaning into the details of the people, places, things, and events, found in the Bible. Notice the caution used by the writer of *Hebrews*, how he drew only broad lessons from the pattern of the Tabernacle (9:1-5). As St Augustine said in one place –

> To be sure, we must not suppose that all the events in the narrative are symbolical; but those which have no symbolism are interwoven in the story for the sake of those which have this further significance. For it is only the share of the plough that cuts through the earth; but the other parts of the plough are essential to make this operation possible. It is only the strings of the lyre, and of other similar musical instruments, that are designed to produce the music; but to effect the result the other components are included in the framework of the instruments. These parts are not struck by the player, but the parts which resonate when struck are connected with them. Similarly, in the prophetic history (of Israel) some things are recorded which have no prophetic significance in themselves; but they are there for the significant events to be attached to them, moored to them, as we might say. [88]

Despite that piece of wisdom, the same Augustine, like many of the Church Fathers, indulged in some highly fanciful typology based on such items as the names of Noah's three sons, or Esau and Jacob, and other Old Testament

---

between the musical worship-style of the temple and the non-musical style of the 17th & 18th century evangelical churches.

[88] The City of God; Book XVI, Chapter Two; tr. by Henry Bettenson; ed. David Knowles; Penguin Books, 1972; pg. 653.

incidents.[89] Their unhappy example has been followed by many modern teachers.

(C) A BETTER WAY

Careful Bible students will avoid all those extravagant ways, and others like them, of studying scripture. Instead, we should seek for a method that successfully fulfils certain obligations –

(1) We must maintain the unchanging stance of evangelical Christianity across the centuries on the identity of scripture as the sure Word of God –

(a) While the New Testament does not explicitly refer to the inerrancy of scripture, the doctrine nonetheless rests securely upon the foundation of statements like the following: *scripture cannot be invalidated* (Jn 10:35); *scripture must be fulfilled* (Lu 24:44; Ac 1:16); *no iota of the Law will pass away* (Mt 5:18); and the apostles, when citing the Old Testament, use the expression *"it is written"* as an unanswerable argument (Mt 4:4; Ac 15:15; Ro 1:17; 1 Pe 2:6).[90]

(b) The Church Fathers held to the same view –

- *Clement of Rome –*

You should examine the sacred scriptures: they speak with the true voice of the Holy Spirit, and you will find nothing in them that is contrary to righteousness, nor anything that is false. *(To the Corinthians I.45)*

- *Justin Martyr –*

Do you suppose that you can throw doubt upon a passage of scripture, so that I will have to admit that scripture contradicts itself? You are mistaken! I would never dare to say nor even to think such a thing! Even if you could produce a scripture and prove that another passage contradicts it, still I would remain convinced that no scripture is truly contrary to another. Rather, I will confess only that I do not yet know how to reconcile the apparent error, and I will try to persuade others to be of the same opinion as myself. *(Dialogue With Trypho 65)*

---

[89] Ibid., and Chapter 41; plus other places.

[90] Drawn from the Jerome Biblical Commentary, 66.77. The same book (66.78) states that the "first mention in ecclesiastical documents of what is now called the inerrancy of Scripture was made in 1351, in the epistle of Clement VI to the Catholicon of the Armenians . . . "

- **_Irenaeus_** –

I know that we cannot explain all the difficult things in scripture that puzzle investigators. But that is no reason to turn away and search for some god other than the One who truly exists. Unless you want to become guilty of a serious fault, you should leave unanswerable questions with God, who created us. In the meantime, rest assured that the scriptures are indeed perfect. They were spoken by the Word of God himself, and by the Holy Spirit. *(Against Heresies II.28.2)*

        (2)   We need to understand what is reasonably meant by *"inerrancy"* –

- does it refer to the *exclusion of all <u>mistakes</u>*? Or
- does it refer to the *exclusion of any <u>deception</u>*?

If the primary, and in the end the only, purpose of scripture is to show us the way to obtain salvation and to glorify God for ever, then surely *inerrancy* means only that scripture is completely free from any *deception* in its teaching on how to fulfil that purpose. That view leads one to search primarily for the salvific *intention* of each passage of scripture. It leads to a focus on *faith*. By contrast, the other view leads one to focus on the minutae of *fact*, without any hope of ever being able to reconcile with any certainty the many ambiguities, contradictions, and difficulties that lie in the biblical text as we now have it.

So if you ask me, "Do you believe in the inerrancy of scripture?" I will answer "Yes!" – so long as you mean a Bible that contains no falsehood in anything it actually requires me to believe or to obey. But if you mean a book that is free from any mistake of any sort, I must say "No!" – for, no matter what solutions can be offered for them, our present Bibles do contain many textual problems. I mean such things as: missing words; contradictory statements; diverse accounts of various events; inaccuracies in geography, history, astronomy; thousands of variations in the extant manuscripts; and the like.

The point is, the explanations offered by scholars for those discrepancies may or may not be right, there is no way for us to tell, so the problems still remain. We can deal only with the Bible we have, which, whether or not it pleases us, continues to present many difficulties. Nonetheless, apparent errors and all, this is plainly the Bible God wants us to have, and in its salvific power it comes to us absolutely as the Spirit-breathed Word of God.

        (3)   So we should look for a hermeneutic that embraces a sober, sensible, reliable, consistent, and godly approach to the sacred text, one that will bring us surely to the infallible truth that breathes out of every page of these divinely given scriptures. If the open Book successfully brings us to salvation and to the inheritance appointed for us in the heavenlies in Christ, then little else matters. It has done what God intended. We shall then praise God for

ever for the words of life that we met in scripture, and that drew us to Christ and to eternal glory!

(III) SCRIPTURE MUST BE EXPOUNDED

Once the *meaning* of a passage is understood, then its *message* must be grasped: that is, an attempt must be made to determine the doctrines and principles that are being taught, and that have universal significance. For example, is the 23rd *Psalm* a treatise on ancient shepherding practices? Or does it rather teach us something about the unchanging character of God, which we should then express in terms that are more meaningful to our present society? Think also about the food laws imposed on Israel by Moses. Are they mandated for us too? Hardly, for if (as some Christians think) they are still required, then so are all the other rules of Moses, such as

- the laws against wearing mixed-fibre garments and cooking in metal pots
- the regulations dealing with the sale of one's daughter as a concubine, beating one's slave, tithes, jubilees, and many others.

Some try to overcome this problem by arguing that the food laws have a dietary and health value, and therefore should be observed by Christians. Perhaps they do, but no such secondary value can be seen in many of the other laws, so it is hardly a valid hermeneutic to isolate just that one group of rules and try to make them universally applicable. Or, to put it differently, if it is right to make one group of the Mosaic statutes compulsory for the church, then they must all be just as forceful. If Christians are required to keep any of them, then they must be equally required to keep all of them!

Do the ancient statutes have no meaning then for today? Of course they do! The *real* importance of those laws is expressed many times in scripture: they show that Israel was to be a "holy" people (basically, "different"), so that even their houses and their dinner tables had to be spotless and distinct from those of their pagan neighbours. Following Israel's example, we too are to be holy and separate; but we achieve that state through Christ, not by eating or refraining from certain foods. The same kind of eternal principles should be sought in the other laws of Moses. The explicit regulations decreed by the great law-giver will seldom be applicable to us; but the unchanging spiritual and moral principles embodied in those laws must always be obeyed. [91]

(IV) SCRIPTURE MUST BE REVEALED

The word now *written* and *known* must then be **revealed** – that is, our "inner eyes" must be opened to perceive the spiritual reality that lies beyond the written word (Ep 1:15-19; Cl 1:9). Here is a task that the Holy Spirit alone can accomplish, in association with prayerful meditation in the Word of God. But that is the theme of my next chapter.

(V) SCRIPTURE MUST BE APPLIED

We come now to the final stage in this fivefold process, which has taken us along an adventurous path. I have so far imagined you doing these four things –

- the Bible, having been written, gathered into its canon of 66 books, and recognised as the Word of God by the church, is also welcomed by you as sacred scripture

- so you pick up the Book and read it, trying to discover what purpose guided each inspired writer

- then you meditate in the Word of God, comparing scripture with scripture, seeking to grasp the great doctrines and principles it teaches

- then you pray over it, striving for a revelation of what the Holy Spirit wants to say to you through the pages of scripture.

Now comes the end purpose of all this endeavour: *to apply the scriptures to the particular time, place, and circumstance in which you find yourself.* In other words, as you read you should be asking yourself: what is this passage saying to me right now, in my personal need; what promise does it convey to me; what command does it lay upon me; what challenge does it present to me; how does the Holy Spirit want my life to be influenced today by the Word that has come to

---

[91] Some of the Mosaic prescriptions, of course, are repeated in the New testament – albeit in a different form – and are therefore mandatory for Christians. But then we keep them, not because Moses wrote them, but because they are now part of "the law of Christ".

me from God? Why should you do this? Simply because anyone who hopes to be strong in Christ, vigorous in faith, and powerful in spirit, must accept that there is no substitute for such personal work in scripture. But we are not obliged to labour alone. Raising and answering questions like those above is also the special (though not exclusive) task of preaching, and it places high importance upon the pastor's function as a *teacher*. Those who hold such a view of scripture (and pentecostals and evangelicals are in general among them), differ from both the

- Roman Catholic church (where the priest's role is primarily liturgical and sacramental), and from much of
- modern Protestantism (where the pastor's role has become one of counsellor and administrator).

But that too is another subject, which, much as I would like to explore it here, must wait for another place. In the meantime: only when the five steps given above have been completed does scripture become for the person who reads and believes it the glorious power of God for full salvation.

> Now, I am no prophet nor the son of a prophet, but one thing I can predict: That every one of our new converts who goes to studying his Bible, and loves this book above every other book, is sure to hold out. The world will have no charm for him; he will get the world under his feet, because in this book he will find something better than the world can give him. (D. L. Moody)

CHAPTER EIGHT

PRAYING THE BIBLE

Everywhere Christians can be found who are weak when they should be strong, defeated when they should be victorious, fruitless when they should be producing a harvest for Christ. Why? Mostly because they are deficient in either *scripture* or *prayer* or more commonly, both. One way to overcome this deficiency is to merge both of those spiritual exercises – that is, to **pray through your Bible**. Those who effectively combine the Bible and prayer discover a marvellous source of spiritual power.

(I) WHY THIS IS EFFECTIVE

(A) YOUR PRAYER WILL EXPRESS THE WILL OF GOD

Christ taught that the worst enemy of prayer is *"doubt"*. You can *"move mountains"* if you learn to pray without doubt! (Mk 11:22-24) The Greek word translated *"doubt"* in *Mark 11:23* literally means *"to be divided in your own mind"* – so it portrays the kind of person described in *James 1:6-8*, unstable, double-minded, unable to receive anything from God. Why is doubt so ruinous? Because to doubt God, or the promise of God, is to come perilously close to calling God a liar (compare 1 Jn 5:9-10). Can you then be surprised to learn that doubt displeases him? A much better attitude was expressed by the apostle –

> *When God wanted to demonstrate beyond doubt to the heirs of his promise how utterly trustworthy his purpose is, he guaranteed it by an oath. So then through two things that cannot be changed – his promise and his oath – two things in which God cannot possibly lie, we who flee to him for safety are strongly encouraged to grasp firmly the hope that stands before us.* (He 6:17-18)

But how can we overcome the debilitating effects of doubt? The best way is to pray with an unwavering certainty that what you are asking is the will of God –

> *We have this boldness in Christ: if we ask anything according to his will, he will hear us!* (1 Jn 5:14)

But how can you be sure that what you are asking is the will of God? That is easy! Just build your prayer on scripture. When you take hold of a passage of the Bible and address it back to God in prayer, you are actually returning to him his own will. So if your prayer is shaped by scripture, you can be sure that God has heard you and that he has already granted your request (1 Jn 5:15). Here is the basic difference between *"hope"* and *"faith"*, which John expressed in the exciting phrase, *"we know that we (already) have."* If you are not sure about God being willing to give you what you ask, then you can only pray in *"hope"*, waiting to see whether or not your request will be granted. But if you ***know***, even before you ask, that your request will be granted, then you can pray with unhesitating confidence. Your gratitude and joy rises, as if you were someone who already possesses the boon he desired. With perfect assurance you are now but waiting for the *materialisation* of that boon. Real faith leaves no room for doubt; it is characterised by the happiness of ownership, by the contentment of possession –

> *Faith tells you that you already have what you hoped for; it makes you the possessor of things you have not yet seen* (He 11:1).

(B) YOUR FAITH WILL BE ENERGISED

See *Galatians 3:2-5*, where Paul describes two basic things we all need – indeed, in one way or another, these two benefits encompass everything you could truly want: *"the supply of the Spirit, and the working of miracles."* (vs. 5) You could hardly imagine any genuine need, or any promise of God, that is not comprehended in those two gracious gifts! Both blessings, says Paul, can be obtained in only one way: by **faith**. No good work of yours, no law-keeping, no personal effort, can ever put God in debt to you to give you his Spirit or to work a miracle for you. Faith alone is the key to those heavenly benefits. But what better source of faith could there be than scripture mingled with prayer? Paul twice declares this in the striking phrase, *"hearing with faith"* (vs. 2,5); that is, *"faith"* is a product of hearing the promises of God mixed with believing those promises. How can we reach that admirable goal? Prayer is the catalyst that enables this mixing to occur. Prayer turns dull into lively hearing; prayer energises within us the promises of God, which enables us to believe them vigorously. Unless the reading of scripture is intermingled with prayer it is unlikely that the reader will be able to discern the presence of God in the Word. Prayer turns the printed page into *"the lively oracles of God"*. Prayer opens your mind to the Holy Spirit, so that he can implant the Word deep within your spirit (compare Ja 1:23). Prayer helps us to yield to the commands of scripture. Prayer enlarges our spiritual capacity and keeps us sensitive to the voice of Christ speaking in scripture . . . and so on.

(C) YOU WILL GAIN A NEW SPIRITUAL AUTHORITY

In the original creation, God gave men and women the right to exercise dominion and authority (Ge 1:26-28). That authority was lost through the Fall, but it has now been restored to us as God's new creation in Christ (2 Co 5:17; Lu 10:19). Can we now use this restored authority to do whatever we like whenever we like? Hardly! We actually have authority only to call into existence whatever God himself has spoken to us. That is, spiritual authority must be channelled through the Word of God, and cannot be exercised outside of the parameters formed by that Word. God himself functions by the same principle – see *Hebrews 1:3*, and note the unusual construction in the original text. The apostle did not say (as we might have expected) that *"God sustains all things by the power of his Word"*, but rather, *"He sustains all things by the Word of his power."* On the one hand you have the power of God, limitless in its awful strength; but on the other you have the Word of God, within which that power is confined. Without the Word you have no vehicle for the power; the power of God is conveyed to us through the Word of God. Those who understand spiritual authority, and who use it rightly, cannot fail to accomplish two things: *(1)* they do the will of God; and *(2)* they call into reality the promises of God. Scripture, when mingled with earnest prayer, is the prime source of knowledge about what God wants us to do for him, and what he is willing to do for us. Furthermore, the Word revealed through prayer prevents the believer from trying to use spiritual authority to do what God has not commanded, or to claim what God has not promised. So spiritual authority, that is, authority to do the will of God and to call into reality the promise of God, can be restored to us only insofar as we are meshed with the Word of God. A major key, then, to dominion over the kingdom of darkness and to releasing the power of the kingdom of God, is to pray over the Bible, and through it, and around it, and by prayer to enmesh the Word with your spirit and your spirit with the Word.

(D) YOU WILL HOLD THE SWORD OF THE SPIRIT

The praying of many Christians lacks a cutting edge because it is separated from scripture. Notice how Paul couples the Word and prayer in *Ephesians 6:17,18* – as though he were saying that the scriptures will be the Sword of the Holy Spirit in your hand, routing the forces of Satan, only when they are drawn out of the scabbard of prayer. It is prayer, then, that causes the promises of God to become a mighty weapon, both of offence and defence, enabling you to overthrow the devil and all his works, and to build the kingdom of God. The Lord God is sovereign of course, and can make his Word come alive to anyone whenever he pleases, whether or not they have approached the Word with prayer; but that does not usually happen. Ordinarily, if the Bible is separated from prayer it will remain a dull and difficult book, and its pages will convey no life to the reader.

(E) YOU WILL GAIN A REVELATION OF THE WORD

Can you conceive a more useful purpose for prayer than to help unpack the hidden treasures of scripture. This is surely one of the major purposes of all prayer (Ep 1:15-19). Why? Because the promises remain fallow until we gain an inner revelation of them, a vision of the reality the promise represents (2 Kg 6:15-17).

(II) HOW CAN YOU PRAY THROUGH YOUR BIBLE?

No doubt many answers could be ghven to that question, but here are a few suggestions –

(A) PRAISE GOD FOR PROMISED BLESSINGS

There are many passages in the Bible that set before us the love of God and the countless benefits he wants to bestow on us. Work your way through those passages, line by line, pausing at each new promise to thank God with all your heart. For example, you could spend a delightful half-hour with the twenty-third Psalm, *"The Lord is my Shepherd"*. It contains twenty-three affirmations about the care of Christ for his sheep. Many people complain that they run out of things to say after only a few minutes in prayer. But suppose you were to take hold of those twenty-three affirmations, and one by one meditate on them, write them down, apply them to your own life, and joyfully praise God for them? You would find that an *hour* would hardly be long enough! Take only the opening phrase, *"The Lord is my Shepherd."* You could thank God that he chooses the role of Shepherd and not of tyrant; ask him to help you to be a true sheep, humble, obedient, dependent upon the Shepherd; rejoice in the certainty of his tender, loving care; ask for a clearer vision of Christ as Shepherd; put yourself in relationship to God as a sheep to a shepherd, following him closely, content to go wherever he leads; and so on.

(B) USE THE BIBLE TO EXPRESS EMOTION

A kind of false piety has developed in the church that prevents us from being truly honest with God. People may be angry with God, hurt and frustrated by what they think he has done (or not done), but they pretend that they are still pleased with him. They put on a facade of worship and hide their tears. By contrast, the scriptures are ruthlessly honest. When the psalmist was furious at heaven, he said so! Indeed, perhaps as many as half the psalms express complaint and bewilderment in place of trust and praise. The same is true of the prophets. They contain many passages of aching lament against God. Some examples can be found in the bitter reproaches in *Psalm 74:1-11; 79:1-7; Je 15:17-18;* or the bleak despair in *Psalm 88; 44:17-26; Lamentations 5:20-22;* etc. There are passages in the Bible that display every possible human emotion: ecstasy, sorrow, trust, pain, anger, joy, peace, anxiety, love, loneliness, and so on. If you are timid about expressing any of those emotions in your own words, turn to your Bible and use the words of scripture. The Father will not object if you turn back to him in prayer the emotion-drenched sayings of the Spirit-wrought scriptures!

(C) PERSONALISE THE PRAYERS OF THE BIBLE

Prayers covering many different situations and needs are scattered through the Bible. You can hardly go wrong if you re-shape those prayers and make them your own. You can expect the same kind of answers from heaven as the original worshippers received. The *Psalms* are a particularly good source of such prayers. Of a different character are the prayers of the apostles in the New Testament. They are not only prayers but also vehicles of incredible revelation about what God wants to do for you in Christ. Suppose, for example, you were to turn to *Colossians 1:9-12*, and not merely read it, but spend an hour praying over every phrase – praying until each mighty affirmation exploded into life within your spirit. You would be powerfully renewed! You might even be transformed, never again to be what you once were! You could thank God for the things that are declared by Paul, plead for deeper understanding of what is revealed, rejoice in what has already been fulfilled in your life, cry out for a greater measure of fulfilment; and so on.

(D) PERSONALISE THE STATEMENTS OF THE BIBLE

Many passages lend themselves to personalisation – that is, read your name into them. For example, the great *"Love"* chapter (1 Co 13). Try praying your way through *verses 6-8,* replacing *"love"* with your own name. You will soon be constrained to stop, and to repent, and to cry out to God to help you more nearly reflect that lovely ideal! Here are two other passages (among scores that could be suggested) that you could personalise: *Jeremiah 17:5-8,* and *Hebrews 13:5-6.* You will be amazed (when you insert your own name into them) how the impact of such scriptures is enhanced. Speak them before God in prayer, both thanking him for what is already true in your experience, and beseeching him to make true what isn't!

(E) PRAY FOR AN INNER REVELATION OF SCRIPTURE

Without this, as we have seen, the Word remains lifeless. But remember that while revelation sometimes comes easily, at other times the scriptures yield their riches only to earnest effort. For example, we are told that on one occasion Daniel received a revelation from God. Although the word was true, Daniel came to an understanding of the vision only after he exerted fierce effort –

> *A revelation came to Daniel ... The word was true, yet only after a great struggle during the course of the vision did he come to understand it.* (Da 10:1)

Daniel himself explained his experience this way –

> *"I Daniel mourned for three weeks ... (after which) I looked up and saw a man wearing a linen robe with a belt around his waist made of the finest gold. His body glowed like a precious gem, his face flashed like lightning, his eyes were like burning torches, his arms and legs shone like polished bronze, and when he spoke his voice was like the roar of an immense crowd. I Daniel was the only one who saw the vision. None of my companions saw it, although they began to shake violently, and then they ran away and hid themselves. So I was left there alone, watching this marvellous vision. All my strength drained away, I became pale as death, not even my closest friend would have recognised me; I was so weak I could hardly stand. Then the angel spoke, and when I heard his voice I fell insensible to the ground, and lay there with my face in the dust. But then a hand*

touched me and raised me, still trembling, onto my hands and knees!" (Da 10:1-10)

That passage follows a typical biblical literary pattern. A short statement is made (about Daniel's revelation and his struggle to understand it), and then the statement is repeated and explained in greater detail (how he had to weep and pray for three weeks before the angel began to clarify the vision). Did you notice that Daniel alone saw the vision? The others knew that something was happening; but they could neither grasp what it was nor what it meant. They were unwilling to search it out in fervent prayer. So while Daniel was meeting angels they ran away and hid! Did you notice also that Daniel never doubted that he had received a *"true word"* from God; nonetheless, at first it made no sense to him? There is a parable here of many Christians. They hold the true Word of God in their hands, but they do not yet grasp its full meaning. Nor will they ever grasp it, unless they are prepared to give time to praying over, and in, and through, the scriptures, crying out to God to *"open their spiritual eyes, and to give them illumination and revelation in his Word!"* (Ep 1:17-18)

CONCLUSION

No doubt the Holy Spirit can show you other, and perhaps better, ways to mingle scripture and prayer. But I will close this chapter by putting before you this spiritual law (which expresses the principle involved in praying through the Bible) –

NEVER COME TO THE WORD WITHOUT PRAYER
- for that will leave the scripture dull.

NEVER COME TO PRAYER WITHOUT THE WORD
- for that will take prayer into presumption.

Here then is a key to a dynamic, balanced, and fruitful Christian life: let prayer keep the promise of God alive in your heart; and let the promise of God determine the boundaries of your prayers.

PART THREE

SIX DIMENSIONS

Make up your mind that you will put some time **every day** in the study of the Word of God. That is an easy resolution to make, and not a very difficult one to keep if the one who makes it is in earnest. It is one of the most fruitful resolutions that any Christian ever made. The forming of that resolution and the holding faithfully to it, has been the turning point in many a life. Many a life that has been barren and unsatisfactory has become rich and useful through the introduction into it of regular, persevering, daily study of the Bible. (R. A. Torrey)

CHAPTER NINE

"COMB" THE BIBLE

Because of ever-thinning silvery locks, combs have a diminishing importance in my personal grooming. But the value of using a "comb" in Bible study has never been greater. This "comb" however is not made of plastic. It is an acronym, "C-O-M-B,"[92] a short-hand way of reminding people to search scripture carefully before jumping to some ill-informed conclusion about what it means. Many have fallen into that hasty error, to their own lasting hurt. The acronym spelled out says –

Context.............. how does this passage fit into the picture of: the whole Bible; the Testament; the Book; the Chapter?

Other .... how does this passage relate to or compare with other scriptures?

Meaning.............. what meaning must be given to the words, ideas, doctrines, commands, promises, contained in this passage?

Background......... what is the historical and cultural background to this passage, and how does that affect its meaning?

The *comb* is a useful device for searching out scripture; but I plan to structure our present study around a different framework. I suggest that within scripture there are *six fascinating dimensions* – [93]

---

[92] I have taken this acronym from my brother Barry's book, <u>The Secret is Out</u>, where it is more fully explained.

[93] Note that two of these six themes will be touched on only briefly in this book, for they properly belong in separate studies. They are: *the formation of the canon;* and *the inspiration of the Bible.*

(1) ***Anthropological*** – everything that can be discovered about the biblical authors, editors, and characters.

(2) ***Historical*** – everything to do with the political, social, cultural, national and international background of the biblical books and events.

(3) ***Literary*** – the literary structure and style of the various books; figures of speech; word usage; and the like

(4) ***Religious*** – the different characteristics of the religious life and experience of Israel and her neighbours during the various stages of biblical history.

(5) ***Divine*** – the nature of scripture as a book "in-breathed" by the Holy Spirit; or, as some would have it, "out-breathed".

(6) ***Practical*** – the formation of the canon of scripture; plus the manner in which the precepts and principles of scripture can best be outworked in daily life in our time.

(I) ANTHROPOLOGICAL

(A) DEFINITION

The word means "the study of mankind", and in the context of this book deals with the human dimension of scripture. It requires us to ask such questions as these –

- who was the author, and when and where did he or she live? [94]
- what place did the author occupy in society?
- what was the author trying to say, and why?
- what experiences did the author have, and how did he or she express the meaning or value of those experiences?
- what example did the author set, and is it one that modern readers should wish to follow?

---

[94] No female writers of scripture are known, but it is at least conceivable that a woman's hand may lie behind some parts of the Bible.

- what information can be discovered about the people who feature in each biblical story or event; what lessons can we learn from them; what part did they play in the unfolding plan of salvation?

(B) ANONYMOUS

Some of the biblical books, of course, are anonymous, so those questions may have only a partial answer. In other cases, scholars are unsure who was the original writer. For example, the book of *Job* – was the hero the author, or one of his friends, or some later poet or editor of genius? Likewise *Ecclesiastes* – was the author Solomon, or another? In fact, there are several books in both Testaments whose authorship is doubtful. Such issues are usually discussed in depth in the various commentaries and study Bibles, and every Bible reader should make as much use of those tools as possible.

(II) HISTORICAL

(A) ESSENTIAL BACKGROUND

(1) Many errors arise because people ignore the historical setting of a passage of scripture. The rule is this: before any text can be applied to modern life the reader must ask such questions as

- what did the passage mean to its original author and its first readers?
- what was its historical, political, social, and cultural setting?
- what is the biblical context of the passage?
- what religious or moral significance did it have when it was written?

(2) For example, consider *The Song of Solomon*, which in its original composition seems to have been a dramatic oratorio, presented by a choir, soloists, and musicians. It celebrated courtship and marriage, and it was presumably written for public performance

- only later was it seen to have spiritual significance, and to contain lessons that could be applied to Israel, and then to the church
- we should not ignore that spiritual message, but neither should we forget that *primarily* the *Song* is a collection of love poems, and that any allegorical or symbolic lessons drawn from it are *secondary*

- those who do forget the first intention of the book (to celebrate human love) usually end up drawing fanciful, sometimes crude, and often unwarranted spiritual images from it.

(B) THE AUTHOR'S INTENTION

(1) The original intention of the writer is the only valid starting point for interpretation, and it must remain the check-point of all other levels of understanding

- this method of looking at scripture, once again, is what we call the *grammatical-historical* rule; that is, the Bible must be read in a way that gives to its words their ordinary *grammatical* meaning, as understood within their own *historical* context.

(2) There is only one way to read the Bible properly, and that is the way you would read any other book – not looking for hidden meanings, but taking words at their face value. The *grammatical-historical* rule is not a piece of exotic protocol. It simply describes the way any intelligent reader, whether consciously or not, should approach any piece of literature, or indeed, any communication from another person. If people did not follow this rule in daily conversation, or in reading a newspaper or a letter, communication would become impossible

- the main proviso, when dealing with scripture (as with any piece of ancient writing), is that attention must be given to the changes that the centuries have wrought in the way people look at things and in the way they use words

- the second proviso is that because the Bible is the Word of God we are looking, not just for factual information, but for divine revelation; nonetheless, whatever heavenly truth we discover in scripture must begin with and be based upon an ordinary and honest reading of the text.

(C) READING SENSIBLY

(1) People have brought great harm upon themselves by refusing to read the Bible in a sensible and practical manner, and especially by giving it an unwarranted and peculiar mystical quality. G. K. Chesterton, in one of his *Father Brown* detective stories gives an illustration of this. Father Brown is explaining how the police had failed to solve a crime simply because too much had been read into a dog's behaviour. Witnesses had given the animal a kind of supernatural prescience, which misled their enquiries, when actually it had done nothing more than follow its natural instincts. Father Brown commented –

> (Here is) something I've noticed more and more in the modern world, appearing in all sorts of newspaper rumours and conversational catchwords; something that's arbitrary without being authoritative. People readily swallow the untested claims of this, that, or the other. It's drowning all your old rationalism and scepticism, it's coming in like a sea; and the name of it is superstition. . . . It's the first effect of not believing in God that you lose your common sense and can't see things as they are. [95] Anything that anybody talks about, and says there's a good deal in it, extends itself indefinitely like a vista in a nightmare. And a dog is an omen, and a cat is a human, and a pig is a mascot, and a beetle is a scarab, calling up all the menagerie of polytheism from Egypt and old India; dog Anubis and green-eyed Paskt and all the holy howling Bulls of Bashan; reeling back to bestial gods of the beginning, escaping into elephants and snakes and crocodiles; and all because you are frightened of four words: *"He was made Man."* [96]

(2) The sensible way to read the Bible is to take off the spectacles of superstition, and treat its words in the most ordinary way possible. We should demystify both the Book and the world in which we live. Readers may eventually discover exalted heights and profound depths in scripture; but the anchor that prevents us from drifting onto the rending shoals of error is to *begin* with a plain and simple reading. Only after the reader has established the *grammatical-historical* sense of each passage should a search begin for possible further insight. [97]

(D) CONSIDER THE CONTEXT

(1) Merely giving to words their obvious sense will not always capture the speaker's intention. Words sometimes do not mean what they say. For example, take the statement, "The wind blows warm." It has a simple literal meaning. But suppose the speaker is using the statement as a metaphor of

---

[95] I would add that too much of the *wrong kind* of belief in God has just the same effect.

[96] The Oracle of God, second-last paragraph. The last phrase, of course, refers to Jesus. Father Brown is saying that Christ, when he became incarnate, stripped the superstitious mystery out of life, and sanctified the ordinary. It is a concept that still evades many Christians, who are prone to look for omens, mysteries, signs, and magic where no such thing exists.

[97] Bible dictionaries, encyclopedias, and commentaries can help here, and Bible-lovers ought to make as much use of such tools as circumstances allow. See also *Chapter Thirteen* below, "Many Treasures", for guidance in building a library.

rising anger? Then it will have nothing to do with warm winds! Or perhaps it is the password of the day in a war zone, or a coded saying, a crossword puzzle clue, an anagram, or part of some other puzzle. In all those cases the intended meaning or use of the sentence has no connection with its literal sense. Many biblical sayings are like that. You have to know something about the setting in which they are found before you can be sure what they actually mean.

(2) So an important part of reading the Bible sensibly is to take account of all dimensions of the passage you are reading – that is, give full weight both to the *grammatical* sense and *historical* setting of the text. It is perilous to pluck a passage out of context, and those who do so usually give to scripture a meaning that never entered the head of either its divine or human authors! Here are some examples –

Joan felt that the words of *2 Kings 9:20* (*"he drives furiously"*) were given to her by God as a promise that he would pay for a car she badly needed. She loved to visit people who were ill, lonely, or troubled, but was obliged to travel by public transport, which was time-consuming and inconvenient. She had prayed fervently for a car, and was now sure that she had received from God permission to go ahead and buy one, though she had no money. Her pastor was not impressed. Reluctantly, she yielded to his warning against purchasing (merely on the strength of Jehu's example) a vehicle she couldn't afford. Some weeks later she came to him saying that a cloud had been lifted from her mind, and she apologised for behaving so unwisely. Soon after, someone *gave* her a vehicle! As a consequence of that generous act by a fellow-Christian, her husband yielded his own life to Christ. How different the result would have been if she had foolishly followed her first plan and so plunged the family into debt!

Andrew was employed as an assistant pastor. One day he approached his superior and said God had told him to take over the church. His justification? The Lord (he said) had drawn his attention to *Deuteronomy 28:13*, *"You will be the head, not the tail!"* So he told the senior pastor to obey God, to resign, and to let him become the new "head" of the church. The result? Andrew was at once sacked! He tried to start another church, which failed, and his threats that God would vindicate him and punish the senior pastor proved vain. His absurd use of scripture achieved nothing except to bring ruin upon himself and his family.

Thomas asked his pastor to marry him to a young lady who was a committed Christian. He said God had shown them they were to wed, by "giving" them *1 Timothy 5:14* (which says that young women should marry and bear children). The pastor argued against such a silly use of Paul's counsel, and also suggested that the couple were unsuited to each other. They insisted that God had spoken to them, and when the pastor refused to conduct the wedding they went off huffily to another church. There they were married; but before a year was gone they had parted from each other in bitterness and violence.

Harry abandoned his wife and five children and became a full time evangelist. When his actions were questioned, he piously quoted the words of Jesus, *"If you come to me, you cannot be my disciple unless you <u>hate</u> your father, mother, spouse, children, brothers, sisters, and yes, even your own life"* (Lu 14:26). He refused to listen to reason, insisting that he had to obey scripture, and went on his way. His unoffending family suffered great misery, and all for nothing, because his ministry proved unsuccessful. His credibility was destroyed, and the family remained divided. Was he obeying scripture? Of course not. He used the words of Jesus in a way that was never intended by the Master. [98]

(3) Those people, like many others, fell into a common fault: the error of plucking Bible passages out of their context and applying them to situations with which, at best, they have only a tenuous connection. But the Bible is not just a string of texts, laced together haphazardly, which people can rearrange however they please. It is not a kind of lucky dip into which someone can plunge a hand and come up with a piece of infallible wisdom. It is not a box of goodies from which believers can pick whatever they feel like at the moment. It is not a Christian equivalent to the Sibylline oracles and entrails so loved by the ancient Greeks and Romans. On the contrary, responsible readers will accept that no passage is properly understood or used until it is fitted into the following framework:

- *first*, the chapter in which it is found;
- *then*, the place of that chapter within the book;
- *then*, the place of that book in the Bible.

Do I mean that God may *never* speak to you through a text that has no specific connection with your problem? Hardly! Can anyone tell God what he may or may not do? In fact, many readers will be able to remember occasions when they discovered a "word" from the Lord in a disconnected passage of scripture. But be careful! A sound hermeneutic cannot prevent God from speaking to his people in any way he pleases, but it can help us to avoid mistaking something else for the voice of God.

(E) A NARRATIVE

(1) The Bible is a narrative, telling the story of salvation, and none of its parts has any divine meaning outside of that story. The *whole* story

---

[98] The incidents described above are genuine, but I have changed the names of the people and some of the details. They prove all too clearly the truth of the adage: ***"A text out of context is a pretext!"***

must be considered before any true meaning (one that does not violate the author's intention) can be given to any one segment. Further, within the entire narrative one part often complements or modifies another. Here are some examples (which could be multiplied many times) of the manner in which one scripture may change the sense of another. The full truth about a matter is known only when *all* the relevant scriptures are compared with each other. As the following examples show, an argument based upon just one passage may sometimes be valid, but frequently it will lead to error –

(a)   The swift and the strong.

Here is an affirmation from *Proverbs* –

> *"Do you see highly skilled people, who work hard? They will be promoted to the highest levels; they will not be obliged to toil among common labourers."* (22:29)

But if that statement is true, then what shall we do with this one?

> *"The swift do not always win the race, nor is the battle always won by the strong. The wise may lack bread, the clever may remain poor, and favour is not always shown to the skilful, for time and chance happen to all."* (Ec 9:11)

Of course, the full truth is that life does not always work out the way we think it will! Often the undeserving flourish while the diligent languish. Though one scripture promises great success to those who are clever and diligent, another shows that life may fail to follow that happy pattern. We must therefore allow one passage to modify the other and not force scripture to promise more than it does.

(b)   Compare Proverbs 12:21 with Job.

Despite the bold confidence expressed in the *Proverb*, many of the righteous (like Job) *are* crushed by sorrow. How can this be? We must recognise that promises of prosperity and happiness are like the "laws" of sowing and reaping. Normally a hard-working farmer can expect an abundant harvest; yet many things may ruin his hopes – a poor season, pestilence, insects; etc. Likewise, many things can interfere with the ordinary rule that blessing comes the way of the righteous. In other words, the "law" of prosperity, like the "law" of harvest, is only generally true; it is not an absolute law. Things both known and unknown can affect its outworking.

(c)   Think about these scriptures:

(i) Would you say that *Proverbs 18:22* is always true, even in scripture, let alone life? (Note *Proverbs 21:9*; etc.) The same question could be asked about many other texts, such as *Proverbs 16:7,13*. Such

statements present ideas that are usually true, yet scripture itself, in other places, shows that there are many exceptions.

(ii) Many parents trust *Proverbs 22:6*, certain that their children will one day commit their lives to Christ. They choose to forget that the Bible contains other passages (such as *Ezekiel 18:5-17)*, which show that a righteous man can sire an ungodly son (note also Pr 17:25; De 21:18-21; etc.; and cp. Mt 10:21; etc.). Scripture and life alike prove that the hopes and prayers of godly parents for their ungodly children are not always realised.

(iii) Would you take *Mark 9:43-48* literally? Perhaps a similar caution is warranted when you are reading other parts of scripture that are not so obviously impossible. What the words of the Bible say, and what the writer intended those words to mean, or how he intended they should be used, may not be the same. So let us be cautious before we leap into action! [99]

---

[99] There have been many cases in church history, including instances in our own time, where people have tragically mutilated themselves in the misguided belief that they had to take Jesus' words literally. One of the most famous in the past was the renowned Church Father, Origen. Eusebius tells his story, which began in the year 202, when he was 17 years of age. He was the son of wealthy Christian parents, and was himself a devout and zealous young man. A persecution had broken out, at the instigation of the emperor Septimius Severus, and Origen's father Leonidas had been arrested –

"As the flame of persecution had been kindled greatly, and multitudes had gained the crown of martyrdom, such desire for martyrdom seized the soul of Origen, although yet a boy, that he went close to danger, springing forward and rushing to the conflict in his eagerness . . . (But God) prevented his desire through the agency of his mother. For at first, entreating him, she begged him to have compassion on her motherly feelings toward him; but finding, that when he had learned that his father had been seized and imprisoned, he was set more resolutely and completely carried away with his zeal for martyrdom, she hid all his clothing, and thus compelled him to remain at home. But as there was nothing else that he could do, and his zeal beyond his age would not suffer him to be quiet, he sent to his father an encouraging letter on martyrdom, in which he exhorted him, saying, 'Take heed not to change your mind on our account.'"

The young Origen apparently found the prospect of rushing naked through the streets far more daunting than a terrible death in the arena! So he was denied his wish for martyrdom. His father was cruelly put to death, and the family's possessions were confiscated. From a position of considerable affluence they were reduced to abject poverty, and Origen had to assume responsibility for caring for his mother and six younger siblings. This adversity, far from discouraging him, inflamed his zeal all the more, and he laboured mightily, studying and then teaching Greek philology and literature, and copying manuscripts. His efforts were rewarded, and he eventually restored the family's prosperity. However, he continued to live very abstemiously himself; indeed, so great was his urge toward holiness, and his desire to serve Christ alone, while he was still a young man (about 25 years old) he acted literally on *Matthew*

Footnotes continued on the next page

(d) There are, of course, promises that are absolute, and remain so within the larger context of the whole Bible, such as the promise of salvation (cp. He 6:18). So a sound principle is the "whole-part-whole" method: that is, study the whole, then the part, then the whole again. Another sound rule is this: "let scripture interpret scripture" – that is, no part of the Bible can be interpreted in a way that contradicts the message of the whole Bible.

(F) SOME EXAMPLES

(1) Here are some examples of mistaken interpretations of scripture –

(a) Deuteronomy 22:5. This passage actually deals with transvestites; it is absurd to use it to ban women from wearing jeans (and other garments) that are specifically designed and cut as feminine apparel. Yet there was a great hullabaloo among some biblical literalists when women's jeans, pant-suits, and other superficially male garments were introduced. But should we ban also women's shirts, shoes, socks, vests, cardigans, ties, etc, which differ little from their male counterparts? If a woman cannot don anything that has the shape of a man's garment, nor a man anything that resembles female attire, then both sexes will be left with virtually nothing to wear!

19:12, took up a knife, and castrated himself – an act of zealous youthful folly that he later ruefully denounced.

He mastered many academic disciplines and became one of the first great Bible commentators, and perhaps the first of the early teachers to produce a systematic statement of all the major doctrines of Christianity. He established a flourishing seminary that became the greatest theological school of its time. It remains the progenitor and model of every Bible college that has since been built. Origen provides a fine example of the godliness, the discipline, the love of learning, that should mark all who wish to be noble teachers of the Word of life.

In the end, after some 55 years of devoted service to Christ, the great man gained the prize he had sought as a youth – a martyr's crown. During the Decian persecution Origen was arrested, put in chains, tortured, burdened with a crushing iron collar, and rabked over a long period.

Eusebius describes his sufferings –

" . . . how many things he endured for the word of Christ, bonds and bodily tortures and torments under the iron collar and in the dungeon; and for how many days with his feet stretched four spaces in the stocks he bore patiently the threats of fire and whatever other things were inflicted by his enemies . . . as his judge strove eagerly with all his might not to end his life."

Throughout the agonies of prolonged and repeated torture, Origen remained steadfast in his faith. His tormentors, since they could not break his spirit, finally released him; but his health was ruined and he soon died, shattered in body, but still mighty in spirit. (The above account is taken from my book, The World's Greatest Story.)

(b) ***Isaiah 3:16-17** and **1 Timothy 2:9**.* Despite the claims of some teachers, those verses do not forbid all use of jewellery and the like, but rather rebuke an excess of vanity and love of this world. Other passages speak quite pleasantly about adorning the body with grace and beauty, so long as it is done with restraint (Ge 24:22,53; Ex 3:22; Ps 45:8-9, 13-15; Is 61:10; Je 2:32; Ez 16:10-14; 40:16,26,31,34,37; 41:15-20,25-26; Ph 4:5, *"let your moderation be seen by everyone"*).

(c) ***Isaiah 28:10*** (KJV) does not provide the excuse that some preachers find in it for slovenly study. They suppose it to mean that the Holy Spirit will inspire them sentence by sentence after they begin preaching, therefore they need put little work into getting their sermon ready at home. But that is an inexcusably inept reading of the passage, and an irresponsible use of it.

(d) ***Jeremiah 10:3-5**.* The prophet was plainly deriding idolaters who cut their gods out of pieces of wood; but I have heard the passage absurdly used to forbid setting up a Christmas Tree. No one who had a proper sense of the *grammatical-historical* meaning of the passage could ever have understood it so foolishly.

(2) Each promise or command in scripture initially has power only in its proper time and place, conditioned by its own environment and by the people to whom it was first spoken. Before plucking a biblical promise off the sacred page, or attempting to obey some command, we need to make sure that it really does belong to *us* in our present circumstances. What was proper for a servant of God three or four thousand years ago may or may not be appropriate for his servants today. Hermeneutics has the task of showing how to make those choices wisely and well.

CHAPTER TEN

WHAT DOES IT MEAN?

"You should say what you mean," the March Hare went on.

"I do," Alice hastily replied; "at least – at least I mean what I say – that's the same thing, you know."

"Not the same thing a bit!" said the Hatter. "Why, you might just as well say that 'I see what I eat' is the same thing as 'I eat what I see'!"

Once again [100] Lewis Carroll [101] raises an intriguing question about the real meaning of words. Do people mean what they say? Do they say what they mean? We have enough trouble bridging this communication gulf among our own friends and neighbours. How then can we, using language in the manner of the 20th century *after* Christ relate to the way people spoke in the 20th century *before* Christ? Reaching for a solution to this problem brings us to the third dimension in the structure of scripture – [102]

---

[100] See *Chapter Two* above.

[101] Charles L. Dodgson (1832-1898), Alice's Adventures in Wonderland, Chapter Seven.

[102] The previous chapter presented the ***Anthropological*** and ***Historical*** dimensions.

(III) LITERARY

(A) FOUR MEANINGS

(1) There are four kinds of meaning in any [103] biblical passage

(a) The meaning intended by the original author, which can be discovered by following the *grammatical-historical* rule described in the previous chapter and elsewhere.

(b) The meaning his or her words gain from the larger context of scripture, which we also explored in the previous chapter.

(c) The spiritual reality implied by the passage –

- Such as when Elisha told his young servant that *"there are many more on our side than there are with the enemy"*, but the youth remained unimpressed until his spiritual eyes were opened and he saw *"the hills covered with horses and chariots of fire all around Elisha"* (2 Kg 6:15-17) The promise spoken by the prophet was empty until the young man saw the spiritual reality that lay behind it.

- All scripture contains those two dimensions: *first,* the spoken or written word; *then* the spiritual reality represented by those words.

- Note however that this spiritual reality will not be, and cannot be, disconnected from the written words. It will do no more than show (as in the case of Elisha and his servant) what those words are describing, or how they are connected with what is happening in the spiritual dimension. I am not in any way encouraging the folly of seeking some hidden, secret, special, or private meaning within the plain words of the Bible.

(d) And the fourth level is the meaning intended for you by the Holy Spirit at the time you are reading – that is, the lesson you should learn, the promise you should believe, the command you should obey, the

---

[103] I pondered my use of the word "any", and was inclined to change it to "many", but finally decided to leave it. Note however that the quantity of spiritual gold lying in each of these four layers must vary immensely from passage to passage.

revelation you should receive – whatever the Spirit may wish to say to you personally through the Word. But again with the proviso that the Spirit will not tell you something that lacks any reasonable connection with the scripture you are reading. The Spirit and the Word always agree with each other, and if there is seeming disagreement then let the Word prevail – most of us are more likely to misread the mind of the Spirit than we are to misunderstand scripture.

(2) All four of those levels must be brought into play before we can be sure that we are *"rightly dividing the word of truth"* (2 Ti 2:15). But let me stress again that the four meanings can be neither opposed to each other nor separated from each other. If there is not a plain link between them, then somehow our reading has gone astray. When I search through my Bible, I am not looking for some esoteric truth discoverable only by myself. Rather, I want to find first just one thing: what the text truly means (which should be the same for everybody); and then, how does the Holy Spirit want me to apply that message to my life today?

(B) COMPARING SCRIPTURE

Each scripture must be compared with other scriptures – no text can properly be used in isolation from the testimony of the whole Bible. This is similar to the idea of "context" that we looked at earlier; but here are some other aspects of it –

(1) Notice how, in the wilderness temptation, the devil quoted a scripture, which Jesus then countermanded with another scripture (Mt 4:3-4; etc.)

- thus the Master demonstrated that texts cannot be read in isolation, but only within the context of the entire Bible.

(2) Specifically, two principles must be remembered –

(a) THE BIBLE IS UNIFIED AROUND CHRIST

- see *Luke 24:27; Revelation 19:10.*

- the Bible speaks with a single theme, and that theme is ultimately Christ
- thus, when a doctrine like "all God's children deserve a luxury car, a mansion, and a yacht" is put at the foot of the Cross, it must cringe in shame, for it is so contrary to the image of Christ presented in scripture.

(b) THE BIBLE EMPLOYS PROGRESSIVE REVELATION

Many early ideas in the Bible are supplanted or changed by later teaching: there is ethical and spiritual development as the biblical revelation unfolds. Later revelation, then, must always have more force than ideas that came earlier. Here are some examples –

(i) GOD AS FATHER

The personal Fatherhood of God was unknown until it was taught by Jesus –

a) Prior to the time of Jesus the Jews thought of God as Father only in a tribal, cultic, or national sense. The idea was much the same as the way "sire" is still used in addressing a king; that is, God was seen as the "sire" of Israel. So "Father" was a term of majesty, of monarchy, rather than one of warm family relationship.

b) Then Jesus came and made the radical statement (for those days), *"This is how you should pray, 'My Father in heaven ... !'"* No one had ever before dared to address God in such an intimate and personal manner. Indeed, that one phrase dramatically changed the nature of human relationships with God, and introduced an entirely new dimension into what the Bible had previously taught about God, his people, and prayer.

(ii) GENTILES IN THE CHURCH

How offended the Jews were by the idea that gentiles were now to be admitted into God's covenant with Israel (Ac 22:21-22). Yet the all-embracing gospel created a magnificent expansion in the vision of the kingdom of God, and the Old Testament must now be interpreted in the light of this enlargement. It gives added meaning to scores of oracles and promises. Not the least of those changes was the almost brazen manner in which the apostles appropriated many Old Testament promises and transferred them from Israel to the church. Even if national Israel still had some part in the promise it was only in conjunction with the church; indeed, in the mind of the apostles, the best part of the promise belonged entirely to the church, God's new spiritual Israel (Ro 9:6; Ga 6:16).

(iii) ENFORCING THE LAW

Compare *Matthew 5:38-40* with *Romans 13:1-5*. We cannot escape the question: which teacher should prevail: *Paul*, or *Jesus*?

- In the main, Paul, giving a later revelation, must prevail over the earlier word of Christ. The apostle shows that the success of the church depends upon an orderly community (1 Ti 2:1-4), and that we are obliged to do all we can to encourage law and order. Therefore we should not assist criminals, nor turn a blind eye to their behaviour.

- Yet there *are* times when Christ's precept will be more appropriate, even if radical – especially when some hurt is being done only to ourselves (cp. 1 Co 6:7-8), or where to leave wrongdoing unrequited will bring no harm upon the community.

- So the rule remains: a later statement must be allowed to modify an earlier one; yet in some circumstances the earlier word may still be fully valid. In any case, earlier statements are still part of the canon of scripture and must always retain some value of teaching or example (1 Co 10:11).

(iv) SELF-MUTILATION

See *Matthew 5:29-30*, a passage I have mentioned a couple of times already, and will come back to again. But now compare it with *Colossians 3:5-10*. Was Jesus wrong? Hardly! Yet how impossible it was to put his counsel into practice! If Paul had not come along with a method of excising the "flesh" by *faith* alone then the terrible words of Jesus would have remained an intolerable burden. But Jesus (as a man) could not know what Paul would write, and in his own time, confronted with a stark choice between heaven and hell, the answer the Lord gave was the best one.

Someone may say: "Surely Jesus knew that his coming death would provide a way of escape from that awful demand to mutilate oneself?"

Perhaps; yet in his humanity Jesus could know only what was revealed to him by the Holy Spirit. Even to him some aspects of the future were dark. For example, he apparently thought there was a *possibility* of avoiding the cross, otherwise his prayer in the Garden would have been pointless (Mt 26:38-44). Had he not been crucified, how differently history would have unfolded! In any case, the revelation Paul gave could not be told until after Jesus' resurrection. That later doctrine provides a way of escape for us that could not have been revealed any earlier, probably not even to Jesus.

(3) Here then is the rule we must follow: the **Gospel** has precedence over and must interpret the **Law**; the **New Testament** must be given supremacy over the **Old**; the **Letters** must interpret the **Gospel**; and so on. God's truth unfolds in scripture step by step across many generations

- as another example, observe how different from the OT is the teaching of the NT on human "immortality" [104]

- on the same principle, the imprecatory psalms are not suitable for Christian worship, except perhaps as parables of the eventual judgments of God. [105]

> If God is a reality, and the soul is a reality, and you are an immortal being, what are you doing with your Bible shut? (Herrick Johnson)

---

[104] Up to the time of Malachi and beyond, the Hebrews had little or no concept of personal immortality. They looked for survival, not in the individual, but in the family, the tribe, and the nation. The Exile, and their contact with the Persians, changed those old ideas so much that by the time of Jesus most of the people had much the same belief as we do about survival after death. However, some groups, such as the Sadducees clung tenaciously to the old ideas and refused to embrace any new concept. Jesus endorsed the popular view, although the OT evidence for it was scant (notice for example what an obscure argument he depended upon in his debate with the Sadducees, Mt 21:31-32).

[105] You will find a discussion of these Psalms in my book <u>Songs to Live By</u>.

CHAPTER ELEVEN

WORD FOR WORD

A good way to explore scripture is to do word studies. If you lack any other tool [106] then a comprehensive English dictionary will display an array of definitions that may be applied to the key words of the Bible. [107] Better still, turn to one of the Hebrew and Greek word books that have been designed for use by readers who have no access to the original languages. Look up the meanings of each word; notice how they are used; try to sense the imagery, emotion, ideas, that each word carries along with it; let the Holy Spirit speak to you as you study. But there are some rules to remember, beginning with one that is important enough for me to keep coming back to it in different ways –

(C) THE IMPORTANCE OF CONTEXT [108]

(1) Words have different meanings in different contexts, such as prose, poetry, colloquial speech, formal speech, parables, proverbs, similes, songs, stories. A word that carries a certain meaning in one context, or in one literary style, may dramatically change when it is used elsewhere. Take, for

---

[106] See *Chapter Thirteen* for more information on various study tools.

[107] For example, my big Webster gives the following definitions for "mercy", which open up a rich source of meditation: "*(1)* a refraining from harming or punishing offenders, enemies, persons in one's power, etc; kindness in excess of what may be expected or demanded by fairness; forbearance and compassion. *(2)* a disposition to forgive, pity, or be kind. *(3)* the power to forgive or be kind; clemency; as, throw yourself on his *mercy*. *(4)* kind or compassionate treatment; relief of suffering. *(5)* a fortunate thing; a thing to be grateful for; a blessing; as, it's a *mercy* he's still alive." Almost every part of those definitions is applicable both to God's mercy toward us in Christ and to the mercy we are commanded to show each other.

[108] The numbering of the headings is continued from the previous chapter.

example the English verb "give", whose multiplied (and subtly different) meanings are explored in these sentences –

"They tell me you are given to gardening?" .... *have an aptitude, liking, or even compulsion for it*
"Now, don't give me that!" .... *a false statement*
"You haven't given it up, surely?" .... *abandon something*
"I gave it away last year." .... *abandon something, or give something to another*
"Don't give up now!" .... *abandon hope, stop trying*
"Give over, will you!" .... *move out of the way; yield the point*
"What gives?" .... *what is happening?*
"It's given over now to lawns and shrubs." .... *devoted to; taken over by*
"And yet I hear it given out that you used
   to give out vegetables to everyone." .... *an announcement; then, a distribution*
"Last year my enthusiasm gave out." .... *resources drained*
"I give in!" .... *accept defeat*
"Give way, will you!" .... *move aside*

"I'm giving all my spare time to the house. I'd been giving it a miss – and then I found the floorboards were beginning to give and the dry rot was giving off an awful smell . . . still, give me one of these older houses any day . . . modern buildings give me a pain in the neck!" [109]

(2) Hebrew and Greek words can be just as subtle in their use and meaning. A significant word in scripture will seldom mean exactly the same thing in each place where it occurs. So the context or setting in which words are found is crucial, along with the way people actually used them in their own time (which sometimes does not have much connection with their original or

---

[109] From an article in the New Zealand Listener (July 7, 1979), by Ian Gordon. The point of the article was to show why the search for a "Basic English" had failed. The first "Basic English" (created originally by C. K. Ogden) had only eighteen verbs, one of them being "give", which then had to do a lot more work than shown even in the examples above. For a foreigner approaching the language for the first time, the complexities were horrendous. It was easier by far to learn more verbs! English contains many other examples of the fine shades of meaning words can have.

strict meaning). Charles Dickens, in his novel *Martin Chuzzlewit* [110] takes up this idea of the individual use of words. Chuzzlewit is the first speaker –

> "A chief ingredient in my composition is a most determined – "
> "Obstinacy," suggested Tom in perfect good faith. But the suggestion was not so well received as he had expected; for the young man immediately rejoined, with some irritation,
> "What a fellow you are, Pinch!"
> "I beg your pardon," said Tom, "I thought you wanted a word."
> "I didn't want that word," he rejoined. "I told you obstinacy was no part of my character, did I not? I was going to say, if you had given me leave, that a chief ingredient in my composition is a most determined firmness."

(3)   The same kind of personalised meaning is not absent from Bible usage. In the end, words mean what their users intend them to mean; which is just as true of the biblical authors as of any other writer or speaker.

(4)   Here is another example from English, showing the different ways in which we use the word "afraid": it can mean *"fear"* (I am afraid of the dark); *"regret"* (I am afraid dinner will be late tonight); *"anxious"* (I am afraid he will be here too late to help); *timid"* (I am afraid to talk in public); *"frightened"* (I am afraid!); and perhaps other things as well.

(5)   Turn to your dictionary and look at the large number of words that undergo a change of meaning when they are used in different settings – try, for example these words that I have picked at random: *bow, square, flight, chase*. Or consider the subtle changes that the word *"good"* can display-

be a good boy	well-behaved
that was good luck	fortunate
I seek the good	a philosophical term
a good thing	desirable
what good news	delightful
that is good for you	beneficial
is that meat still good	fit to eat
he has a good character	morally blameless
what good is that?	useful
I feel good	well, healthy
he's a good worker	trustworthy, diligent
that's a good car	reliable, well-made

---

[110] Chapter Six.

that was a good sermon........ well preached, excellent content

what a good deed! .... commendable, noble – *etc, etc.* [111]

(6) The point is, none of those meanings are entirely interchangeable, and some of them can be used only in a single context. It would be absurd to apply all those meanings of *"good"* to every use of the word in a piece of English literature. Indeed, one needs a deep familiarity with the language to know in each case which shade of meaning is intended. Someone for whom English is a foreign tongue would need to be guided by a person thoroughly at home in the language. Much the same is true of the languages used in the Bible. Failure to recognise the subtlety of words has led to many foolish sermons, which travel a long way from the real meaning of their text. I hope never again to hear such silly effusions; but I doubt that I will be so fortunate!

(7) The multiple meanings that words possess increase the difficulties of translating and understanding the Bible. Those difficulties are not insurmountable, but they should make us cautious. Consider the fine distinction we make in our use of *which* and *what* –

"What door?"
- *means, "I don't see any door; where is it, how can I open it?"*

"Which door?"
- *means, "I see several doors, but don't know which one to choose!"*

- in English, both words may function either as a <u>pronoun</u> *(standing instead of something)* or as an <u>adjective</u> *(describing something)*, which sounds very confusing; yet in practice English-speaking people seldom choose the wrong one

- but think how well, how instinctively, one must know the language to be able to make such distinctions without thought or effort!

(8) Another example. In English, what do you suppose the word "let" means? That depends on where you happen to find it:

---

[111] The list is my own compilation and is not exhaustive.

- in older literature, it means "hinder or obstruct"; but in modern literature it has the opposite sense of "permit, or allow"
- in legal jargon ("without let") it means an impediment
- in the game of tennis, it means an illegal serve
- in the phrase "let be" it means to leave something alone
- in real estate it means to rent a piece of property; etc.
- a good dictionary will list several other uses; but notice how in some places it means quite the opposite to what it means in others – all the way from allowing something to happen to preventing it!

(9) Like the word "let", hundreds of other English words have changed their meanings over the centuries: thus *prevent* used to mean "arrive early"; *conversation* was once "behaviour"; *awful* signified "awesome"; *cunning* meant "pleasing"; and so on. Readers who find such words in older English documents make nonsense of them if they give them a modern meaning. Old sayings must be understood in the sense they had for the people who used them. So too, biblical words were prone to undergo shifts of meaning across the centuries. The way Malachi uses a word may not be the same as the way Moses used it! Paul may not use a word in the same way as John. Alert readers will be aware of these things, and will not jump to hasty conclusions.

(D) WORKING WITH WORDS

We can summarise the above by saying that anyone who starts to work with words should keep in mind the following rules –

(1) Words stem from a root expression, which may sometimes shed light on their underlying meaning and significance –

- thus the word *"help"* in *Hebrews 4:16* comes from a nautical term, "frap", which means to stiffen a wooden ship when it is being battered by a storm, by running a heavy cable right around the vessel and twisting it tight with an iron rod – which leads to some fascinating spiritual applications
- many other Bible words have similar colourful backgrounds, which can add a dramatic depth of meaning to them.

(2) However, the root meaning (or *etymology*) of a word can sometimes be misleading, for (as we have seen) words tend to change as the years roll by

- a brief check through an English dictionary will show you how a word may lose all connection with its root; thus
    - *fool* comes from the Latin *follis,* a bellows; hence a windbag
    - *lady* comes from a Latin root meaning a sacrificial cake
    - *dollar* comes from the German *thaler*, a coin worth about 3 marks
    - *focus* comes from the Latin word for fireplace
    - *amazed* comes from a Norwegian word meaning bewildered
    - *gaudy* comes from a Latin root meaning joyful
    - *share, short, skirt, score* all come from the same OE root, *to cut*
- likewise, the familiar word *with* once meant exactly the opposite of its present meaning, for it was used in the sense of *against, opposed to, on the opposite side*, echoes of which still exist in <u>with</u>stand, <u>with</u>draw, <u>with</u>hold
- and never forget how Queen Anne, when she was taken in 1710 to view Sir Christopher Wren's magnificent new St Paul's Cathedral, exclaimed: *"Oh, how awful, amusing, and artificial!"* [112]
- to build a dogma upon the root meaning of those words, and to ignore their quite different current meaning would be nonsensical; yet that very folly is often committed by the unwise when they turn to the Hebrew and Greek words used in the Bible.

(3) Words have a meaning for the people who use them, which may differ from the way their neighbours use them

- among the Greeks contemporary with the apostles, the verb *agapao* (to love) was used as widely and as carelessly as we use its English equivalent; but the apostles took it up, adapted it, and made it descriptive specifically of the benevolent love of God in Christ, and

---

[112] "Awe-inspiring! Amazing! Artistic (highly skilled)!"

therefore of the quality of love we Christians should offer each other [113]

- so it has a meaning in the New Testament distinctly different from its common contemporary meaning; as a result, neither the way the word was used in the pagan world nor its etymology has much bearing on the way it was normally used by the apostles

- so while the root meaning of a biblical word may illuminate its use in a particular text, it is a fallacy to suppose that some deeper sense can be discovered in every word by tracing etymologies; yet I have often heard preachers make that foolish mistake

- note too that the apostles did not feel confined to one meaning for each word, so that even in the case of *agapao* they did not hesitate to use it in an ungodly setting (Lu 11:43; Jn 3:19; 2 Ti 4:10; 2 Pe 2:15; 1 Jn 2:15; etc.)

(4) Nonetheless, since most people use most words in a way that is common to their culture, the meanings given to words in the contemporary society – that is, in non-biblical documents – must be taken into account

- thus the word *"Saviour"*, which in the New Testament belongs exclusively to Christ, in the larger Greek and Roman world was usually applied to the Roman emperor, because the empire had brought universal peace and prosperity to nations that for centuries had been riven with wars and tyranny

- *"Saviour"* was applied also to noble benefactors, and to tutelary deities, and those secular uses of the word add a special dimension to its meaning in scripture.

(5) So words must be studied not just in their grammatical or dictionary sense, but also in their larger historical and cultural context

- words gain a pile of baggage as they travel through a culture; they pick up a cluster of associated ideas and images that no dictionary

---

[113] "The etymology of *agapao* and *agape* is not clear. The verb *agapao* appears frequently from Homer onwards in Greek literature . . . (and) is often quite colourless as a word, appearing frequently as an alternative to, or a synonym with, *ereo* and *phileo*, meaning to be fond of, treat respectfully, be pleased with, welcome." (Dictionary of New Testament Theology Volume Two; ed. Colin Brown; Zondervan Pub. House, Grand Rapids, 1979; article, "Love".)

can adequately convey, and indeed that no later culture can hope to grasp fully [114]

- we will therefore never know *all* that the biblical authors had in mind when they wrote those 66 books; but the more nearly we can *feel* the times in which they lived the more closely we will come to catching the full sense of their words

- indeed, the meanings of significant words are always more *felt* than they are reasoned; their emotional force is stronger than their cool dictionary definition; they gain their impact in a user's life from their association with places, events, relationships, happiness, sorrow, pain, joy, friends, foes and so on

- no one can approach the true meaning of a word without some awareness of those associations; so the more vivid the world of Bible days becomes in your imagination the more riches you will draw from the sacred writings.

(6) Another way of expressing this idea is to say that the meaning of words is rooted, not in a dictionary, but in the culture out of which they arise; [115] which shows the folly of those who argue that the only valid translation is one that is as literal as possible

- some have condemned any translation that departs even a little from a word-for-word carry-over of the original text into English; but such an attempt is doomed to fail from the beginning

- any good translation must be in part at least a paraphrase as the translators try to capture the *feel* of the original, not just its grammatical or dictionary meaning

- any good translation, too, will involve a degree of *interpretation*, for no two languages have exactly the same vocabulary, grammar, sentence structure, idioms, and the like; hence translators have to do the best they can when they bring ideas from one language across into another

---

[114] See again *Chapter Two* above.

[115] That is why their meanings keep on changing, and why an English dictionary written 100 years ago has scant value today, except as an historical curiosity; nor will today's dictionaries be much use 100 years from now.

- indeed, as Sirach's grandson long ago discovered, there are always things that can be said in one language for which there is no exact equivalent in another –

I do ask you to read this work with diligence, but also with goodwill and generosity, for despite the hard work I have put into it, I have probably done a poor job in some places. Things that were originally written in Hebrew do not have exactly the same sense when they are translated into another language. Not only my grandfather's book, but even the Law itself, the writings of the Prophets, and the rest of the sacred Books sound quite different when they are read in their original language. [116]

- we are in the happy position of having a wide array of translations available: all the way from those that stick as closely as possible to the wording of the original documents, to those that try to give the best sense of the original, to those that are full paraphrases

- by comparing these various translations we may hope to come very close to the intentions of the original authors.

(7) Later users of a word may give it a substantially changed meaning

- as we have seen, any major English dictionary contains scores of words that have come to mean something far removed from how our forefathers understood them

- careful readers will watch for the same kind of changes in the Bible; they will not suppose that possession of some original-language *Concordance* has suddenly turned them into Hebrew and Greek scholars!

- in our case, of course, our translators have done the job for us, mostly dependably, yet not always, and sometimes you may wish to quarrel with them; but none of us should pretend to either knowledge or expertise that we do not have.

(8) Words may have *technical, specialist,* or *religious* meanings that differ from their everyday use

- Paul, for example, uses a word *tithemi* (to set, appoint, ordain, put in place) in *1 Corinthians 12:28*, which had a technical religious use

---

[116] From the Prologue to The Wisdom of Jesus Son of Sirach (or *Ecclesiasticus);* circa 132 B.C.

among the Greeks, describing the solemn moment when an idol was installed on its pedestal for the first time, thus turning a mere building into a temple

- knowing this technical use shows the importance placed on the *charismata*, which have been "set" in the church by the Holy Spirit; they are not optional extras, but essential to the very purpose for which the church has been brought into being.

(9) Note that the languages used in the Bible were not composed of some special religious jargon, nor were the books of the Bible written as technical or scientific treatises. The biblical writers used the ordinary speech of their day in its ordinary manner to express their wonderful revelations of God and of his dealings with men and women. Their words should be treated as you would statements made in any other writing. The Bible is not shrouded by some mystic aura, it is not a book of magic, nor is it weirdly written. It will therefore yield its best meaning to anyone who approaches it with careful, intelligent, sober, and diligent study.

(10) Through this entire process we are seeking for just one thing: what did this expression mean for the speaker at the time and in the place where he or she used it? Despite other meanings that may be drawn out of the text, all reliable research must at least begin with contemporary usage, and must remain grounded in it. Any other approach leads to folly.

CHAPTER TWELVE

MIXED UP METAPHORS

The folly of mistaking a paradox for a discovery, a metaphor for proof, a torrent of verbiage for a spring of capital truths, and oneself for an oracle, is inborn in us. [117]

Metaphors, analogies, similes, paradoxes, idioms, [118] and the like must be treated with care, especially when someone tries to make a dogma rest upon them. Figures of speech are illustrations, not arguments. They are difficult to carry from one language to another, and they can be troublesome to interpret. Think of such English expressions as

> *you are a pig*
> *face the music*
> *he put his foot in it*
> *walking on air*
> *don't lose your head*
> *a bee in his bonnet*
> *bats in the belfry*
> *the other side of the black stump*
> *we're already breaking our necks to finish it*

---

[117] Paul Valéry (1871-1945), French poet, mathematician, and philosopher; Introduction to the Method of Leonardo da Vinci (1895).

[118] ***Metaphors***: carrying across to one word the meaning of another (Mt 16:18, where "rock" means a spoken statement). ***Analogy***: explaining one thing by comparing it at length with another (Ps 80:8-17, where Israel is compared with a vine). ***Simile***: likening one thing to another, but differing from a metaphor because the comparison is explicitly stated (Mt 3:16, "the Spirit descended like a dove"). ***Paradox***: a statement that seems absurd, yet is actually true, or where two ideas seem mutually exclusive (Mt 8:23; 10:39; Lu 14:26; Jn 11:25; 12:24-25). ***Idiom***: the particular way in which the users of a language choose to form their ideas (such as Paul's custom, unique to him in the NT, of softening bold statements by using *"charis"* (grace) in an expression of thanksgiving to God (Ro 6:17; 1 Co 15:57; 2 Co 2:14; etc).

> *raining cats and dogs*
> *cool it!*
> *it was touch and go;* [119] *we barely made it*
> *I've got the blues*
> *lock, stock, and barrel*
> *we'll come to the party*
> *he won't come up to scratch*
> *take a high jump off a long jetty*
> *it was touch and go;* [120] *we barely made it*

- and hundreds more. Any attempt to understand such sayings literally simply makes nonsense of them; and the same can be said of many biblical expressions. Figures of speech usually mean less than what they actually say (as in, *"I wish I were dead!"*). They are colourful, vigorous, dramatic ways of expressing otherwise sober and formal ideas. So when Jesus spoke about *"hating"* one's father, mother, wife, children, brothers, sisters, and even one's own life, he was using a vivid figure of speech. To take his words with sombre literalness is to falsify them. Many follies are committed by Bible readers who fail to recognise figures of speech, and so force into scripture far more than it actually means. Before rushing into action, careful readers will first ensure that the scripture they are depending on does in fact say what they think it does.

Bible readers who fail to tread warily often stumble also into the quicksands of *idioms* and *poetry* –

(E) IDIOMS [121]

Idioms are particularly awkward to carry from one language to another. Sometimes there is no exact way to say in the new language what the original could say with ease – the idioms employed in various cultures are seldom identical. Translators usually have to be content with finding an expression or phrase that reflects the original as nearly as possible.

---

[119] Originally a nautical term, describing a ship whose keel had touched bottom, yet managed to keep sailing and get itself out of trouble. It now means, of course, any situation that could have had one result as well as another.

[120] Originally a nautical term, describing a ship whose keel had touched bottom, yet managed to keep sailing and get itself out of trouble. It now means, of course, any situation that could have had one result as well as another.

[121] Note again that the heading numbering is continuous from the previous chapter.

There is a story that a computer got mixed up when it tried to put a sentence into Russian, and then back again into English. "The spirit is willing but the flesh is weak" came back as "The vodka is strong, but the meat is rotten." Or how would some distant translator, long after English is dead, work out the intended sense of "Go jump in a lake!" or "Go fly a kite!"?

Here are two expressions, which, if one looks only at their dictionary meaning, appear to say the same thing; yet how different their real meaning is! –

> "She has a face that makes time stand still!"
> "She has a face that would stop a clock!"

Neither statement has anything to do with actual time; and they have opposite meanings – one describes a beautiful woman, and the other an ugly one. Some future translator will have to be very familiar with our idioms to get those two statements right! Only careful attention to the context can bring a correct understanding – and even then, if the context is sparse (as it sometimes is in the Bible) the matter may remain unsure.

Here is a more subtle example, from Jane Austen's *Emma*, [122]

> "Mr Frank Churchill (had to endure) the sad evil of sleeping two nights on the road ... "

– that is, in a lodging house or hotel. *We* know what it means; but how will a translator 2000 years from now handle it, when English as we know it will have long vanished from the earth? Only someone who has thoroughly mastered a language can hope to translate such idiomatic expressions sensibly.

Consider a phrase like *"my foot"*, which somehow in English has come to be used as a term of scorn, as in, "A peaceful house, my foot; they never stop quarrelling!" [123] An editor in the distant future will probably think that the expression is a misprint and emend it to something more sensible – a practice that some Bible translators and commentators are much addicted to.

Mind you, the translators deserve our sympathy. Anyone who has travelled in Europe or Asia, or even read a set of instructions printed overseas, knows what mayhem foreigners can commit upon the English language – yet they live in the

---

[122] Chapter 23.

[123] Nor should we forget other idiomatic uses of "foot", as in: you must <u>foot</u> the bill for that mistake; <u>foot</u> up that column of figures; put your <u>foot</u> down; now you've put your <u>foot</u> in it; put your best <u>foot</u> forward; he's got one <u>foot</u> in the grave; go to the <u>foot</u> of the line – and there are more.

same world we do, with access to every imaginable translation help! No wonder translators struggle to get it right when they have to reach across several thousand years to a long-lost culture and a long-dead language! Here are some modern examples of the mutilation of our language

- A Rumanian hotel had the following notice fixed to the outside of its elevator door: "The lift is being fixed for the next days. During that time we regret that you will be unbearable."
- Another hotel put up the sign, "Ladies are requested not to have children in the bar."
- Or a Czech tourist service announced: "Take one of our horse-driven city tours. We guarantee no miscarriages."
- Or on a Bulgarian lift: "Attention please: Automatic doors. They open by themself." [124]
- Then I found this in the instructions attached to an audio amplifier: "If you put in or out the power plug with amplifier volume set at high this causes the fear of breaking it."

I am sure that you too have seen many such examples, some of them probably even more ludicrous.

What is wrong with those statements?

Their grammar, spelling, and sentence structures are mostly correct – why then do they read so strangely? Because their *idiom* is wrong. Indeed, developing a sense for correct idiom is the most difficult thing to master in any foreign language. How little connection there is, for example, with normal grammar and the ordinary meaning of the words in an expression like, "I made friends with them, so I am not at all likely to hurt them." The structure is probably so familiar to you, that you will have to stop and think about it for a moment, before you begin to realise how odd it is! Yet all languages are full of such curious patterns. They represent the familiar way a language is spoken, independently of what a strict adherence to grammar might require or allow.

Another example: "As far as I am concerned, he can go hang!" – which grammatically should be, "go and hang himself," or "go and get himself hanged;" but the saying would then be too strong, and probably offensive. As it is, the

---

[124] The first four of these items were culled from a magazine article; provenance unknown to me.

idiom expresses little more than a mixture of annoyance and unconcern. How foolish too is the introductory phrase, "It goes without saying . . . " – for if that is so, then why say it? Yet we all know what it means, and often there is no better way either to introduce a theme, or to provide a safe transition from one idea to another. But it will surely puzzle a translator twenty centuries from now! Bible translators face the same problems when they try to bring the idioms used in scripture safely into English. For example, *Psalm 41:3* reads literally, *"you change all his bed"*, which is plainly a Hebrew idiom. But what does it *mean*? Is there an equivalent idiom in English? Here are some of the choices made by translators; but which one, if any, is correct, is another matter –

> *In their illness you heal all their infirmities* (NRSV)
> *You restore him from his bed of illness* (NIV)
> *You will turn his bed when he is ill* (NEB)
> *You will soothe their pains and worries* (TLB)
> *To all his illness on his bed Thou wilt bring a change* (Berkeley)
> *You transform altogether the bed where he lies sick* (Jerusalem)
> *Thou wilt make all his bed in his sickness* (KJV).

A search through the footnotes or the marginal references in your Bible (if it possesses such things) will show you many other places where the translators have had to guess at the meaning of a Hebrew, Aramaic, or Greek idiom. Mostly those guesses can be trusted, but they may be wrong, so a degree of caution is wise.

(F) POETRY

(1) A large part of the Bible is poetry – most of *Job*, the *Psalms*, *Proverbs*, the greater part of the *Prophets*, and many other portions. Poetry cannot sensibly be read as if it were prose. All poetry abounds in what we call "poetic licence" – that is, poets take freedom to do things with language that would not be acceptable in writing prose. The Hebrew poets did not stand outside that rule. They expected their readers to make full allowance for the nature of poetry when their words were read or studied. How astonished any poet – including the biblical authors – would be to find his or her words being treated as if they were a piece of formal argument!

The truth of a poem lies not so much in the actual words and imagery used, but in the intention of the poet. Ask yourself, what is the poet trying to *tell* me in these lines? How does he set about achieving that goal? How literally does he expect me to take his words? How much of the poem must be seen as metaphor, simile, analogy, a figure of speech, a piece of poetic exaggeration or colour?

Consider this sonnet by William Shakespeare –

> How oft, when thou, my music, [125] music play'st,
> Upon that blessed wood whose motion sounds
> With thy sweet fingers, when thou gently sway'st
> The wiry concord that mine ear confounds, [126]
> Do I envy those jacks, [127] that nimble leap
> To kiss the tender inward of thy hand,
> Whilst my poor lips, which should that harvest reap,
> At the wood's boldness by thee blushing stand!
> To be so tickled, they [128] would change their state
> And situation with those dancing chips,
> O'er whom thy fingers walk with gentle gait,
> Making dead wood more bless'd than living lips.
> Since saucy jacks so happy are in this,
> Give them thy fingers, me thy lips to kiss.

Would anyone be so foolish as to search that sonnet for some teaching about harpsichords? Is it a poem about music, or about love? Does it even prove that the young lady who was the swain's desire was an accomplished harpsichordist, or that she played any instrument at all? In the end the poem truly says only one thing: the poet is envious of anything that his sweetheart touches, and wishes instead that she were touching him, especially with her lips! To find anything else is to find more than the poet intended, and to make him say what it was never in his mind to express.

Something the same may be said about the poetry in the Bible. Don't be too hasty about plucking one phrase out of a poem and hanging an entire argument upon it. You may well end up with falsehood rather than truth.

(2) Let me put a provocative example before you. See *Joshua 10:12-14*, which tells about the day the sun and the moon stood still. Is that a piece of prose *history*, or is it dramatic *poetry*? The words that Joshua spoke, we are told, came from the *Book of Jasher*, which may not have been composed until the time of David (2 Sa 1:18). If that is so, then the lines were added to *Joshua* by a later editor as a kind of poetic summary of what happened on that great day of victory. But if it is poetry then should it be literally

---

[125] The young lady the suitor is courting, whom he imagines as playing a harpsichord.

[126] The harmonies produced by the wire strings.

[127] "Jacks" in a harpsichord are akin to the hammers in a piano.

[128] His lips.

understood? Perhaps no more so than similar vivid images that are scattered through scripture:

> *The stars fought from heaven, they leaped out of their appointed paths to fight against Sisera!* (Jg 5:20); ... *The heavens were torn asunder* ... *Lebanon skipped like a calf, and Mount Herman leaped like a wild bull* ... *The mountains leaped like rams, and the hills fled like young lambs* (Ps 18:9; 29:6; 114:4,6) ... *The mountains and the hills burst forth into song, and all the trees of the field clapped their hands!*

If those poetic descriptions of nature cannot be taken literally, perhaps the same is true of the story in *Joshua*. Further, if you refer to the various commentaries you will learn that the Hebrew text is open to different readings. The actual event may have been some kind of heavenly eclipse, or a darkening hailstorm, or some conjunction of the heavenly bodies that was seen as a sign of Yahweh's favour. Then again, the event may have been exactly what is described: the sun and the moon obliged to stand still at the command of Joshua! The point I am making is simply this: *(a)* we are dealing with poetry, which should at least make us cautious; *(b)* the meaning of the Hebrew text is uncertain, which should squash dogmatism. The story contains only one indisputable element: on that never-to-be-forgotten day God gave Israel a marvellous victory over her enemy.

(3) The basic hermeneutical rule is to read each passage of scripture literally as far as it is possible or reasonable to do so. But in passages like those that talk about trees clapping their hands, who can doubt that a figurative sense is required? Equally, there are many other places where a literal reading is inescapable. But in between lie a large number of texts where the choice is difficult. What one reader may easily accept as literal another insists is figurative or symbolic. In those places, special attention must be given to

- the *context* in which the passage stands
- the literary *style* of the passage – is it prose? poetry? prophecy? parable?
- the probable *purpose* of the whole segment
  - and the like.

By such means the number of disputed passages has been greatly reduced; yet there remain many verses (like the poem about the sun standing still) where sincere commentators differ. Readers who are not scholars must avail themselves of as much help as they can find, and then try to make a responsible decision about how they should read the passage.

(4) Happily, no doctrine of any significance depends upon any of those uncertain passages. Whatever is truly necessary for Christian faith and practice, and for a secure grip upon eternal life, is written plainly and largely in scripture, so that even the simple may read, believe, and be saved. Indeed, the kinds of problems I am raising in these pages seldom become evident until a reader has grown deeply familiar with the Bible, from *Genesis* to *Revelation*, and begins to notice the anomalies, discrepancies, and contradictions, that do seem to exist in its pages. Any lover of scripture who becomes aware of these problems at once desires an explanation, or a solution of them. If you are such a person, then I hope that these pages will show you some reasonable answers and bring satisfaction to your spirit.

(5) Some problems, of course, are bound to remain, which keeps the Bible endlessly exciting, always challenging, ever provoking, and drives devout readers to an untiring quest for more insight, more revelation, more understanding, and, above all, more faith. Undoubtedly, that is precisely what the Holy Spirit planned. How dull it would be if he had given us a Book – like some child's primer – that yields all its secrets to one careless reading! Instead, like countless others before me, after a lifetime of pouring myself into scripture, and pouring scripture into myself, I still find in the Bible a never-diminishing joy and ever-increasing wonder. If Jesus is the living *Logos* of God (Jn 1:1), then this Book is the written *Logos*, and like the Saviour it represents (for Christ is in all the scriptures – Lu 24:27), it too is *"filled with wisdom, the grace of God, and truth"* (Lu 2:40; Jn 1:14).

Moses lifted his eyes and saw the sun radiant in the sky above him, conveying to the earth light and life, health and prosperity. Do your eyes see a different sun? Does it not shine now as it did then, with the same beneficent result? Time has not diminished its splendour. Nor can time dim the Bible. Across the changing ages it remains unchanged, ever brilliant with divine truth, with healing in its rays, ready to beam its lustre into every soul that turns toward it. (Anonymous)

CHAPTER THIRTEEN

MANY TREASURES

We are still exploring the <u>six dimensions</u> that lie within any passage of scripture. So far we have looked at three of them –

> ***Anthropological***
> ***Historical***
> ***Literary.***

We now come to the fourth –

(IV) RELIGIOUS

Suppose you are studying a passage of scripture. You should ask yourself some questions. What theological principle can be drawn out of this passage. What doctrine does it teach, highlight, or support? What religious experience stands behind it? What promise does it offer, what command does it speak? What does it tell me about God, or about the kingdom, or about heaven or hell, life and death, the church and the world, and so on?

Those questions lie beyond the scope of this book. Many fine Bible commentaries are available to assist students in their quest for answers. I propose here only to offer some practical help in the matter of building a religious library. People often ask: which is the best Bible; what commentaries should I trust; what other books do I need? – and the like. If you have been puzzled by such questions, then here are my suggestions about what books to buy. With only these on your shelf, you will have enough resources to keep you busy in Bible study for the rest of your life! The books are listed in order of priority; that is, buy the ones at the top of the list first; and then work through to the end, as your finances permit, or as your interest guides you.

(A) THE BIBLE

You should have

    (1)   an accurate translation for formal use, [129] especially if you are a teacher or preacher; then

    (2)   a free translation (or paraphrase) for private and devotional reading; [130] and also

    (3)   various other translations and paraphrases for comparison, as many as you can afford to buy

- there are at least 20 major translations on the market at present
- they all have some strengths and some weaknesses; there is no perfectly reliable English translation
- so you should be aware of what to look for; which means, you should especially read the *Preface* that stands at the front of all modern translations, and discover:

    (a)   ***What master-text is this translation based upon?***

Earlier I said that before translators can begin their task they must create a master-text. They do this by comparing the hundreds of ancient manuscript copies of the Bible that are now available. To those documents they add scripture citations culled from the works of the Church Fathers, and any other source material they can draw upon. All this material is compared, sifted, collated, and finally organised into a single Hebrew, Aramaic, and Greek text of the Bible. Only then can the task of translation begin. Each translation is therefore based upon a particular "text", and that text reflects the scholarly preferences, and sometimes dogmatic prejudices, of the translators. Some scholars prefer one text, others another; but in any case, the *Preface* will usually tell what master text has been chosen and why.

    (b)   ***What is the underlying philosophy of this translation?***

---

[129] Such as the *New International Version* or the *New Revised Standard Version*.
[130] Such as the *Revised English Bible*, the *Good News Bible*, or the *Living Bible*.

(i)   No one, no matter how objective he or she may try to be, can approach any piece of literature with complete neutrality. We all read within a particular social and cultural context, which means that we all bring to our reading a set of pre-conceived ideas about what words mean. Our understanding is deeply influenced by upbringing, learning, experience, and a thousand other things – sometimes known, sometimes unknown. Every word we meet comes to us freighted with a thousand images, rich colourings, ideas, associations, memories, and the like. Before we open any book (including the Bible) we possess a certain world-view, a philosophical framework, within which we spend our lives, and which shapes our interpretation of everything we read and of all that happens to us.

Translators are not immune from such influences. Indeed, they are so well aware of them, that they deliberately spell out their philosophy of translation before they approach the first line of the Bible. That is, they create a particular framework in which they choose to do their work; or, if you prefer, they devise a set of rules that will control their choices and shape the result.

(ii)   Here are examples of what I mean, taken from the *Prefaces* of three versions of the Bible –

a)   *The New King James Version*

> Bible readers may be assured that the most important differences (between the different versions) . . . are due to the way in which translators view the task of translation: How literally should the text be rendered? How does the translator view the matter of biblical inspiration? Does the translator adopt a paraphrase when a literal rendering would be quite clear . . . ? The *New King James Version* follows the historic precedent of the *Authorised Version* in maintaining a literal approach to translation except where the idiom of the original language cannot be translated directly into our tongue . . . The *NKJV* has been based on the 'Received Text,' thus perpetuating the tradition begun by William Tyndale in 1525, and continued by the 1611 translators in rendering the *Authorised Version*.

b)   *The New American Bible*

> (It) has become increasingly desirable that contemporary translations of the sacred books into English be prepared, in which due reverence for the text and strict observance of the rules of criticism would be combined. *The New American Bible* has accomplished this. . . . From the original and oldest available texts of the sacred books, it aims to convey as directly as possible the thought and individual style of the inspired writers. . . . (However) the problem of marked literary peculiarities must be met. . . . (The) limited vocabularies and stylistic infelicities

of the (writers) cannot be retained in the exact form in which they appear in the originals without displeasing the modern ear. . . . Similarly, the syntactical shortcomings of Paul, his frequent lapses into anacolouthon [131], and the like, are rendered as they occur in his epistles rather than 'smoothed out'. . . . The *Gospel according to John* comprises a special case. Absolute fidelity to his technique of reiterated phrasing would result in an assault on the English ear that would be almost unendurable.

c) *The Living Bible – The Way*

The present volume departs radically from (the past) history of Scriptural translations. It is born out of a sincere desire to have the Word of God reach as many people as possible, and in a language that is our own. Perhaps more than other translations, this translation cannot be used as a basis for doctrinal or traditional disputes. More than other English versions of the Bible, this one freely departs from a literal translation from the original languages. . . . Most readers of the Bible who choose this translation will not be interested in . . . technical, theological considerations. They will be looking for spirit and life from the Word of God."

(iii) I hope you already do this, but if not, then do read carefully the *Preface* to whatever Bible(s) you use, and be aware of the choices the translators have made. Try to sense what influence those choices have made upon the result that you hold in your hands. You are not obliged to agree with the translators. You may dislike their choices. If so, put that version aside, and choose another. I have above twenty translations on my shelf; some (having read them right through once) I seldom use, others I refer to occasionally, while two or three I use constantly. Why are they my favourites? Simply because *first*, I agree with the translation philosophy that stands behind them; *second*, I have found them accurate; and *third*, I like the way they read.

(B) CONCORDANCES

(1) Bible concordances are available for the various major English translations; but be sure to purchase a *complete* concordance; an abridged or incomplete volume has little use in serious study

---

[131] Also spelled "anacoluthon". It means starting a sentence in one way and finishing it in another, or mixing grammatical constructions, or leaving phrases or clauses unfinished. "Why would you want – oh! just do it!" "Who will deliver me from this body of death? Thanks be to God – through Jesus Christ our Lord!" (Ro 7:24-25). See also Ro 5:12-13; 2 Co 7:5-7; Ph 1:29-30; Cl 3:16.

- *note*: the concordances that are printed at the back of some Bibles have a limited scope; they are necessarily shortened, and must omit hundreds of words and references
- I think you would do better to buy a plain Bible (that is, with no concordance), plus a separate complete concordance.

(2) You should probably first purchase key items from the other categories listed below; then when you have done so, you may want to come back to this place and begin adding to your library some Greek & Hebrew reference tools, such as the following –

(a) *The New Englishman's Greek Concordance*, to give you access to the Greek text of the NT.

(b) *The Englishman's Hebrew & Chaldee Concordance*, to give you access to the Hebrew text of the OT.

(c) For adequate Greek and Hebrew study, you will also need *lexicons* that explain the meanings and roots of each word

- for example, *Vine's Expository Dictionary* is an excellent tool for those who have no knowledge of the original languages

(d) then various other one-volume or multi-volume lexicons are available for those who know the Greek and Hebrew alphabets and can decipher Greek and Hebrew words.

(C) BIBLE DICTIONARIES OR ENCYCLOPAEDIAS

(1) These books will give you masses of information about people, places, events, flora, fauna, background summaries of biblical books and ideas, historical and geographical data, etc. Two kinds of "dictionaries" are available –

- Single-volume: such as *The New Bible Dictionary*, and many others.
- Multi-volume: such as the Zondervan Pictorial Encyclopedia of the Bible, and many others.

(2) Books produced by an evangelical publisher are preferable; but in this field the works of almost any major publisher are probably reliable enough.

(3) A good Bible dictionary and/or encyclopaedia will add immense depth, colour, and reality to your study of the scriptures. This is an indispensable tool.

(D) TOPICAL CONCORDANCE

This is not a list of *words* but of *topics*. For example, a topical concordance not only lists the occurrences of the *word* "love", but also all the places in scripture where the *idea* of "love" is found. It will show you not only the places where the Bible contains teaching about love, but also where people behave lovingly.

Some study Bibles, like the *Thompson Chain Reference Bible* and others, are useful, but inadequate. A comprehensive *topical concordance* (e.g. *Zondervan*) will give you a much more extensive list of the passages in which a given theme can be found.

Another very useful volume is a concordance of parallel passages keyed to the biblical text (eg, *The Treasury of Scripture Knowledge*). Once again, this book contains a far more extensive list of cross-references than any study Bible can find space for.

(E) COMMENTARIES

There is an almost endless choice! Your task will be made easier if you recognise that there are four kinds of Bible commentary:

(1) Critical

(a) These determine and clarify the text of scripture; that is, what did the author actually write; what was each passage intended to *say*? These works are necessary because of the tens of thousands of variations that exist in the ancient manuscripts, including missing words, misplaced phrases, expressions whose meaning is unknown, and the like. Thus, in the following fictitious illustration, a letter and a word are missing from the text. It is the task of the critic, using as many tools as possible, to arrive at a correct solution. So, in the example, the missing letter could be either *"t"* or *"w"*, and the missing word might therefore be either *"hot"* or *"on"* –

"he was (t)alking (hot) air!"
"he was (w)alking (on) air

(b) For the sake of our argument, we will say that our critic, [132] after examining all the available evidence, has concluded that the text should read: *"he was walking on air"*. Does that settle the matter? No, for there are opponents, who insist that the correct reading should be, *"he was talking hot air"*. Which of them is correct? Perhaps the arguments of one scholar will prevail over all others; perhaps the issue cannot be resolved, and the reader will simply have to make a choice. And that is what happens as scholars labour to create an authentic text of the Bible –

- sometimes in biblical criticism the evidence is sufficient to make a reading either certain or fairly certain
- but from there certitude descends through various levels of probability all the way (in the case of some words or lines) to a pure guess!

The footnotes and/or marginal references in your Bible usually draw attention to these deficiencies in the text, and to alternative readings. If the quest interests you, however, and you want to pursue it further, then turn to a critical commentary – for example, *The Anchor Bible*; or *The Word Biblical Commentary*.

Once the text is more or less fixed, so that we are fairly sure what the original author *wrote*, then a second kind of commentary becomes necessary –

(2)   Exegetical

(a)   These **_interpret_** the original sense of the text; that is, what does each passage **_mean_**? In our example *("he was walking on air")*, an exegete (hopefully familiar with English idioms) would suggest that the phrase describes a man who is one of several things: *happy, unburdened, lively, exalted.* Which choice is correct? The context in which the statement occurs should suggest the probable answer. Since we lack a context for our example, we cannot resolve the problem – which sometimes occurs in scripture too, especially in books like *Proverbs*, where the context is either brief or non-existent. That is why the various translation may vary quite startlingly in their rendering of those passages.

---

[132] This is technically known as "higher criticism", and despite the bad press that "higher criticism" tends to have among some fundamentalists, it is an inescapable task. *Someone* has to do the job of creating a biblical text that is as near to the original writings as it is possible to come.

(b) Suppose, however, the translators are not aware that they are dealing with an idiom? [133] Imagine what strange meanings they might put into the text! What a miracle! A man walking on air! How did he do it? Can I do the same? Such mistakes, sometimes tragic, are not lacking in biblical interpretation. [134] Be careful! A misunderstood idiom can bring disaster!

(3) **Expository**

(a) These ***expand*** the theology of the text; that is, what does each passage ***teach***? In the case of our example, an expositor would probably expand it to mean *the possibility of a joyful and free life.*

(b) In the case of a biblical text, the commentator would also set the statement within the larger context of the Bible, showing how it relates to or modifies other scriptures, plus what it might say about Christ and the believer's union with him, and so on.

(4) **Homiletical/devotional**

(a) These ***apply*** the text to life; that is, what does each passage ***preach***; what ***practice*** does it enjoin; what ***promise*** does it offer, and so on?

(b) Using our example, the preacher might argue that it is wrong for a Christian to walk around gloomy, dispirited, cut off from the joy of Christ!

Many commentaries contain elements of all those categories; others more clearly belong in one domain.

You should probably begin with a general one-volume commentary that is primarily *exegetical* and *expository*; then you could advance to multi-volume commentaries in all categories.

---

[133] See again my comments on "idioms" in the previous chapter.

[134] Some religious people are capable of any madness. Just a day or two before I penned the above lines a report appeared in the newspaper about the drowning of a dozen or so young people. Incited by a priest, they had stepped out of a boat in the middle of a lake, intending to emulate Peter and Jesus, and walk on water. Instead, both they and their priest went straight to the bottom. Should God have intervened? Of course not! They should have been more sensible in their use of scripture.

(F) FURTHER BOOKS

Serious students, teachers, preachers, will include in their library the following:

(1) *Systematic Theologies*, which present the whole body of Christian doctrine in a coherent and orderly form. But note the *plural*: you should not lock yourself into one way of looking at doctrine. Remain open to different perceptions of the great themes of the Bible.

(2) *Studies on Ethics*, dealing with proper behaviour at home, in the church, and in the world.

(3) *Groups of books* that reflect diverse viewpoints on various topics (e.g. eschatology, the church, history, church history, healing, salvation, faith, God, etc.)

(G) VOCABULARY

(1) Anyone who intends to use words professionally in speaking or writing will need:

- a good *English dictionary*, one that has extensive definitions, including the etymology of at least the major words

- a *thesaurus*, that is, a dictionary of synonyms and antonyms

- books on *correct English usage*, explaining the rules of grammar, sentence construction, and anything to do with using the language vividly and effectively

- books of *popular quotations*, to give you access to what some of the greatest thinkers and writers have said about a multitude of themes; and also to help you track down the source of a familiar saying.

(2) You should also set yourself a reading programme in good literature (see the recommended list in *World Book* encyclopaedia). There is no better or more enjoyable way to develop a lively vocabulary and to enrich life.

> A book is good company. It is full of conversation without loquacity. It comes to our longing with full instruction, but pursues us never. It is not offended at our absentmindedness, nor jealous if we turn to other pleasures — of leaf or dress or mineral, or even of books. It silently serves the soul without recompense — not even for the hire of love. And, yet more noble, it seems to pass from itself and to enter the memory, and to hover in a silvery transformation there, until the outward book is but a body and its soul and spirit are flown to you, and possess your

memory like a spirit. And while some books, like steps, are left behind us by the very help which they yield us, and serve only our childhood or early life, some others go with us, in mute fidelity, to the end of life — a recreation for fatigue, an instruction for our sober hours, and solace for our sickness or sorrow. Except the great outdoors, nothing that has so much life of its own gives so much life to us.
(Henry Ward Beecher)

(3) Do include *poetry* in your reading programme, for nothing else can give you a better encounter with the noblest and deepest human aspirations.

(H) HOMILETICS

(1) If preaching is part of your God-given task in life, then do study the sermons and outlines of great preachers. Make sure to read C. H. Spurgeon's *Lectures To My Students*.

(2) Purchase from time to time the latest books on techniques of sermon preparation and delivery (styles change across the years, even within one lifetime). You might also read my book, *The Pentecostal Pulpit*. It is the distillation of my own experience, after more than 40 years of constant preaching.

(I) COMPUTER SOFTWARE

You probably know that an ever-increasing abundance of computerised material is now becoming available for Bible study: many versions of the Bible; concordances; indexes; topical concordances; Christian classics; outlines on every imaginable theme; and the like. Some disks contain the full text of several hundred volumes, complete with various search tools. The array is almost endless. I use these disks myself, and sometimes they are the best source; but in the main, I still prefer to pull a book off my shelf. There is a tactile pleasure, a delight, in handling a well-made book that no CD I have yet seen can equal. The books too are often easier to use, and quicker to handle. Nonetheless, I will buy more CDs, because I am eager to draw upon anything that will enhance my access to and understanding of God's wonderful Word.

(V) DIVINE

The fifth dimension in scripture is found in its divine inspiration. Here we ask: what level of inspiration underlies the pages of the Bible; in what sense is it the Word of God; what heavenly revelation did it convey to its first readers; what level of authority exists in the various parts of the Bible? Some answers to those questions have already been spoken in these pages, beginning with the *Statement of Faith* at the very beginning. But the question of *inspiration* rightly belongs in a separate study, so I will not say anything further about it here. Let me put before you only these propositions –

- we believe in the plenary inspiration of scripture
- the Bible is an infallible self-revelation of God
- it is his divinely given word, inerrant in all that it truly affirms
- in all matters of Christian belief and practice it speaks with absolute authority.

(VI) PRACTICAL

Under this last heading, if space permitted, we would ask the questions: what response from me does this passage of scripture call for; what action does it demand; what release of faith does it require?

Other books in the *VCC* series deal with such questions, spelling out what it means to be a Christian in all of one's relationships, lifestyle, worship, morals, practice, and indeed, every aspect of Christian character and conduct. We can go no further along this path here, but must turn now to the next part of our study.

> Set yourself to study these words, so full of wisdom.
> They will fill you with knowledge.
> They will ensure that you are well-trained. [135]

---

[135] The Wisdom of Amenemope, Ch. 30; Egyptian sage, 11th. Century B.C. Several segments in *Proverbs* seem to be drawn from or at least influenced by this earlier writing.

PART FOUR

LONG, LONG AGO!

O Sir, what a commendation is this of your doctrine! . . . Is it the same person? this spiteful, morose, touchy man? Alas, what has *"the knowledge of the truth"* done? What a deplorable change has it made! Sir, I love you still; though I cannot esteem you as I did once. Let me entreat you, if not for the honour of God, yet for the honour of your cause, avoid, for the time to come, all anger, all spite, all sourness and bitterness; all contemptuous usage of your opponents, not inferior to you, unless in fortune. *"O put on again bowels of mercies, kindness, gentleness, long-suffering; endeavouring to hold,"* even with them that differ from you in opinion, the *"unity of the Spirit in the bond of peace!"*

- John Wesley, in a letter to a former friend who had become a strict Calvinist, and, in Wesley's view, intolerant and objectionable.

CHAPTER FOURTEEN

THE PROTESTANT PRINCIPLE

> No matter how much the golfer with a sand wedge and cleated shoes wants to play squash, the squash court expects something else: rubber-soled shoes, a squash racquet, and a player who's come to play squash. Does the Bible also expect a certain sort of reader? Is the (Bible) both an open book for all to read, and in some sense a closed book, with a distinct readership in mind? Does the Bible conform to a genre that has been externally imposed by coercive readers and hard misreadings, or is its genre a reflection of the will of the communities that produced it, assented to its ongoing word of address, and handed it over to new communities of faith, of which we are one? [136]

Just what is the Bible? How should it be read? Can anyone read it and fully understand its message? Or is true understanding limited to a certain group of people? Does the Bible speak equally to all readers, or does it disclose its message in different ways to different classes or kinds of people? Or again, how much scholarship is needed before one can feel qualified to read and interpret the Bible? The answers to those questions are not obvious, and they have been a source of much argument among Christians. Whose opinion is correct –

- those Protestants who say that every believer is adequately equipped by God to be his or her own interpreter of scripture; or

- those Roman Catholics who insist that the church alone (through its teaching magisterium) has the right and authority to explain the meaning of the Bible; or

- those others who adopt some kind of middle position between the two?

---

[136] Christopher R. Seitz; art. "The Changing Face of O.T. Studies"; <u>The Christian Century</u>, Oct. 1st, 1992.

In the main, my own position is the third one. That is, while I agree heartily that every Christian should, and indeed must, read the Bible for himself or herself, in the end the major burden of interpreting scripture must belong to those whom God has gifted as teachers in his church. Why this mixture? Because of the following –

(1) THE FAILED CATHOLIC PRINCIPLE

Those, such as the Church of Rome, who deny the right of private judgment in the interpretation of scripture, and who insist that the church alone has authority to determine how the Bible should be understood, have hardly been consistent in their dogma over the centuries. Occasions are not lacking in history when sundry popes or patriarchs furiously denounced each other as heretics. The steamy record of ecclesiastical squabbles gives us scant encouragement to put *all* our trust in church pronouncements.

(2) THE FAILED PROTESTANT PRINCIPLE

In reaction against the failures of Catholic dogma, the Protestant leaders of the 16th century argued vigorously for the right of each believer to exercise his or her own judgment and to follow his or her own conscience in studying the Bible. They also urged a thorough dependence upon the Holy Spirit (1 Jn 2:27). No doubt those are valid principles, and they are in general still part of Protestant dogma; yet they have brought no final agreement among evangelical Christians, who to this day differ markedly in their views on many important issues. [137]

If the church can't get it right, and scholars can't get it right, there is not much chance that ordinary believers will be able to do so without a lot of help!

(3) THE MIDDLE WAY

So while all Christians should fervently love and constantly read scripture, we cannot escape the need for skilled teachers, excellent in wisdom, filled with knowledge of the Bible, and called by God to impart his message to the church. I do not mean, of course, that you should altogether surrender your conscience to some ecclesiastical authority. God forbid! No one has any right to tell you what you must believe. In the end each person will be answerable only to God for the way their lives were shaped by the dogmas they embraced (1 Co 3:10-15).

---

[137] For example, the church, the eucharist, baptism, the charismata, eschatology, heaven, hell, etc.

You and I alone are responsible for our beliefs; we cannot cast that burden onto another. Nonetheless, how arrogant it would be for anyone to suppose that he or she possesses all the wisdom, knowledge, or understanding needed to read and interpret the Bible correctly! I am not so foolish. Therefore, I gladly draw on the learning of gifted teachers, and measure my beliefs against what they tell me – yet always reserving to myself the right to say "no"!

Some critics, keen to maintain a Protestant stance, are opposed to that half-Roman position. They insist that every believer fully can be and should be his or her own interpreter of scripture, and that no pastor or teacher can claim any higher right. But something is wrong. For while they may hold to the doctrine of *private judgment* in *theory*, it is seldom their *practice*. Suppose you were to apply for membership in one of their churches? What will happen? You will be handed a statement of faith, and your application will be accepted only if you give full adherence to it. Not much freedom of private judgment there!

Nor do *pastors* enjoy any higher liberty. Most if not all Protestant and Pentecostal denominations rigorously impose their body of doctrine upon their clergy. How much freedom of belief lies inside those structures? Very little! Surely it is sophistry for a denomination, while it refuses to trust its *pastors* to interpret scripture privately, to insist that every *believer* has the right to do so? That seems suspiciously like preaching one doctrine while practising another!

Similarly, there are evangelical *seminaries* that hold as one of their basic tenets the right and the duty of every Christian to exercise private judgment in the interpretation of scripture. Yet those same colleges every year require all the members of their faculties to renew *in writing* their personal commitment to a particular body of evangelical dogma! What wonderful independence of interpretation they allow! It is like the car merchant who said that you can order any colour you please, so long as it is black! So in church they say you can believe any dogma you like, only it must agree with ours!

Clearly, no church in practice (whatever its theory about private judgment may be) freely allows either pastor or people to do their own unaided, unguided, uncontrolled work in scripture. Freedom of conscience is inevitably confined by the need for ecclesiastical uniformity. People of like mind gather together, and cannot help but exclude troublesome dissenters!

DENOMINATIONAL DIFFERENCES

Consider also how many Christian denominations there are, each with its own statement of faith, each sure that its reading of the Bible is the best one. Let us narrow the field, and think only about the various Pentecostal groups (to one of which I belong myself). Here are sincere, devout Christians, mature in faith and strong in understanding, yet how much they differ in the way they interpret scripture! Surely it becomes obvious that the task of hermeneutics is a far from easy one!

Let me cite here an example of just one of those awkward places where honest interpreters will differ strongly. It is a text that seems to be historically incorrect, or even to contradict other passages – *Mark 2:26*, where the name of the priest should be *Ahimelech* (Abiathar's father, cp. 1 Sa 21:1-6). Commentators and textual critics provide various ways of solving this problem, which do not concern me here. My purpose in drawing attention to the apparent error is simply to show the need for a scholarly appraisal of scripture. [138]

The Bible is not an easy book. The claim that any person is as competent as another to interpret scripture is irresponsible, except in the case of those passages that are indeed plain and simple enough for a child to understand. Even then there are traps for the unwary, as the following pages will show. In many places the true meaning and message of the Bible for our time can be found only after diligent study, careful research, responsible thought, humble prayer, and out of a background of profound and wide knowledge of the whole Bible. And since there will always be people who know more than I do, I must remain humbly willing to learn from them, and not arrogantly suppose myself to be a fountainhead of all wisdom!

DARK AND DIFFICULT

Scripture itself acknowledges that it contains things that are *"dark and difficult to understand"*, which the *"uneducated"* misuse and so cause untold harm (2 Pe 3:16). Indeed there are several places where the Bible openly admits that many people (for various reasons) may find it a hard book to interpret properly – see *Isaiah 6:10; Jeremiah 5:21; Ezekiel 12:2; 2 Thessalonians 2:2; Hebrews 5:11-14*. So almost as soon as the canon of the Old Testament was completed (around the time of Ezra), scribes appeared whose task it was to preserve the sacred scrolls and to expound them to the people (Ezra 7:10). The first instance of the public reading and teaching of scripture from a wooden pulpit occurred under the auspices of Nehemiah, prince and governor of the Jews (Ne 8:1-12). Notice how a passage of scripture was first read by Ezra, then explained by the Levites (vs. 7-

---

[138] I have compiled a list, based simply on my own reading of scripture, of perhaps a hundred similar problems.

8) – and they persevered with their expositions until *"everybody understood the reading . . . and there was great joy among them because they now understood the words that had been spoken"* (vs. 8,12). Neither Ezra nor Nehemiah believed that the people could be trusted to do this work by themselves. They knew that *some* scripture would be readily understood by all the people; but they also knew that those same people would find other scripture dark – which is an idea that Sirach echoed – [139]

> A scribe gains wisdom because he can devote time to getting it. Only those who have few things to distract their attention can become wise. How can someone become wise who has to walk behind a plough, cleverly wielding a goad, driving oxen, and working hard all day? He has to concentrate on making a straight furrow, and he is worried about having enough hay for his stock. . . . *(the rabbi goes on to talk about builders, architects, painters, jewellers, smiths, potters, and then says)* . . . These people all rely on their hands; in their own trade they are highly skilled. No matter where they live they will never go hungry, for without them the city would soon become desolate!
>
> Yet they are not the ones that people turn to for advice about weighty matters, they are not chosen to sit among the elders . . . How different are those who devote themselves to studying the law of the Most High! They take time to reflect upon the gathered wisdom of the fathers; they examine the prophetic oracles, searching out the sayings of famous people, and revealing the hidden meanings of parables and proverbs. . . . They must discipline themselves to get up early, to seek the Lord their Maker in prayer . . . and if the great Lord is willing they will be filled with spiritual understanding, able to pour out wise sayings of their own, while giving heartfelt thanks to God. Their learning will be directed by the Lord, according to his own wisdom, and they will take delight in discovering his divine secrets. Their knowledge will fill their words with wisdom, for their only boast will be the Word of the Lord and his covenant.

Little has changed. The people of God still need teachers who, obedient to the call of God, devote themselves to the study and exposition of his word. Let us pray for such men and women; and add a petition that they might work in grace, and with truth.

DOCTRINAL HEDGES

Let me approach the matter from another direction. If well-instructed teachers are not needed, why do we spend such vast sums of money on our many Bible

---

[139] Sirach 38:24 – 39:11.

colleges and seminaries? Why do we insist upon an educated clergy? Why are we so particular to spell out our doctrinal stances, and to print our mandatory statements of faith? We hedge both our clergy and congregations inside a multitude of pre-determined dogmas. Nor can we do anything else. Chaos would result if a church, or group of churches, were to allow the people to believe anything they like, or to interpret scripture in any way they please. The very identity and mission of a church depends upon establishing some theological boundaries beyond which it cannot allow its people to trespass. Those who do go too far have no choice except to withdraw from the fellowship of that church.

Think also about the labour scholars and commentators must undergo before they can call themselves competent interpreters. Many disciplines must be mastered, of which hermeneutics is only one –

> The study of the **canon** confirms which books should or should not be called scripture. The study of **historical criticism** reveals the social, cultural, and political framework in which each book was written. The study of **textual criticism** determines as nearly as possible the original wording of each passage. The study of **hermeneutics** provides the rules for trustworthy interpretation of each passage. The study of **exegesis** teaches how to apply the above rules and so draw correct doctrine from the sacred canon. The body of truth known as **biblical theology** is the eventual result. [140]

So let us be done with the fiction that people can get along quite well without teachers. God himself has placed instructors in the church for the express purpose of guiding it into sound doctrine. Even honest and intelligent readers of the Bible cannot always be trusted to grasp its message properly. Indeed, neither can gifted teachers – which shows just how much we need each other as a balance against error! And of course, the best antidote against error for both pastors and people is a sound hermeneutic, which is what I am hoping to arrive at in these pages. Have I succeeded? I think so; but you will have to make your own judgment. In any case, if error can be found here, I am most willing to be shown where I have gone wrong.

Too much dogmatism should be avoided by all, for even the cleverest among us can boast no more than fragmentary knowledge (1 Co 13:9). Yet it remains true that a good hermeneutic will remove many difficulties, and bring the church ever closer to consensus in its beliefs.

---

[140] From an unpublished set of lecture notes. Author unknown to me.

CHAPTER FIFTEEN

FARM BOYS AND SCRIPTURE

In 1516 the renowned Greek scholar and translator Desiderius Erasmus wrote in his *Greek New Testament,*

> I vehemently dissent from those who are unwilling that the sacred Scriptures, translated into the vulgar tongue, should be read by private persons . . . I wish that the husbandman may sing parts of them at his plough, that the weaver may warble them at his shuttle, that the traveller may with their narratives beguile the weariness of the way.

A few years later the great English reformer and martyr William Tyndale echoed the same idea in his ringing declaration to an angry priest, who said that the pope's word was greater than the law of God –

> I defy the pope and all his laws; if God spare my life, ere many years I will cause the boy that driveth a plough shall know more of the scripture than thou dost!

Those words became one of the great themes of the 16th-century Reformation, and enormous energy was put into making the Bible accessible to everyone who wanted to read it. Nearly half a millennium later we are still benefiting from their labours, with an abundance of translations in many low-cost editions. Every attempt by civil and church authorities to keep the Bible out of the hands of the people has been thwarted, and we may truly rejoice in its universal availability.

However, there remains an element of untruth in Tyndale's claim that he would cause a farm boy to know the Bible better than a bishop. Why? Because *the Bible itself presupposes a literate readership* – that is, people skilled enough to understand poetry, prophecy, sacred history, and narrative, along with an acquired knowledge of the history, culture, and chronology of the larger world in which the Bible was written. For the first readers of the various biblical documents, of course, many of those environmental factors were part of their daily lives, and they understood them without effort. But for us, such knowledge cannot be gained without considerable labour.

Thus the church must maintain a balance between the need for good teachers to guide the people into the truth, and the requirement for each believer to accept his or her own duty in scripture. The church cannot cast aside its obligation to be a guardian and promulgator of the truth; but neither can I (as a believer) deny that I am personally responsible for all that I believe and do. Others may guide and instruct me, but I alone am answerable for my own conscience, both for its decisions and its actions. None will be able to stand in the day of judgment and point a finger at another as the cause of some faulty doctrine or wrong practice. Instead, you and I must each apply ourselves to the tasj of reading the Bible properly, of understanding it wisely, and of applying its teaching sensibly.

A PERSPICUOUS BIBLE

With these things in mind, the Reformers coined an expression. the *"perspicuity* [141] of scripture". It is sometimes taken to mean that the full message of the Bible is clear to any reasonably intelligent and literate person. But that is not quite right. Even the Reformers wrote many volumes of theology, comment, and explanation, and insisted upon their followers adhering only to the approved dogmas! Rather, when they called the Bible "perspicuous", they meant only that a normal reader could readily meet with Christ in the pages of scripture, and discover salvation, without need of priest or even church. For that reason alone, even if there were no others, we should urge every Christian to meditate continually in the Word of God, and to dwell there in the Master's presence. Yet still the most earnest believer will need guidance in mining the treasures of that Word. [142]

So we come back to the notion that the most sensible approach is to find a balance between the right of each person to read the Bible and interpret it himself, and the right of the church to call on its highest scholarship to establish and impose sound doctrine. [143]

But whether the sacred page is under view by a teacher or a student, both of them, to guard against error and to ensure the truth, will need a good

---

[141] "Perspicuity" comes from the Latin for "transparent", and means free from obscurity, clear, unambiguous, lucid.

[142] *1 John 4:6* may be appropriate here, as an apostolic confirmation of the principle.

[143] For example, note what a heavy burden Paul places upon local church leaders to ensure that **sound doctrine** is both taught and preserved among the people (Ro 6:17; Ep 4:14; 1 Ti 1:3,10; 4:6,13; 5:17; 6:3; 2 Ti 4:2-3; Tit 1:9; 2:1,7).

hermeneutic. Too often one encounters ideas that are inconsistent, or that read more into scripture than what is actually meant, or apply scripture in ways that are false.

INTELLECTUAL ELITISM

A certain peril hides in the shadows of these ideas; I mean, the risk of an intellectual elitism. We must beware of feeling that only learned scholars can grasp the true message of the Bible. There is nothing in a good hermeneutic that any reasonably literate person should find difficult to understand. No prior level of rare academic attainment is required by the Bible, nor does it presume any elevated doctrinal or theological learning. A good background knowledge of the historical, social, political, and cultural setting in which each part of scripture was composed can be gained by any normal person who is willing to male the effort.

In the end, a truly sound hermeneutic rests upon little more than a comparison of scripture with scripture, an interpretation of the Bible based upon what the Bible itself says. It will also deal bravely with questions that many intelligent people who have become thoroughly familiar with the Bible over many years might be likely to ask. Serious Bible readers who are not preachers or professors will inescapably meet these problems. They are not issues of scholarship, but simply quandaries that need to be faced and solved. I am certainly not the only Bible student who has pondered them, nor will I be the last! Whether or not my answers are the best ones is, of course, another matter. That is something each reader will have to determine personally.

But this coin also has another side; this ocean is not always shallow; this river plunges into

SOME DEEP POOLS

Jesus once spoke about a well-instructed scribe, who, being rich in knowledge of the kingdom of God, was like a wealthy man who brought out of his treasures things both new and old (Mt 13:52). That is what I am aiming for. So far we have seen that parts of the Bible are plain enough, simple enough, for even a child to understand and to find the way of life (2 Ti 3:15). But other parts are sufficiently profound or difficult to stretch the loftiest intellect, and to leave even the most learned scholar with a sensation of being condemned to wade only in the shallows of wisdom. We cannot help but notice how thinkers of the most towering skill still differ in their reading of some parts of scripture. Even that great divine St Augustine, for example, despaired of explaining satisfactorily the *Six Days of Creation* –

> What kind of days these are is difficult to imagine, hard to understand, and nearly impossible to describe! [144]

Who then is that *"wise scribe"* Jesus mentioned? Where shall we find such a paragon? What shall we look for? Certainly not for infallibility, for no one save Jesus embodies all truth. But there are *some* qualities that do mark out a teacher who deserves the honour of the church, the kind of instructor at whose feet any godly person might be content sit and learn. Here is a list (which I found among my notes) of some of those qualities. I think the list is one that I compiled myself, but if not, then my humble apologies to the unknown author –

- ***a sanctified mind*** – pure and holy in worship of God, fixed on things above, not on things on earth (Cl 3:1-3).
- ***an open eye*** – able, like Zechariah, to penetrate the veil and see into the spiritual dimension (for he *"looked up and saw"* – 1:8,18; 2:1; 3:1; 4:2; 5:1,2,5; 6:1).
- ***an illumined spirit*** – echoing Paul's prayer for inner enlightenment, revelation, wisdom, and knowledge (Ep 1:15-19; Cl 1:9-10).
- ***a disciplined soul*** – devoted to wide study and hard labour in order to *"rightly divide the word of truth"* (2 Ti 2:15).
- ***a humble heart*** – ever willing to be corrected, to be taught, eager always to learn, ever on the journey, never supposing that the end has been reached (Ph 3:13-14).
- ***a reasonable attitude*** – tolerant of other views while ardent for truth; able to engage in debate without acrimony (Is 1:18; Ga 5:26; 1 Ti 6:20; 2 Ti 2:16; Tit 1:10; 3:9).
- ***a tender conscience*** – not arrogant in knowledge nor conceited in learning, but gentle, persuadable, still able to be convicted of sin and of error (Ac 23:1; 24:16; Ro 9:1; 2 Co 1:12; 1 Ti 1:19; 3:9; He 13:18).
- ***a yielded life*** – eager to hear the command of God, ready to obey the Spirit without hesitation, willing to function under the disciplines of the local church (Ac 5:29; 26:19; Ro 2:8; 2 Th 3:14; He 13:17).
- ***a quickened faith*** – ready to grasp and believe every promise of God, motivated and governed by faith rather than by sight (2 Co 4:18; 5:7; Ga 2:20).

---

[144] The City of God, Book XI, Chapter 6, last sentence.

- *a prayerful demeanour* – a life, a ministry, a service, bathed in constant prayer, for only thus can the Word of God be illuminated to the searching eye (Ps 119:18; Is 62:6; Ro 1:9; Ph 1:4; Cl 1:3; 1 Th 1:2; 5:17).
- *a Christlike character* – this perhaps should have come first; yet a person can be thoroughly Christian without having any gift as a teacher – so let it be the crowning glory of the true interpreter, that his or her life radiates the beauty of Jesus (2 Co 2:15-16).

CHAPTER SIXTEEN

AN OBSOLETE BOOK?

> It is not unremarkable what Philo first observed, that the Law of Moses continued two thousand yeares without the least alteration; whereas, we see the Lawes of other Common-weales doe alter with occasions; and even those that pretended their originall from some Divinity, to have vanished without trace or memory. I beleeve, besides Zoroaster, there were divers that writ before Moses, who, not withstanding, have suffered the common fate of time. Men's Workes have an age like themselves; and though they out-live their Authors, yet have they a stint and period to their duration: This (Bible) onely is a Worke too hard for the teeth of time, and cannot perish but in the generall Flames, when all things shall confesse their Ashes. (Sir Thomas Browne, op. cit. Part One, Sec 23.)

This book of mine, too, will perish. Some may think it should have perished before it was written! They dislike it when attempts are made to put the Bible into its historical context. They feel that stressing the antiquity of the Bible has the effect of making it "obsolete", of robbing scripture of its relevance for our own time. But how can that be? No hermeneutic worth considering will deny that the Bible has a powerful and wonderful message for the modern world. The Bible remains, as it has always been, the only wholly reliable source of God's truth. No one deserves to be heard who denies the veracity of scripture as the revealed Word of God, in which the face of Christ is mirrored on nearly every page!

Yet after agreeing that scripture speaks truthfully today, every Bible reader still faces the task of discovering what is _actually_ God's word to _us_. To do that, we must modify its words – its surface meaning – in a thousand places. People may differ in the rigour with which they apply that modifying rule, but apply it they do, as must every intelligent reader of the Bible. Indeed, a good hermeneutic simply puts into a consistent form what everybody (including the most fervent literalists) does in practice – that is, we all adjust our understanding of scripture in a way that suits our environment. We do this by adjusting (whether consciously or unconsciously) the way in which we read various parts of the Bible –

- some passages of scripture we embrace and apply without question, never doubting that they belong to us word for word (e.g. Jn 3:16)
- some passages we utilise only after much modification (e.g. Mk 9:43-47; [145] Lu 14:33; 17:6; etc)
- some passages that cannot conceivably be applied to modern life, we ignore, except to draw a spiritual lesson from them (e.g. Nu 5:11-31; Le 14:33-53).

Since those modifications are undeniably practised by all Bible believers, certain conclusions seem inevitable –

LOCKED INTO A DILEMMA

Surely no one can sensibly deny that there are customs and laws enjoined in different parts of scripture that are not valid for our time? Even those who insist upon reading the Bible literally do not obey those laws, nor do they follow those practices. Indeed, they would be appalled if they found anyone attempting to do so.

But now see what a dilemma exists. Here is someone who plucks a text off the sacred page and insists that it must be obeyed exactly as it stands, but then serenely declares that another command found in the same passage must be strongly modified

- for example: some writers quote *Matthew 5:31-32*, insist that Jesus' words must be strictly obeyed, and then forbid any re-marriage after divorce
- yet those same pundits refuse to apply the same literalness to the two verses immediately previous (vs. 29-30), for if they did, it would certainly cost them one or more of their bodily parts!

That seems unconscionable to me. On what valid basis can the first two verses be treated symbolically, while the next two are read literally? All four verses are part of the same discourse. Jesus made no distinction between them. They differ

---

[145] Even in our own time there have been sad cases of people taking these words literally, and mutilating themselves – tearing out an eye, cutting off a hand, castrating themselves. Tragic though such incidents are, the victims were at least consistent in their reading of scripture. Having been taught to take the Bible literally, they did so, with terrible consequences.

not at all in grammar, literary form, context, style, or in any other meaningful way. So what governing rule controls those arbitrary judges of the literal and the symbolic? Convenience? Culture? Civil law?

We should rather aim for a consistent way to read every part of scripture, one that does not involve us in arbitrary or capricious choices. We should search for the message each passage contains for our time, and strive to apply that message wisely in daily life. So the Bible must first be read as an ancient book, and then the question asked, "What is the meaning of this book for today?"

A DISCRIMINATING EYE

Some readers may perhaps be troubled by such an approach. Yet how can it be thought improper? The Bible *is* an ancient book! Its antiquity *must* be taken into account. Every preacher does that to some degree – we would be in a terrible mess if we didn't! I simply argue that we ought to be consistent in our view. Error must arise when people choose haphazardly to read some bits of scripture as if they were written yesterday, but others as if they come from the mists of history. How can any hermeneutic be valid unless it teaches us it teaches us

- *first,* to learn what the biblical authors were saying in their own time, and
- *then,* to search for the meaning the Holy Spirit intends the church today to find in each passage.

The fact that sometimes the meaning of a passage for us will prove to be exactly the same as it was for its first readers does not invalidate the general rule. The Bible does not always speak to us in the same way as it did to the ancients. We had better teach people to read it with a discriminating eye, to read it intelligently, and from a background as historically well-informed as possible, otherwise they will soon fall into many kinds of bizarre behaviour.

BETTER OR WORSE?

In the following pages you will find several comparisons drawn between our culture and that of the Hebrews. I do not mean to imply that our social structures are invariably better than those of the past. On the contrary, there may well be areas in which *they* were ahead of *us*. For example, consider the matter of spiritual discernment, in which the Hebrews seem to have been more advanced than contemporary western people ordinarily are. Thus, we constantly struggle to discern whether certain events have a natural or demonic origin; but godly Jews apparently could make the distinction with ease. Nonetheless, whether better or worse, there *is* a large cultural difference, and it must be taken into account before scripture can be reliably imported into modern life.

INFALLIBLE INTERPRETATIONS?

In 1627 George Hakewill wrote an *Apology* for the Christian faith, in which he said –

> Though I am bound steadfastly to believe what St Paul affirms, yet am I not bound to believe your affirmation that St Paul affirms it, and for any such convincing infallible demonstrations (as you speak of) that he so doth, I confess as yet I cannot find it. [146]

That counsel from a preacher who lived four centuries ago is often forgotten – which is a problem mentioned at the beginning of this book. It is worth repeating here. There are many who confuse an infallible Bible with their *understanding* of it! To maintain the authenticity and authority of scripture is one thing; but to claim the same authority for one person's interpretation is something quite different. Like Mr Hakewill, we should happily believe everything scripture affirms; but we are not obliged to believe what someone alleges it affirms! Only the Bible speaks with the authority of God. We do not. So humility and a willingness to admit error are useful additions to the scholar's toolbox!

You should always keep inviolate the right to read and understand the Bible according to your personal conscience. But then all who claim that *right* must also accept the *responsibility* of applying themselves as earnestly as possible to the study of scripture, so that they may hope to come very close to what the Bible really does teach.

---

[146] Quoted in Christopher Hill, op. cit.; pg. 349.

CHAPTER SEVENTEEN

DANGEROUS SECRETS?

> Your cannons moulder on the seaward wall;
> His voice is silent in your council-hall
> For ever; and whatever tempests lour
> For ever silent; even if they broke
> In thunder, silent; yet remember all
> He spoke among you, and the Man who spoke;
> ***Who never sold the truth to serve the hour,***
> ***Nor palter'd with Eternal God for power.*** [147]

Are there times when, spurning the noble example of the Duke Wellington, one should indeed "sell the truth to serve the hour"? Are some things too dangerous to tell? Surely there are situations when it is wiser to be "economical with the truth"? [148] Perhaps too, Oscar Wilde's warning is valid? "If one tells the truth, one is sure, sooner or later, to be found out." Or is it more a case of, "Questions are never indiscreet (but) answers sometimes are"?

This problem (is it better to tell or not to tell?) is one that has often vexed philosophers and divines. Henry Fielding touches on it in his epic comedy *Tom Jones*. [149] He quotes Lord Shaftesbury, who "somewhere objects to telling too much Truth". In fact, the worthy earl said –

---

[147] Alfred, Lord Tennyson; Ode on the Death of the Duke of Wellington (1852); lines 173-180; emphasis mine.

[148] A comment first made by Sir Robert Armstrong (circa 1986) in response to an accusation that a letter he had written told a lie: "It contained a misleading impression, not a lie. It was being economical with the truth."

[149] Book XIII, opening lines; Fourth Edition, published in 1750. Tom Jones is often called the progenitor of the modern novel, although it should probably share that honour with Samuel Richardson's *Pamela* – see Chapter. Three above.

> We can never do more injury to Truth, than by discovering too much of it, on some occasions.[150]

The "occasions" referred to by the earl occur when hard things are spoken in the presence of people who have a limited or undeveloped understanding. Truth may be to them a nut too hard to crack, or may even appear as error. That is the quandary we face here. We are about to look at some particular difficulties that hinder an easy interpretation of scripture, and I cannot help but ask: how far should this disclosure be taken? Am I raising too many questions? Are the problems too far ahead of the experience and learning of readers who are young or undeveloped in faith?

Tennyson grappled with the dilemma in another of his poems. He refers to the supposedly innocent and uncluttered faith of Mary (the sister of Martha and Lazarus) who, while Martha was busy with many things, chose to sit at Jesus' feet, happily listening to his words. The poet warns the reader against disturbing her childlike trust with troublesome questions –

> Her[151] eyes are homes of silent prayer,
> . . . . .
> All subtle thought, all curious fears,
>   Borne down by gladness so complete,
>   She bows, she bathes the Saviour's feet
> With costly spikenard and with tears.
> Thrice blest whose lives are faithful prayers,
>   Whose loves in higher love endure;
>   What souls possess themselves so pure,
> Or is there blessedness like theirs?
>
> O thou that after toil and storm[152]
>   Mayst seem to have reach'd a purer air,
>   Whose faith has centre everywhere,
> Nor cares to fix itself to form,
>
> Leave thou thy sister[153] when she prays
>   Her early heaven, her happy views;

---

[150] Anthony Ashley Cooper, Third Earl of Shaftesbury (1671-1713). From his "Essay on the Freedom of Wit", Sec. II, par. 2; in *Characteristics of Men, Manners, Opinions, Times* I.62. Cited in <u>Tom Jones</u>, edited by Sheridan Baker; W. W. Norton & Co., New York, 1973; footnote on pg. 564.

[151] Mary.

[152] Of much debate, reasoning, questioning and argument.

[153] Mary.

> Nor thou with shadow'd hint confuse
> A life that leads melodious days.
>
> Her faith thro' form is pure as thine,
> Her hands are quicker unto good.
> O, sacred be the flesh and blood
> To which she links a truth divine!
>
> See thou, that countest reason ripe
> In holding by the law within,
> Thou fail not in a world of sin,
> And even for want of such a type. [154]

Charles Dickens, too, struck the same note in his tale about a church antiquarian, known as the Bachelor, who fudged the truth a little by preferring a charming legend to the dull facts of history –

> He was not one of those rough spirits who would strip fair Truth of every little shadowy vestment in which time and teeming fancies love to array her – and some of which become her pleasantly enough, serving, like the waters of her well, to add new graces to the charms they half conceal and half suggest, and to awaken interest and pursuit rather than languor and indifference – as, unlike this stern and obdurate class, he loved to see the goddess crowned with those garlands of wild flowers which tradition wreathes for her gentle wearing, and which are often freshest in their homeliest shapes – he trod with a light step and bore with a light hand upon the dust of centuries, unwilling to demolish any of the airy shrines that had been raised above it, if any good feeling or affection of the human heart were hiding thereabouts. Thus, in the case of an ancient coffin of rough stone, supposed, for many generations, to contain the bones of a certain baron, who, after ravaging, with cut, and thrust, and plunder, in foreign lands, came back with a penitent and sorrowing heart to die at home, but which had been lately shown by learned antiquaries to be no such thing, as the baron in question (so they contended) had died hard in battle, gnashing his teeth and cursing with his latest breath – the Bachelor stoutly maintained that the old tale was the true one; that the baron, repenting him of the evil, had done great charities and meekly given up the ghost; and that, if ever baron went to heaven, that baron was then at peace. [155]

Certain critics have pressed the Bachelor's complaint (and Tennyson's) against some of the propositions offered in this book. They argue that some questions

---

[154] In Memoriam, Sec, 32 & 33.

[155] The Old Curiosity Shop, Chapter 54. I cannot aspire to the genius of Dickens, but I will at least boast this: I have never inflicted on my readers any sentence nearly as long as the two in the above quote (150 & 128 words respectively)! I think the longest sentence of mine you will find here would scarcely exceed 70 words, and there are few that approach even that length.

should not be asked, and some issues should not be aired, lest they disturb the faith of more simple souls. I cannot deny that the temptation to allow people to stay happy in a pleasant delusion is a strong one. There is a certain charm, albeit perilous, in the innocence of ignorance, as Tristram Shandy's father once cried to Uncle Toby –

> Gracious heaven! cried my father, looking upwards, and clasping his two hands together, — there is a worth in thy honest ignorance, brother *Toby*, — 'twere almost a pity to exchange it for a knowledge. —— But I'll tell thee. —— [156]

Now there's a piece of ambiguity! Whatever the worth of ignorance, Mr Shandy was still resolved to speak up! Likewise, I am loth to think that there is a level of knowledge accessible only to an initiated group of divines, as if one has to join the "club" before one can be told these hidden secrets. Surely truth belongs to everyone, and it is better to be informed than uninformed, even if at first the truth is troublesome?

LETHAL LEARNING?

Still, I am mindful of the peril of too much knowledge. If, as Alexander Pope said, "a little learning is a dangerous thing," then the added saying of the English comic writer Tom Sharpe might be equally true, "a lot is lethal!" Tristram Shandy certainly thought so. In a piece of biting sarcasm, Tristram describes how his Uncle Toby was trying to calculate the flight path of a cannon ball –

> — He proceeded next to *Gallileo* and *Torricellius*, [157] wherein, by certain geometrical rules, infallibly laid down, he found the precise path to be a PARABOLA, — or else an HYPERBOLA, — and that the parameter, or *latus rectum*, [158] of the conic section of the said path, was to the quantity and amplitude in a direct *ratio*, as the whole line to the sine of double the angle of incidence, form'd by the breech upon an horizontal plane; — and that the semi-parameter, — — stop! my dear uncle *Toby*, — stop! — go not one foot further into this thorny and bewilder'd track, — intricate are the steps! intricate are the mazes of this labyrinth! intricate are the troubles which the pursuit of this bewitching phantom, KNOWLEDGE, will bring upon thee. — O my uncle! fly — fly — fly from it as from a serpent. — Is it fit, good-natur'd man! thou should'st sit up, with the wound

---

[156] Laurence Sterne, op. cit. Volume Three, Chapter XVIII.
[157] Two mathematicians who wrote about parabolic flight.
[158] Straight line.

upon thy groin, [159] whole nights baking thy blood with hectic watchings? — Alas! 'twill exasperate thy symptoms, — check thy perspirations, — evaporate thy spirits, — waste thy animal strength, — dry up thy radical moister, [160] — bring thee into a costive habit of body, impair thy health, — and hasten all the infirmities of thy old age. — O my uncle! my uncle Toby. [161]

The Bible itself gives a warning about those who are ever learning but never arrive at a knowledge of the truth (2 Ti 3:7). Somewhere there must come a resting point for faith. Is it then wise, is it an act of love, to disturb sincere people who, no matter how ill-informed they may be, are content in their faith? Thus Paul adds his own admonition –

> *Knowledge inflates; love edifies. Do you claim to know something? Perhaps xou know nothing! Do you think you possess liberty? Be careful that your freedom does not become another person's chain! Suppose you assert your rights and succeed only in destroying some weaker person for whom also Christ died? Do you really want to sin like that against a fellow Christian? Worse still, when you wound the conscience of a weaker brother or sister, then you actually sin against Christ himself!* (1 Co 8:2-12, abridged).

FOCUS ON THE WISE?

Other thinkers have presented an opposite view, insisting that knowledge is too precious to hide away. Among them was Maimonides, a famous medieval Jewish philosopher, who in his last and greatest book, *Guide to the Perplexed* (a commentary on the *Torah*), and near its beginning, wrote –

> When I am dealing with a difficult subject . . . if I can see no other way to teach a truth that cannot be denied except to please one intelligent person, though it displeases ten thousand fools, then I will ignore the accusations of the multitude and focus my attention on the one who is wise. [162]

I have some doubts about the morality of that saying. It seems ethically dubious. Yet if difficult truth must always be hidden because there are people who either cannot grasp it or cannot handle it wisely, then nothing perplexing will ever be

---

[159] He had been wounded in battle, struck by a cannon ball.

[160] The moisture inherent in all plants and animals, and essential for life.

[161] Laurence Sterne, op. cit., Volume Two, Chapter Three.

[162] Jewish Literacy, by Rabbi Joseph Telushkin; William Morrow & Co. Inc., New York, 1991; page number lost.

known. So what shall we do? I am disposed to be cautious, and for good reason. Like the psalmist, I worry about causing harm to the children of God –

> *If I were to say such things, I might become an offence among your people. When I tried to solve this problem, I found that it was too hard for me!* (Ps 73:15-16)

But then I notice, despite his hesitation, the poet still went on to tell the doubts that were troubling him. He did however protect himself by revealing a solution he had later found to his problem (vs. 16-17). Here then may be our escape: not just to pose conundrums, but also to provide answers that are true to scripture, reason, and faith. That too is how Paul handled the situation. Despite his good words (quoted above) about never allowing *"knowledge"* to supplant *"love"*, he still declared his own position clearly enough. Nor did he hesitate to use the adjective *"weak"* (1 Co 8:7,10-12) in connection with believers who were fearful about eating meat that had been offered to idols. Having insulted them with that epithet, one wonders how impressed they were when Paul later agreed to sit down with them to a vegetarian meal! His hope of course was that those same *"weak"* believers would, through greater knowledge and better understanding, become *"strong"*. In the meantime, he loved them deeply in Christ, and endeavoured to bring them to a tougher level of faith.

JESUS WAS BRAVE

Suppose we turn to the gospels? How did Christ handle this problem? At once we observe how boldly the Master announced the toughest things, and how little he cared for public opinion –

- he made many enigmatic pronouncements, which provoked people to bewilderment, anger, or both (Mk 9:43-48; Jn 2:18-22; 6:41,52,60,66; etc)

- without offering any clarification or answers, he asked awkward questions, leaving his hearers puzzled and disturbed (Lu 20:41-44)

- he did not hesitate to countermand Moses, which was almost unthinkable behaviour for a devout Jew (Mk 7:19; etc).

- he made the most shocking demands, adding neither qualification nor explanation (Mk 9:42-48; Lu 14:26; Mt 5:39-42) – although sometimes he privately explained to his disciples the meaning of sayings that deeply offended his wider audience (Mt 19:10-12; Jn 6:60-65; Mk 7:17; Mt 15:12,15)

- he spoke perplexing things that certainly make me (and I think you too) feel very uncomfortable (Lu 6:20, 24-25) [163]

- he used obscure parables, deliberately hiding his meaning from all except those who had earned the right to understand him (Mk 4:10-12)

- he frankly told his disciples that they were not yet ready to hear some of the things he wanted to teach them (Jn 16:12-13)

- and think how many scholars (and countless others) have torn out their hair trying to penetrate the mysteries of his prophetic oracles, which students are no closer to solving now (except in broad, undetailed pictures) than the Church Fathers were in the beginning [164]

- perhaps even more astonishing, he spoke some of his most aggravating and bewildering words in the presence of a mixed audience, predictably arousing an indignant protest (Jn 6:59-60), which was occasionally violent enough to threaten his life (Lu 4:28; Jn 8:55, 58-59; 10:30-31, 38-39)

---

[163] In comparison with most of the inhabitants of this planet, are we not rich, are we not well-fed, do we not live in much comfort? Must we then pronounce ourselves wicked, deserving only woe?

[164] The Puritan commentator Matthew Henry described the *Olivet Discourse* (Mt 24:3-51) as "dark and difficult", and reckoned that Jesus preached it, not *ad populum* – to the people, but *ad clerum* – to the clergy (Commentary, in. loc.). William E. Biederwolf says that across the centuries opinions on the first part of the *Olivet Discourse* have fallen into four groups –

- "Those who think it was all fulfilled in the past at the time of the Destruction of Jerusalem.
- "Those who think it is all yet to be fulfilled during the time of the great tribulation just before the coming of the Lord in glory and in judgment on the antichristian forces of the world after the Church has been caught up according to the fourth chapter of *1 Thessalonians*.
- "Those who think it is being fulfilled in this present dispensation and is to find its final and more awful fulfilment in the great tribulation through which the Church herself will pass in the time of the end.
- "Those who see part fulfilment in the Destruction of Jerusalem and the other part in the Parousia (the second coming of Jesus) which is still in the future." (The Second Coming Bible, Baker Book House, 1972; pg. 327.)

I would add a fifth common interpretation: the *idealist* view, which holds that the oracle must be read in a figurative and symbolic sense, with continual fulfilments across the centuries. Which is the correct view? Only heaven knows! That is why St John Chrysostom (5th century) thought it safer to focus on the moral and ethical aspects of the *Discourse* than on any attempt to pinpoint the meaning of its details – an opinion with which I heartily concur *(Homilies on Matthew 24).*

- the result was that even his disciples sometimes failed to understand him or gave his words a wrong meaning (Mt 16:6-7; Mk 9:32; Lu 9:45; 18:34; Jn 10:6; 12:16; 16:17-18).

- in the end, the disciples had to acknowledge that Jesus spoke the truth boldly, deferring to no one, allowing no excuses for ignorance or disobedience, showing special favour to none (Lu 20:21).

Of course, *everything* Jesus said, both easy and hard, whether in private or in public, now stands openly on the pages of the New Testament. There his words are freely accessible not just to the learned but also to the ignorant; they are read by the immature as well as by the mature. Surely this is dangerous? Yes it is, and many follies have been committed by *"silly and unstable people who have twisted the scriptures to their own destruction!"* (2 Pe 3:16). But the Lord is apparently prepared to tolerate such abuses for the sake of the benefits that millions of sensible people can gain from a wise use of the Bible.

You and I can join that company of the wise by

- applying the remedy in which Jesus himself reposed much confidence: the teaching skill of the Holy Spirit (Jn 16:13-15); and by

- developing a sensible hermeneutic that will guard us against wresting a lie out of the truth, so that we *"rightly divide the word of truth"*. (2 Ti 2:15, KJV)

JESUS' HERMENEUTIC

What hermeneutic did Jesus follow? Notice how he looked for the *divine* rather than the *literal* meaning of many passages of scripture. For example –

- he apparently did not expect *Elijah* to return in a strictly literal sense, despite the clear statement in *Malachi 4:5* (see Mt 11:14; 17:10-13; and cp. Lu 1:17)

- he rebuked the Sadducees because their view of scripture was too narrow and too literal: *"You are wrong, because you do not know either the scriptures or the power of God!"* (Mt 22:29)

- he himself suffered the same abuse that was done to scripture: he was constantly misunderstood by those who insisted upon taking his words too literally (Jn 2:20-21; 3:3-4; 4:10-11, 31-34; 6:51-54; etc.)

The above preamble means simply this: I am aware that some of the questions raised in the following pages carry a risk of disturbing people whose faith is simple and uncluttered, whose eye has never discerned the difficulties raised here, and into whose mind such questions have never before entered. Yet it is hard to believe that even such innocent souls, if they continue to search out the scriptures, will not eventually be confronted by these problems. What will they do then? Some, having never discovered a way to cope with them, may have their faith shattered; others will limp along, plagued by doubts they cannot resolve. It seems better to be forearmed – that is, to develop a hermeneutic that will provide a universally reliable method of understanding scripture, and of applying its message to life.

DR JOHNSON'S SOLUTION

Dr Samuel Johnson, the great 18th century raconteur and lexicographer, offered a solution to the problem of handling vexing questions –

> To play with important truth, to disturb the repose of established tenets, to subtilise objections, and elude proof, is too often the sport of youthful vanity, of which maturer experience commonly repents. There is a time when every wise man is weary of raising difficulties only to task himself with the solution, and desires to enjoy truth without the labour or hazard of contest. There is, perhaps, no better method of encountering these troublesome irruptions of scepticism, with which inquisitive minds are frequently harassed, than that which Sir Thomas Browne declares himself to have taken: "If there arise any doubts in my way, I do forget them; or at least defer them, till my better settled judgment and more manly reason be able to resolve them: for I perceive, every man's reason is his best Oedipus." [165]

That passage is not entirely appropriate, for I am no sceptic, nor (at 63 years of age) can I be accused of indulging in "youthful vanity", nor am I raising clever questions merely for the sake of a debate. Rather, the questions already exist, and I am hoping to offer a fair answer to them. Nonetheless, for some readers the task of confronting these problems may be too disturbing. If so, heed Sir Thomas Browne's advice, and put them aside for a later occasion. My goal is never to weaken faith, but rather to strengthen it by giving it a better foundation upon which to build. In the end, I think that goal can best be reached by adopting the attitude expressed by Richard Nixon –

---

[165] Op. cit. pg. 505-506. "Oedipus" solved the riddle of the Sphinx.

Let us begin by committing ourselves to the truth, to see it like it is and to tell it like it is, to find the truth, to speak the truth and live with the truth. That's what we'll do. [166]

AN AWESOME TASK

Anyone who loves scripture (as I do), and who believes that the Bible is the authoritative Word of God, inspired by the Holy Spirit, and given for our correction and training in righteousness, [167] must tremble at the thought of failing to *"teach the word of truth correctly"*. [168] Let us then approach the Bible with humility, for here we meet God face to face. Yet the very presence of divine truth in the pages of scripture demands a high level of honesty and diligence from every interpreter. Some things in the Bible are simple, like the shallows at the edge of a vast ocean that a little child may safely splash in. But other parts of scripture, like the deepest seas, yield their treasures only to swimmers who are well trained, strong, persistent, gifted in their art, and who have developed their skill to the highest degree. My prayer is that this book will help readers who are floundering to swim comfortably, both in the shallows and in the deeps of scripture.

> If there is anything in my thoughts or style to commend, the credit is due to my parents for instilling in me an early love of the Scriptures . . . If we abide by the principles taught in the Bible, our country will go on prospering and to prosper; but if we and our posterity neglect its instructions and authority, no man can tell how sudden a catastrophe may overwhelm us and bury all our glory in profound obscurity. (Daniel Webster)

---

[166] From his speech in response to his nomination for the U.S. presidency, given in Miami in 1968. He would have fared better if he had stuck to the principle of truth, which he himself acknowledged (in 1977) three years after his resignation: "I brought myself down . . . I let down my friends. I let down my country. I let down our system of government." To which he later added, "You can't put the toothpaste back in the tube!"

[167] *2 Timothy 3:16-17.*

[168] *2 Timothy 2:15; 1 Corinthians 3:10-15*, which refers primarily to teachers of scripture.

CHAPTER EIGHTEEN

SPARE THE ROD!

A young mother in Melbourne was put on trial for child abuse. She had beaten her two young children (aged 7 years and 3 years) with a metre-long rosewood cane. She argued in court that "the Bible says the hand is only for love, and a child should be disciplined with a rod." [169] Her lawyer supported her case by quoting *Proverbs*, [170] whose message can be summed up in the 17th century English aphorism, *"Spare the rod and spoil the child."* [171] However, she was found guilty, and was fortunate to escape only with a fine. The cane was confiscated by the police and solemnly destroyed.

A hundred years ago people would have been astonished to find the state urging such gentleness in handling children. In those days, boys and girls alike were regularly beaten with both whips and rods, not only by their parents but also by schoolmasters and other authorities. Sanction for this adult savagery against the young was of course found in the Bible. Those 19th-century floggers never doubted that they could best please God by not sparing the rod. Confident in the correctness of their reading of scripture, they were determined that no one would ever accuse *them* of unbiblical leniency!

It was not uncommon for boys (and sometimes girls) to be bent over a stool and to receive thirty stripes from a bundle of birch rods upon their bare buttocks. The beatings left them deeply bruised, lacerated, and bleeding. A child might be punished in this way two or three times in a week. Lord John Lawrence, who became the governor-general of India (1863-1869), lamented that he had been

---

[169] The first of those two claims of course has no biblical warrant, it is a piece of fiction. The second, as the following paragraphs will show, may have scarcely any more validity.

[170] For example, 13:24; 19:18; 22:15; 23:13,14; 29:15.

[171] Coined by Samuel Butler (1612-1680), paraphrasing *Proverbs 22:15; 23:13-14*; etc.

"flogged every day of my life at school, except one, and then I was flogged twice." [172] Numerous similar accounts pepper the annals of school life during the 18th and 19th centuries.

Charlotte Bronte, probably remembering her own harsh school days, describes such a scene in *Jane Eyre*. A teacher at a girls' school, being displeased with one of her pupils, commanded a 14-year old girl, whose name was Helen Burns, to fetch a bundle of birch sticks and make herself ready for punishment –

> Burns immediately left the class, and going into the small inner room where the books were kept, returned in half a minute, carrying in her hand a bunch of twigs tied together at one end. This ominous tool she presented to Miss Scatcherd with a respectful curtsey; then she quietly and without being told, unloosed her pinafore, and the teacher instantly and sharply inflicted on her neck a dozen strokes with the bunch of twigs. Not a tear rose to Burn's eye; and, while I paused from my sewing, because my fingers quivered at this spectacle with a sentiment of unavailing and impotent anger, not a feature of her pensive face altered its ordinary expression.
>
> "Hardened girl!" exclaimed Miss Scatcherd; "nothing can correct you of your slatternly habits: carry the rod away."
>
> Burns obeyed: I looked at her narrowly as she emerged from the book-closet; she was just putting back her handkerchief into her pocket, and the trace of a tear glistened on her thin cheek. *(Chapter Six).* [173]

---

[172] The Age of Scandal, by T. H. White; The Folio Society, London, 1993; pg. 83. The same chapter contains several similar accounts, along with a general description of the almost unbelievable brutality that was common in schools at that time, on both sides of the Atlantic.

[173] In the same book (Chapter Twenty One), Jane Eyre visits her dying aunt, and as she enters the bedroom, describes the scene: "There was the great four-post bed with amber hangings as of old; there the toilet table, the arm-chair, and the footstool, at which I had a hundred times been sentenced to kneel, to ask pardon for offences by me uncommitted. I looked into a certain corner near, half-expecting to see the slim outline of a once dreaded switch which used to lurk there, waiting to leap out imp-like and lace my quivering palm or shrinking neck." These severe penalties were inflicted on a six-year old child (!), but were not uncommon for the time (early 19th century). There are instances on record of young women up to 20 years of age being flogged with a whip or a bundle of birch rods simply for refusing an eligible marriage. Believing that they were sanctioned by scripture, the general community approved such beatings. (See Perfecting Fiona, a Regency novel by Marion Chesney, but based upon meticulous research, in which the heroine was so treated by her guardian.)

Similarly, I can still remember when I was a child being distressed by reading (in Arthur Mee's Children's Encyclopedia) an early 19th-century nursery rhyme that echoed the harshness of school life in those days –

    Dr Faustus was a good man,

Footnotes continued on the next page

The girl's fault was minor, and any teacher behaving today with such despicable cruelty would be rightly charged with criminal assault. Surely not even the most fervent modern quoter of *Proverbs* could wish a return to those brutal days.

But why not?

The Bible has not changed. The wisdom of *Proverbs*, which advocates quite vicious penalties, was cited in Victorian times as full justification for inflicting violent beatings on the young. Yet what ardent fundamentalist today would not bitterly resent his or her daughter being flogged by a teacher with a bundle of birch sticks?

But again I ask: "Why?"

It is certainly not because the wording of scripture has been altered, for it is just as violent today as it was then. If we do shrink from such cruelty it is not because the *Old Testament* has become kinder; rather, it is our *culture* that has become more gentle. So people today read those texts literally only so far as it suits them, which is scarcely an honest way to handle the words of God. Let us instead find an interpretive rule that allows us to treat the Bible with full seriousness, neither softening nor toughening its teaching merely because of some cultural pressure.

NICE PEOPLE AND GENTLE MANNERS

Why is the culture more gentle? There are many reasons, but among them are the continuing changes since the English Civil War [174] in the way people read the Bible. Those changes were themselves accelerated during the 19th century by two other major factors –

(1) The American Civil War

> He whipped his scholars now and then;
> When he whipped he made them dance
> Out of England into France,
> Out of France and into Spain,
> And then he whipped them back again.

The violence of the poem (which is open before me as I write) is emphasised by a surround of lively drawings of a schoolmaster furiously shaking a bundle of twigs as he chases a group of school boys. It is set to music, which makes it seem even more cruel. (Volume Seven, pg. 73. The <u>Children's Enclopedia</u> was first published in 1908. The nursery rhyme, in the form given above, first appeared in print in 1842, but is certainly several decades older.

[174] See again *Chapters Four* and *Five* above.

On one side were the slave owners, demanding the right to buy and sell human beings, because, as they said, slavery was nowhere condemned in the Bible; rather, it was sanctioned by the laws God had given to Israel. The only way to countermand that claim was to develop a different hermeneutic, one that stripped those old statutes of any validity for the church. But if the passages that approve slavery are no longer in force, then all the other rules and regulations scattered through the Old Testament (at least in their literal application) must also be reckoned inadmissible. But if the approvers of slavery were right, then no just grounds exist for ignoring any of the brutal statutes that were part of the Mosaic law.

So the dreadful spectacle of supposedly devout Christians using scripture to support the merciless exploitation of their fellow creatures had one good effect: it drove other right-thinking Christians to a new way of reading and understanding the Bible.

That process was still further hastened by the horrifying privations suffered by

(2) Children in the Factories

Unless you have done extensive reading in the history of the Industrial Revolution, it is almost impossible to grasp the unspeakable miseries that tens of thousands of children had to endure. They worked eighteen hours a day, six days a week, in the awful factories, compelled by poverty to toil at the looms and in the mines. Helpless, foully exploited, they were beaten constantly with whips and rods to force them to work ever harder. Their masters allowed them only a few moments of infrequent rest, and they had to survive the cruelly long day on nothing more than a crust or two of bread with a little water. Even when they were ill the children dared not slack. To lose even a day meant losing their job, which could bring ruin upon a household, for the wretched pittance the children earned was frequently the only protection their families had against dying from starvation.

Here is how one visitor described the conditions in a cotton factory –

> It was the most ghastly place I've ever seen. It was like being in the middle of Dante's Inferno. The heat, the noise, the suffocating atmosphere couldn't be matched by anything designed by Lucifer. And the children . . . oh! the children. . . . Some of them are only seven or eight, perhaps less. They work up to eighteen hours a day on a small piece of rancid bread. They can only relieve themselves when the foremen take it into their heads to let them go. Their clothes are so thin and torn that it's easy to see the welts and cuts which the straps make on their bodies. One small boy had heavy pieces of metal screwed to his ears because he'd made some trivial mistake. He kept shaking his head but that made it worse and he couldn't stop crying. Another was immersed in a tank of icy water because he was still sleepy at five o'clock in the morning . . . . The noise was greater than (could

be) imagined; the smell was frightful; the air so impure it was hard to breathe. It was terrible to see (the children) scurrying back and forth, pale as little ghosts, bones sticking through their flesh, and very much afraid. [175]

Another reference describes the scene thus, and states that religious authorities, church leaders, were among the leading advocates of forcing idle children to work – [176]

> Conditions as bad as those imposed on pauper children rapidly developed in enterprises employing non-pauper children. Often with the approval of political, social, and religious leaders, [177] children were permitted to labor in hazardous occupations such as mining. The resultant social evils included illiteracy, further impoverishment of poor families, and a multitude of diseased and crippled children. . . .

> The shortage of adult male labourers, who were needed for agriculture, contributed to the exploitation of child labourers. In addition, the majority of adults, ostensively imbued with puritanical ideas regarding the evils of idleness among children, cooperated with employers, helping them to recruit young factory hands from indigent families.

No attention was given either to hygiene or safety, consequently the mortality and accident rate among the children was appalling. Little ones often fell into an exhausted sleep, so that they tumbled into the unprotected machinery and suffered shocking injuries. Their hurts were given at best minimal medical attention, and then, if no longer fit for work, they were thrown out of the factories to perish.

Notice again that there were not lacking Christian literalists who insisted, citing the Old Testament, that this was all agreeable to scripture. Christian factory owners were entitled to do what they pleased with their own property, which

---

[175] Ruby, by Pamela Bennets; Ulverscroft Foundation, 1994; pg. 221, 233.

[176] "Child Labor," *Microsoft® Encarta® 96 Encyclopedia.* © 1993-1995 Microsoft Corporation. All rights reserved. © Funk & Wagnalls Corporation. All rights reserved.

[177] For example, in response to attempts by starving mill-workers in 1795 to demand better and safer working conditions for themselves, their wives, and their children, Bishop Horsley said only, "The people have nothing to do with the laws but obey them." (Beau Brummell, by Kathleen Campbell; Hammond, Hammond & Co, London, 1948; pg. 43. Ms Campbell describes the workers: "They lived or existed on starvation wages, exploited, with their wives and children, by employers who cared only to obtain labour as cheaply as possible, and under conditions of which it horrifies us even to read today. . . . Brutalised by misery, denied any semblance of social justice, housed in street after street of filthy slums, without any alleviation but drink, or any hope but for death . . .")

included their workers, and all attempts by gentler voices to bring these horrors to an end were fiercely resisted, not just in the places of commerce, but also from many pulpits. "Idle hands make mischief," was the stern cry of the preachers as they piously quoted *Proverbs*, while children were beaten into cowed and tear-drenched submission [178]

In reaction against both this manifest abuse of scripture and the dreadful spectre of those emaciated, maimed, and weeping children, godly men and women took another look at the Bible and began to see a different way of reading its inspired pages. William Wilberforce (1759-1833) was one such man –

WILBERFORCE & SHAFTESBURY

British statesman, humanitarian, and devout Christian, Wilberforce laboured, despite bitter opposition (often from other Christians), to suppress the slave trade and to abolish slavery throughout the British Empire. He was joined by other like-minded reformers, who strove to improve conditions for all workers in the work-houses, prisons, and factories, whether child or adult.

One of the greatest of the social reformers was Lord Ashley, the seventh Earl of Shaftesbury (1801-1885). He was an Anglican evangelical, with a sound view of scripture and of Christian morality. Under his vigorous patronage astonishing changes were implemented –

> He first directed attention to the alleviation of the conditions of the insane, obtained complete reform of the Lunacy Acts, and remained chairman of the Commission until his death. He was largely responsible for legislation in behalf of employees in mills, factories, collieries, and mines, and especially for abolishing the apprentice system and the employment of women and small children in the mines. Under his auspices, and after a long battle, the Ten-Hours Act (1847) was passed, which regulated working hours and conditions. He secured still further improvements with the passing of the Factory Act (1874). He brought about the abolition of the system of apprenticing small children as chimney sweeps, who until then had been driven up the chimneys by whips, and by lighting fires under them. He helped to remedy many evils in connection with the slums, securing

---

[178] For example: *"A diligent man deserves to have power; but the lazy must be turned into slaves"* (12:24); *"Those who are rich will surely rule over the poor"* (22:7); *"To an employer, a lazy worker is like vinegar on the teeth and smoke in the eyes"* (10:26). So the rich ruled, and made sure the children were neither idle nor lazy, by working them to death in their grim pits of hell, while the church (much of it), believing that the merciless owners had a biblical mandate, applauded.

great improvements in the housing conditions of the poor, with better lodging house regulations, and new and better tenement houses. He supported the emancipation of Roman Catholics from the legal restraints that had been imposed on them for two centuries, and assisted Florence Nightingale in her efforts for army welfare. Some of his other interests were the British and Foreign Bible Society, the National Society for the Prevention of Bruelty to Children, the Pastoral Aid Society, the Protestant Alliance, the London City Mission, the Church Missionary Society, and the Young Men's Christian Association. During the mid-19th century he acted virtually as the conscience of a nation, and by his incessant labours vastly improved the living conditions of tens of thousands of people. Even today multitudes of working people stand in his debt. [179]

What an amazing man!

THE PITS OF HELL

Conditions in the factories were outrageous, but they were even more vile in the mine tunnels, where children as young as five or six had to squat alone in a tiny dark hole for fifteen or sixteen hours each day, opening and closing a gate. Older children, boys and girls together, stripped naked to the waist, and fastened to each other by ankle chains, had to crawl on their hands and knees along pitch black tunnels, often less than a metre high, hauling trucks loaded with as much as 250kg of coal. They were compelled to do this in slave-labour conditions for as long as fourteen hours a day on privation wages. If they lived, they were kept at this brutal toil until they were-full grown, when they "graduated" to equally harsh adult tasks. Groaning, sobbing, and struggling in midnight darkness through those endless hours, savagely whipped if they slackened, poorly fed, never earning more than a few pennies, thousands of them soon sickened and died. Those who did reach adult years, crippled, emaciated, worn out, could scarcely hope to gain their thirtieth birthday. Their lives were so wretched that mostly they were glad to die. Some found relief by suicide; others were held back from death only by the awful threats of damnation that were furiously hurled at them from the pulpit. They knew too that a suicide's fate was to have a stake driven through the chest and to be buried at a crossroad, without any tombstone,

---

[179] Compiled from the *New International Dictionary of the Christian Church*; the *Wycliffe Biographical Dictionary of the Church*; and *Chambers Biographical Dictionary*.

so that the soul might lose its way and be forgotten forever. Thousands found what solace they could in drunken oblivion and sexual debauchery. [180]

SYDNEY SMITH

Lord Ashley did much to remove those sufferings from women and children, and he was aided by other humanitarian and Christian voices. Among them was Sydney Smith (1771-1845), an English clergyman, essayist, and wit. In numerous magazine articles and pamphlets he campaigned vigorously against the transportation of criminals, the dreadful conditions in the jails, slavery, the foul abuses practised in the factories and mines, and many other matters. He delivered a series of influential lectures on moral philosophy, and for a time suffered social ostracism for his outspoken views, being banished to a tiny rural parish in distant Yorkshire, where he was obliged to remain for nearly twenty years. He said it was "so far out of the way that it was actually twelve miles from a lemon." But his writings, and his efforts for reform, continued unabated. Religious bigotry, hypocrisy, and cruelty, especially when done in the name of God, were his special targets. He reckoned that Bible-quoting literalists were joined together in "one general conspiracy against common sense" – and against true Christianity. He said of one offending divine that "he deserves to be preached to death by wild curates." His humane and generous voice, added to that of others who had espoused a new style of Christian morality, so stirred the conscience of the nation that a great cry for change began to rise on every side.

ELIZABETH FRY

Elizabeth Fry (1780-1845), a devout Quaker, was another reformer whose gentler reading of scripture drove her to rectify the appalling miseries she observed around her. In 1813 she visited Newgate prison, where she found more than 300 women and children herded together in squalor and neglect. Many of them were naked and starving, they were helpless against sexual assault both by other prisoners and by the prison officers. If possible, the state of the children, both boys and girls, was worse. At once she devoted her life to prison reform. She also founded hostels for the homeless, and various other charity organisations. She provoked bitter opposition, of course, from the establishment (including much of

---

[180] For an account in fiction of these iniquitous conditions, see Barbara Cartland, The Temptation of Torilla; Robert Hale, London, 1990; pg. 9 ("Author's Note"), 27-28, 31, 74-75, 96-97.

the church), which argued that it was *"casting pearls before swine"* to take an interest in such human "refuse". Undeterred, she visited the prisons daily, taught the women various hand-skills, read the Bible to them, and did all she could to ameliorate their misery. She campaigned for the separation of the sexes in prison, for female warders to supervise women prisoners, for an adequate provision of food and clothing, and for secular and religious education for the inmates. Her efforts were eventually successful, and, despite fierce hostility, various acts were passed that implemented most of the reforms she had advocated. She continued her work unwearied until her death.

Notice again, however, that to maintain their case Smith, Wilberforce, Shaftesbury, Fry, and the other reformers had to turn to a hermeneutic that enabled them to nullify the quoters of the Old Testament, and to give dominant force to the gentler ethic of the New Testament. When the strength of their voices was enhanced by a growing number of enlightened and humanitarian thinkers, and by the outcry of the people, reluctant legislators were forced to pass the various social reform laws of which we today are the happy beneficiaries. The protests of the "Christian" opponents of the reformers, after a long struggle, were finally silenced, and now not a preacher in the land would dare to echo the sentiments that so many of their colleagues in the 18th and 19th centuries expressed so strongly.

It would be pleasant if this uniform *attitude* of the modern pulpit toward such crimes as slavery and child labour arose from a uniform *hermeneutic*. Unfortunately it does not, for although modern *practice* has changed, among many fundamentalists and evangelicals the old *hermeneutic* still prevails. This seems to me to involve them in an unacceptably capricious selection of which passages they will or will not obey literally. Then at the other extreme stand the liberals, whose altered practice arises simply from a cavalier abandonment of the entire authority of the Bible. Surely there is a better way? We ought to be able to read all scripture as the Word of God, with a hermeneutic that enables us to discover in its pages, not just some "proof-texts", but a message that is as valid for our time as it was for every previous age.

HARD TIMES

Two prisoners, manacled together and released from the Marshalsea [181] where debtors were held, begged for alms for themselves and other poor unfortunates. [182] Athelstan threw them some pennies, moved to compassion by their ice-blue feet. [183] ... Outside the hospital of St Thomas a baker had been fastened onto a hurdle [184] as a punishment for selling mouldy bread. Athelstan ... watched as the unfortunate was pulled along by a donkey. A drunken bagpipe player slipped and slid along behind, playing a raucous tune to hide the baker's groans. In the stocks a taverner, wry-mouthed, was being made to drink sour wine, whilst a whore, fastened to a stake, was whipped by a sweating bailiff who lashed the poor woman's naked back with long thick twigs of holly. ... (Athelstan intervened, and when she was released) the woman collapsed in a bloody heap on the ice." [185]

Such was the harsh treatment of even petty criminals in the late 14th century. Other common penalties in those days were –

- for a clergyman guilty of sexual offences, to be castrated

- for an obdurate person who would not confess, to be stretched on the rack; to the *first degree*, which caused dislocation of the shoulders and muscle tearing; then, if that failed, to the *second degree*, which dislocated other joints, and left the victim maimed for life; or to the *third degree*, which left the victim dismembered and paralysed, and always resulted in death

- for various offences, a specified number of hours suffering the excruciating torment of a thumbscrew

- for pederasty, to be slowly boiled to death in a large cauldron of water

---

[181] One of the chief prisons for debtors in London. Entire families were often incarcerated there, frequently for life.

[182] Prisoners were expected to buy their food. If they could not do so, they had to beg for it, or starve to death an act of judicial murder that continued until the early 19th century.

[183] They were shoeless, and London was in the grip of a deep winter freeze.

[184] A wooden frame upon which the naked victim was fastened, and then dragged through the streets, with his body scraping over the cobble-stones.

[185] The House of the Red Slayer, by Paul Harding; Headline Book Publishing, London, 1992; pg. 32,33. Athelstan was a monk.

- for treason, or for an act of violence against any member of the royalty, to be flayed alive

- for forgery, to be pressed in the Iron Maiden, which was a metal coffin equipped with spikes that penetrated the body, but not fatally, so that death was prolonged across two or three days of unceasing torment

- for larceny, libel, or blasphemy to have one or both ears, or the nose, cropped, and sometimes cut away entirely

- for witchcraft and similar offences, trial by ordeal, which might take the form of plucking a pebble out of a pot of boiling water, or plunging a hand into a burning brazier, trusting that innocence would protect the accused from any harm

- for women accused of various offences, the ducking stool, in which it was believed the guilty would float (to be hauled out of the water and punished), while the innocent would sink (and often drown before the stool was lifted)

- and other punishments equally gruesome, or worse, were inflicted for a wide range of crimes, both great and small.

I mention these unpleasant things to countermand any suggestion that I am entirely blaming the Bible, or at least a false reading of the Bible, for the savageries of the past. Undoubtedly much of the cruelty that was so endemic across many centuries of European history must be attributed, not to scripture, but to a barbaric culture. Their violence had little to do with either a right or a wrong way of handling the Bible. They were people of their time, just as much as we are and as the ancient Hebrews were, and they behaved accordingly. Nonetheless, as later developments showed, a wiser way of understanding the Bible does inescapably lead to a gentler and more just society. The tragedy is that it took so long for that better hermeneutic to achieve a place of dominance in western thought and practice.

But that raises another problem. Could Moses and David (if they had properly understood the ways of God) have arrived at the position taken in this book? Should they have done so? Why was the worldview expressed in the Old Testament never questioned within its own pages? Why did people in the Middle Ages accept the brutality of their society? We call their behaviour foul; but was it then sanctioned by God? No criticism is expressed in the Bible against Moses' harsh laws, nor is there any complaint about Joshua's pitiless slaughters, nor about David's merciless depredations. [186] Were those men at fault because (as one reader has put it) "they failed to glean out the real message of God from the cultural baggage that accompanies it in scripture"? Must we call them reprehensible criminals (the same reader asks) because of the awful things they did, and if so, how can we say that they were men approved by God?

The question is perplexing, and I can hardly attempt to answer it here in any length. The simple answer seems to be that God himself has chosen to take people and cultures as he finds them, and to work from there. [187] That is, he never expects to find a later mentality among people of earlier times. Even within the Bible (especially in the transition from the Old Testament to the New) there are marked changes in worldview, while God kept in step with each new social setting as it developed. Thus we know that behaviour he was willing to tolerate (or even approve as necessary for the time) centuries ago, the Lord would sternly condemn today. Polygamy provides an example of this principle. It was certainly tolerated (if not actuallx endorsed) in ancient Israel, but is now recognised as unacceptable for Christians.

How far then can we excuse our church forefathers who shared so enthusiastically in the atrocities of their age? Plainly, we must allow that they could no more *entirely* shake off the influence of their culture than we can. Yet we must also be guided by the New Testament, and at once we notice that the apostles, although they were obliged to live in a violent, malevolent, and horridly unjust world, nonetheless set out to change it. Contrary to the culture, their writings flowed with gentleness, they enjoined tolerance, they urged mutual honour and love upon the saints, they commanded mercy and preached kindness. Their words, after a millennium [188] of misunderstanding, became the source of inspiration for the gracious social reformers of the last century, who themselves had to stand firm against fierce opposition from both secular and sacred authorities.

---

[186] *Joshua 9:24*; and cp. *Deuteronomy 7:2; 20:16*; etc; *1 Samuel 27:7-12.*

[187] Cp. *Acts 17:30*, "In the past, God was willing to overlook ignorance, but now he commands men and women everywhere to repent."

[188] The barbaric punishments, and the savagery, that were so prevalent during the Middle Ages were little known during the previous centuries. They seem to have arisen out of a combination of social and cultural factors that are only partly understood. Having been established, the violence prevailed with rising and falling force until well into the last century. Torture, for example, was finally abandoned as a legal instrument in Europe only at the end of the 18th century.

CHAPTER NINETEEN

WHIP YOUR SLAVE

A few pages back I raised the question: *"Can parents quote Proverbs to justify caning their children?"* My purpose was not to decide the rights or wrongs of corporal punishment – which is a matter for family experts, or the law of the land, to determine – but to say something about hermeneutics. I think that people who flourish their canes, straps, sticks, or wooden spoons, while they piously intone, *"Spare the rod and spoil the child,"* [189] are guilty of three hermeneutical faults –

- To quote *Proverbs* to justify beating a child, while refusing to apply the text in its full rigour, is **_capricious_**. The passages in *Proverbs* refer not to a few mild smacks, but to *flogging* with a whip, a bundle of sticks, or a heavy rod. [190] If scripture must be obeyed *literally*, then it should be obeyed *fully* – or else a better way should be found of reading it.

- To quote *Proverbs* to justify beating a child, but then to ignore the many barbarous penalties enjoined both in that book and in other places in the Old Testament, is **_dishonest_**. The faults for which

---

[189] One reader wrote to me and complained: "I reckon you overdo the use of the proverb relating to beating your kids. At first, I started to wonder if you had any other examples. Indeed, a good number of your other illustrations come from *Proverbs,* which could easily make the reader sceptical as to your own use of scripture. Perhaps the problems you pose are only relevant to *Proverbs*?"

I sympathise with the reader's complaint, for I had already noted the problem myself. My response is threefold: <u>first</u>, by the time you get to the end of the book, you will find that I do employ many other examples from various parts of scripture; <u>second</u>, while I was writing this book, laws were enacted banning the use of corporal punishment in all schools, both state and private, which made the cane then (as indeed it still is) a lively issue; and <u>third</u>, while few Christian would attempt to obey literally (say) the fierce laws in *Deuteronomy*, millions of them *do* read *Proverbs* as if it were a rule book for the church, written only yesterday.

[190] Note the ferocity implicit in such passages as *Proverbs 23:13-14; 19:18; 22:15.*

scripture prescribes those harsh punishments are still prevalent; so if one sentence (beating a child) must be applied, why not the others?

- To quote *Proverbs* to justify beating a child is **_superficial_**, because it fails to recognise the position children held in the ancient world. There is an enormous difference between the status children hold in our society and the way they were viewed in the past. [191]

The first two of those ideas I will take up again below; but here let me develop the third: *the false assumption that children held the same place in the social structure of ancient Israel as they do in our culture.* Rather, children held a status nearer that of slaves, and were treated accordingly. Hence the same punishment (severe flogging) was prescribed for rebellious children and for recalcitrant slaves. For example, here is the opinion of a Jewish rabbi who lived about 200 years before Christ –

> You should never be ashamed of frequently punishing your children, nor of drawing blood from the back of a stubborn slave. . . . A man who loves his son will whip him often . . . for just as an unbroken horse runs wild, so an unbridled son will become unruly. If you pamper your child he will grieve you, if you play with him he will take advantage of you. Do you want to share his pain? Then go and share his laughter! But if you dislike gnashing your teeth, then give him no freedom in his youth. Never excuse his errors; crush stubbornness while he is still a child; beat him black and blue while he is yet a boy. If you don't, he will grow up lawless, and break your heart when he disobeys you. So discipline your son, and put a slave's yoke on him. Then perhaps he will not shame you by some disgraceful act. (Sir 42:1,5; 30:1,8-13)

In another place the rabbi insists that a son must "serve his parents as a slave does his master" (3:7), and he tells how livestock, slaves, wives, sons, daughters, should all be treated equally and dispassionately as a man's private property (7:22-26). The same whip prescribed for rebellious slaves should be used, he says, on wayward sons (33:25-30). But, you may rejoin, none of that is scripture. No, it is not. Nonetheless, the master-and-slave language used by the rabbi is a

---

[191] We need to distinguish between what is normal in a given *culture* for good child-rearing, and what is actually required by *scripture*. So in answer to the question, "Does the Bible **_command_** the use of the rod in Christian homes?" I would reply, "No!" Then to the question, "Does the Bible **_permit_** the use of the rod in a Christian home?" I would reply, "Perhaps! But only if the punishment is moderate, fair, and stays within the limits tolerated by society. It must also conform to Paul's stricture against provoking children to bitter anger" (Ep 6:4). We cannot ignore the insights of sociology or psychology, which at most allow moderate corporal punishment, and which also seem to agree with Paul. Violence against children is sanctioned only in the Old Testament. The New Testament presents a milder rule.

clear echo of the ideas embedded in the various references in *Proverbs* (13:24; 19:18; 23:13-14; etc). We are left in no doubt about the lowly status of children in ancient Israel. How distant those attitudes are from what is acceptable in our time! But in the pages of scripture we are not viewing the modern world. Instead, we are looking at the culture of a small nation three thousand years ago, and the references in *Proverbs* must be given the meaning they had for the people of those primitive times.

Perhaps there is someone who still wants to take the *Proverbs* references literally? Then I must ask: do you apply them with full vigour? It is not honest to lessen their force merely to conform with the dictates of our culture. So then, away with the wooden spoon, and out with the whip, or the bundle of birch rods! Anything less is dealing falsely with scripture! Of course, a far better solution is to find a hermeneutic that can give due weight to each verse yet also extract from it only what it means for our time. In the case before us, we can agree that the Old Testament texts do teach the harsh flogging of naughty children. Should we then obey them? No, we cannot do so. Why? Not because it would get us into trouble with the law and probably earn a prison sentence. Rather, because Christian behaviour should be shaped by the loving rule of the New Testament, which forbids parents to incite their children to resentment and welcomes the little ones into the kingdom of God. What then do we learn from *Proverbs* about the punishment of children? Within the context of our present discussion, only one eternal and unchanging lesson: *the need for a proper level of discipline to be maintained in a godly home.* What shape that discipline should take, however, must be determined by factors outside of scripture, for the Bible is silent on the matter. [192]

THINGS DID GET BETTER

The position of children in Israel had improved by the time of Jesus, but not much. When Christ stood a little child in front of the people and bade them gaze upon him (Mt 18:2-4), what do you think they saw? Certainly not a picture of charming innocence such as our eyes might catch. Looking at that scene today, we can hardly view it any other way. But what did Jesus have in mind? He used the child, not to display enchanting artlessness, but to provide an example of helpless weakness. Here was a small human without any rights, lowly in status, dependent upon others, born only to serve. To his hearers that image was both

---

[192] *Proverbs* and of course other biblical texts say many other things about raising godly children, but I am not concerned with those matters here.

familiar and acceptable; they understood what Jesus meant, for it is the picture they themselves saw. Indeed, they had never thought any other way about children. But then Jesus shocked them. He said, *"If you hope to gain the kingdom of God then you too must become like this child."* No wonder they were angry! To burden a child with helpless vulnerability, humble dependence, and meek service was perfectly agreeable. But how dare he impose the same debasement upon an adult! Never! The very idea was outrageous. They were ready to kill him for it! Should we be surprised by their reaction? Hardly! We may view children more sweetly than they did, but are we any more ready than they were to emulate the humble dependence of a child? Judging by the squabbles that so often rend the church, the jostling for power, the scant observance of the Christian demand for selfless sacrifice for others, and for unflagging service of Christ, there are not many *"little children"* among us!

Only in gradual response to Paul's teaching did the outlook for children begin to improve. With an almost breath-taking audacity the apostle took up the cause of the three lowest levels of society – *wives, children,* and *slaves* – who were all in those days treated as hardly better than material possessions. [193] He insisted that they must from now on be given full honour and receive fair dealing. We can hardly imagine how radical his words were to the people who first read them. Their impact was revolutionary! They still are in many parts of the world!

Because of the social upheaval implicit in Paul's teaching, obedience by the church to his precepts has varied across the centuries. Indeed, it is probably fair to say that only in our time have they at last come to some measure of fruition. [194] Nonetheless, despite his noble new ethic, even Paul could not wholly escape thinking like a man of his time. So he did not hesitate to use slave imagery in relation to children (Ga 4:1-5), thus unconsciously echoing the common opinion held by his contemporaries, which itself simply reflected the culture of ancient Israel as displayed in *Proverbs*.

ON FLOGGING FOOLS

In case someone still wants to insist that we can use *Proverbs* to sanction corporal punishment, consider an even more surprising fact: the same harsh

---

[193] See, among other references, *Colossians 3:18-4:1*.

[194] At least in the Western world, with its now almost universal laws protecting the interests of children; elevating women to a status of equality; social welfare benefits for the poor, the infirm, the elderly, and the like.

penalties prescribed for naughty children and slaves were also prescribed for those who were merely *"fools"* (see 10:13; 14:3; 17:10; 18:6; 19:25,29; 20:30; 26:3.) What an amusing dilemma now confronts the literalist! Here, say, is a pastor who loves to quote the texts about beating children, and urges his congregation to stand firm against society and to keep on applying the rod to their offspring. Will he also take these other injunctions literally? Suppose he begins to insist upon his right to use the stocks and the whip upon troublesome parishioners? How can the people complain? If they allow him to quote the one group of texts they can scarcely forbid him to quote the other!

Someone may say, "That is absurd!" But why? Less than 200 years ago those very scriptures *were* quoted to justify flogging adult miscreants almost to death. What has changed? Not the Bible, only the culture! But is my reading of scripture to be determined by some social dictate, or by the authority of the Word of God alone? The issue is inescapable: any literalist hermeneutic that requires obedience to the texts about corporal punishment of *children* must equally require the same for *fools*. But if (for whatever reason) I am unwilling to quote the Bible to support the flogging of an *adult,* how can I then turn around and quote from the same Bible to justify beating a *child*? Why don't the rod-wielders quote those passages about *"fools"*? Why too do even the most fervent of today's thrashers apply the rod so much more gently than their great-grandfathers did? The answer has far more to do with fear of social disapproval than with any literal understanding of the Bible. Those problems vanish when they are confronted with a wiser hermeneutic.

WICKED SLUTS

In this sense (of using all of *Proverbs* literally, not just the convenient bits) people in the 18th and early 19th centuries were more consistent than many modern readers. Our forefathers *did* treat both sets of instructions in the same way, and therefore were just as keen to flog *adults* as *children*. They never doubted that they had a biblical warrant for both cases. In *Tom Jones* there is a story that shows the fierceness of the time. An honourable squire, Mr Allworthy, finds a baby left in his bed by an unknown mother. The infant is obviously base-born, and therefore deemed an outcast; nevertheless, flouting custom, the squire calls an elderly servant, Mrs Deborah Wilkins, to carry it to her room and care for it. The lady is horrified. With affronted indignation she condemns the unwed mother, and says to Mr Allworthy –

I hope your Worship will send out your Warrant [195] to take up the Hussy its Mother . . . I should be glad to see her committed to Bridewell, [196] and whipt at the Cart's Tail. Indeed, such wicked Sluts cannot be too severely punished." [197]

To be "Whipped at the Cart's Tail" was the ordinary punishment for a "bawd" into the early 19th century. The unfortunate woman was stripped to the waist, tied to the end of a cart, and then as she stumbled along behind the moving vehicle from one end of the village to the other, was severely flogged, either with a cane or a whip. In the 17th and 18th centuries she was often branded as well with a hot iron. These savage punishments, of course, were all inflicted in the name of justice supposedly shaped by scripture. So a clergyman would usually be in attendance, calling the "slut" to repentance and to renounce her wicked ways. How cruel! Yet given the even harsher penalties prescribed in the Bible for no worse sins, the magistrates of the 18th century probably thought that they were behaving with mercy. At least, there were not wanting biblical literalists, like Mrs Wilkins, who urged a return to more severe chastisement. There are many today just like her. The mistake they all make is a refusal to allow the splendidly higher ethic of the New Testament to inform their understanding of the Old. So we encounter the weird scenario of someone saying –

> "*I am a Christian*, so of course I oppose flogging a *grown-up* person! *I am a Christian*, so of course I believe in whipping a *child*!"

Both stands are justified from scripture! How can they do it? How can they show such deplorable caprice in reading the Bible? Hermeneutics ought at least to make us consistent! In the case before us, it is not reasonable to use *Proverbs* to sanction the use of a rod on children unless one also approves its use on adults – including grown-ups who are merely *"fools"*. [198] Further, if it is proper to read the child-beating verses literally, then consistency demands that we obey also the injunctions to

- **stone to death** drunken sons (De 21:18-21);

---

[195] The squire was a magistrate.

[196] The common name for a house of correction for women of loose morals.

[197] Henry Fielding; op. cit. Book I, Chapter Three.

[198] I think the sentiment expressed by the American author and humorist, Finley Peter Dunne (1867-1936), is appropriate. Taking the part of an Irishman ("Mr Dooley"), Dunne is conversing with a fellow Irishman, Mr Hennessy: "Spare th' rod an' spile th' child," said Mr Hennessy. "Yes," said Mr Dooley, "but don't spare th' rod an ye spile th' rod, th' child, an' th' child's father." (From Dissertations by Mr Dooley: On Corporal Punishment (1906).

- ***burn at the stake*** adulterous daughters (Le 21:9; and cp. 20:14; Ge 38:24); and
- ***summarily execute*** not only adulterers but also: blasphemers (De 22:20-24; Le 24:15-16); rebellious sons (De 21:18-21); immoral daughters (22:20-21); parent-abusers (Ex 21:15,17); kidnappers (vs. 16); heretics and deviates (vs. 19-20); sabbath breakers (Nu 15:32-36); and even those who were guilty only of refusing to *"seek the Lord, whether young or old, men and women alike"* (cp. 2 Ch 15:13); etc.

You will notice that the death penalty (often by stoning) was exacted for a wide range of crimes, including minor religious infractions.

Those very laws were the basis upon which Pontius Pilate was able to order the flogging and then the crucifixion of Jesus; without them, he could not have done so. If Christians continue to insist upon the authority of the Old Testament in such matters, then there is nothing (except the tender heart of society) to prevent such penalties being once again imposed by religious authorities who think their dogmas are under some threat. [199] Consider also the other gruesome punishments that are prescribed in scripture for various crimes. [200] Why do the literalists not demand *their* inclusion in our penal code? Should they not insist upon the restoration of death by stoning for drunkenness, blasphemy, backsliding, irreligion (2 Ch 15:13), or filial rebellion? How absurd! But if those sanctions cannot be literally obeyed today, why is the command to flog a naughty child given such immutable authority? Either give *all* or *none* of them authority, but at least be consistent.

THE REASON WHY

Once again, I have not raised these questions about using the "rod" in order to solve (as Hamlet might say) the problem of whether "to beat or not to beat?" We should look outside of scripture for guidance on appropriate methods of discipline for our time. Rather, the issue facing us here is *hermeneutics*. I am

---

[199] Remember the unspeakable horrors of the Inquisition! If religious zealots were again able to seize power there is little doubt that the shrieks of tortured infidels would soon be heard across the land. Note the savagery that is occurring this very day in lands where a fundamentalist Islam rules supreme.

[200] Such as mutilations, brandings, harrowings, and the like. For an example see De 25:11-12; along with Ex 21:25; Le 24:19-20; De 19:21; etc. See also below, *Chapters Twenty-Three, Twenty-Four, Twenty-Five*.

using *Proverbs* simply to expose an interpretive problem that arises in many parts of scripture. I mean *the fault of forcing upon the Bible a meaning that differs from its own God-born intention.* That fault occurs because people fail to recognise how far we are separated from biblical events, especially those of the Old Testament. No one can reliably interpret scripture who fails to take that gap into account. Yet at once another problem arises: how can we locate and then bridge the hiatus that exists between Bible days and our time? The following pages will suggest some answers.

> The Bible is a window in this prison-world through which we may look into eternity. (Timothy Dwight)

PART FIVE

CROSSING THE GAPS

Historical
Linguistic
Cultural
Philosophical
Cognitive
Spiritual

CHAPTER TWENTY

THE MISTS OF TIME

PART FIVE – 1. THE HISTORICAL GAP

How difficult it is to cross the gulf of history and gain a realistic sense of the way people in former times felt and thought! Most people are prone to imagine that the ancients were much the same as we are, that their world-view was identical, that their motivations and ideas were similar to ours, and that they enjoyed a common life-style. Naturally, they *were* like us in many ways (as the Bible itself clearly shows). But the centuries have wrought many dramatic changes in the way people think and feel, which means that the world they saw each day differed greatly from the one that greets our eyes.

LIFE WAS TOUGH

Archaeology has shown that in early times the people of Israel were (by our standards) diminutive, averaging probably about 160cm (5ft 3in) in height. You can be sure that Gideon and his friends, or even David and his mighty men, did not look much like the modern Hollywood image of them! On the contrary, to our eyes they would seem almost stunted in growth. They were probably undernourished, suffering from an inadequate variety in their diet, which limited them to an average life-span of hardly more than 50 years. [201]

---

[201] Note how the priests had to retire when they reached 50 (Nu 4:3; 8:25), which in those days represented old age. The information in this paragraph, and in the one following, was largely drawn from an article "A Visit With Ahilud", by Joseph A. Callaway, in <u>Biblical Archaeology Review</u>, Sep – Oct 1983.

The culture of the land was generally rough and primitive. Excavations at the site of ancient Ai (one of the towns captured by Joshua) have revealed something of the uncouth life of those times. None of the roof beams of the excavated houses is more than 168cm (66 inches) above the floor. The ruins show that the people lived in simple mud-brick homes, with no more than two or three rooms, into which adults, children, servants, and livestock alike were crowded. Their furniture was simple, rough-hewn, and sparse, with round stones often providing the only seating. Since there were no kitchens in the houses, the villagers cooked at communal ovens, and several families probably ate together, mostly outdoors.

Across the whole nation, in fact, few people had any of the conveniences that we take for granted. Water had to be carried to most homes from a well or nearby river, and was often in short supply. Since many settlements, for protection against attack, were set on a hill or prominence, the task of carrying water up to the homes was laborious, and depended mostly upon the shoulders of the women. So except for their hands and possibly faces they seldom washed. Standing in the rain, or plunging occasionally into a river or pond, was probably the nearest they came to a bath.

Except in the wealthiest homes toilet facilities were non-existent. Where did they go? Outside, anywhere that was convenient. Moses had indeed made some rules about camp hygiene during the wilderness wanderings (De 23:13,14); but how well those laws were obeyed after Israel had settled in Canaan is unknown. Presumably some piece of land was sequestered for the purpose, but they were probably careless about the matter, especially in rural areas. Few people enjoyed the luxury of a separate bedroom. Everybody slept together in the one room, along with their animals, on pads on the floor, depending only on their rough blankets for a little privacy. The floors had little or no covering, being mostly packed dirt, and the only inside heat came from an open fire, with nothing for a chimney except a hole in the roof. For most of the inhabitants of ancient Israel life was crude, hard, smelly, laborious, and monotonous. Across the centuries conditions gradually improved, but even the time of Jesus the daily life of most people (by our standards) was still harsh, and offered few pleasures.

SCANT LEARNING

By any modern measure the clothing of the early Israelites was rough and ill-formed, Their manners were crude, and their notions about the world appallingly narrow. The men had a peasant's pragmatic knowledge of how to work the fields and flocks, and perhaps some skill for other simple tasks in the house or on the land. The women too had little understanding of anything beyond their homes. Few people had an education that would equate even with the knowledge we expect to find today in a primary-school child. Most of them knew almost nothing about life beyond their own village or near neighbours. The daily labour of all the people, men and women, young and old, was long and hard. They rose at dawn, they went to bed with the sun, for only the wealthy could afford to brighten the night hours with lamps. The level of sophistication and learning in Hebrew society of course rose over the centuries, especially as the people came into ever greater contact with the surrounding more advanced cultures. Nonetheless, throughout the span of the Old Testament the way of life of the common people, their levels of understanding, their manners and methods, would have seemed raw and primitive to modern eyes.

A FRIGHTENING WORLD

Further, the world to them was a frightening place, fraught with mystery, redolent with peril, clouded with superstition (Ge 30:37-42). The natural explanations we readily ascribe to such awesome cataclysms as a lightning-threaded thunder storm, the rattling hail, a shrieking tornado, or a ravaging flood, did not occur to them. The ancients deeply felt that behind all such phenomena there must lie some kind of spiritual entity, whose purpose might be good or evil. Forests and deserts were haunted by demons (De 32:10), and hideous dark spirits infested ancient ruins (Is 13:21; 34:14). [202]

Our western world is so different. [203] It has been almost totally demythologised, so that we no longer believe in ghosts, ghouls, or any other gruesome denizens of earth's shadowy corners. When you and I look out of our windows what do we see? Simply a natural vista of trees, rocks, mountains, or other ordinary things made by the hand of God or man. But the ancient Hebrews viewed everything through a prism of mystery, and wove into every scene some benevolent or malevolent spiritual power. We observe an effect, and at once look for a *natural* cause; but the Hebrews, observing the same effect, looked instead for a *preternatural* cause. Israel too was a small nation, surrounded by mighty empires, which constantly sent their brutal armies tramping across the land. An endless threat of invasion, of being either killed in battle or sold into lifelong slavery, placed its perpetual shadow over every town and village. Even within the

---

[202] Notice the references to "howling creatures" and "goat demons", along with the Babylonian night-hag, "Lilith". I will come back to these ideas later.

[203] In many parts of Asia, Africa, and South America, the common people still see a world fraught with mystery, haunted by spirits of various kinds, unpredictable, capricious, magical, in which happiness depends upon placating the dominant ghostly powers.

nation, among their own kin, the rule of law was imperfectly understood and applied, so that the rich and powerful could generally do whatever they pleased. Hence ordinary people lived with a constant peril of oppression, either by their own or foreign tyrants. [204]

Their world, then, and ours, were coloured very differently. The environment in which they lived bore only a superficial resemblance to the modern (western) world, and inevitably their worldview took a shape different from ours. Some attempt must be made to bridge this span of many centuries before the reader can enter accurately into the motives of those men and women of long ago. They spoke and acted in ways that often seem to us strange, superstitious, or even horrible. But we cannot judge them honestly, nor interpret them properly until we are able to climb into their skin, sense their particular joys and sorrows, and look at their life through their own eyes. Those who fail to do this make the mistake that C. S. Lewis condemned in certain literary critics. He scorned the crazy ideas that scholars sometimes draw out of what they read, and he insisted that anyone who picks up a piece of ancient writing must follow this rule –

> You must, so far as in you lies, become an Achaean chief while reading Homer, a medieval knight while reading Malory, and an Eighteenth Century Londoner while reading Johnson. Only thus will you be able to judge the work "in the same spirit that its author writ". [205]

Would you know not only what the biblical authors wrote but what they *meant* by what they wrote? Then, as Lewis said, you and I must "as far as in us lies" try to cross the gap of centuries and feel what they felt. We need to stand inside their skin and view the world through their eyes. Doing this creates an environment within which we can be reasonably sure of *not* doing violence to scripture, and of reading it sensibly.

---

[204] This scene is made very clear in the prophets, who continually preached (with little effect) against the tyranny and extortion practised by the rich upon the poor.

[205] From his <u>A Preface to Paradise Lost</u>, pg. 63. Quoted by A. N. Wilson, op. cit. pg. 173. Wilson goes on to say: "Lewis does present in his *Preface* . . . a very convincing impression of having read the poem which John Milton set out to write and meant us to read. If that seems like faint praise, you should read the dozen most recent books on *Paradise Lost*." The same may be said of many Bible commentators. One wonders if they are reading the same Bible, so weird are the meanings they draw out of its pages. Let us at least *try* to read the Bible God intended us to read!

CHAPTER TWENTY-ONE

THEY TALK STRANGELY

PART FIVE – 2. THE LINGUISTIC GAP

Taylor Caldwell, in her splendid novel *Glory and the Lightning,* set in the Golden Age of ancient Greece, invents a conversation between Pericles, the ruler of Athens, and the philosopher Anaxagoras. They are discussing the problems of communication –

> "Our minds," said Pericles, "approach the universal but our tongues are the gross tongues of apes. We communicate with each other in the meagre language of the jungle, even while our thoughts are afire. That is the tragedy of mankind."
>
> "We must find a different mode of communication, then, Pericles. Mind to mind, and not tongue to tongue. For, despite what Socrates has said, there is no defining of terms which are relevant to every man. Our emotions intrude." [206]

"There is no defining of terms which are relevant to every man." This takes us back to an idea I touched on in *Chapter Two* – the fuzzy nature of words, and how they can mean subtly different things to different hearers. Several hurdles are placed in our way by this linguistic barrier. They are not insurmountable. The main thing is to be aware, and take enough care not to trip over them.

---

[206] Fontana Books, Glasgow, 1977; pg. 289.

FIRST CHOICES

No one can read any piece of writing intelligently without first deciding several things:

- what kind of literature is this?
  - *poetry, history, fiction, prophecy, didactic, inspirational; etc*
- what meaning did the terms it uses have for the author?
  - *did he or she use words as we do, with the same meaning and intention, or were there factors that give an altered sense to the writing?*
- what meaning did it have for its first and later readers?
  - *did they give it the same sense as the author planned, or did some change of time or place compel them to understand it differently?* [207]
- how does it convey its meaning to a modern reader?
  - *should we read it literally, symbolically, metaphorically, figuratively, prophetically, spiritually, personally, collectively?* – and the like.

Every reader makes some of those choices instinctively, mostly without being aware of it. No one ever does or can pick up a piece of writing and simply read it, in a state of perfect neutrality, free of any bias. We are all pre-conditioned by a host of factors that shape the way we approach a book, begin to read it, and start to understand it. Upbringing, education, environment, culture, and a host of other factors all pre-cast us to bring a certain prejudice to every line we read, and to apply its words in a certain way. [208] If those influences are allowed to remain wholly unconscious, then they may well lead the reader astray. The more deliberately and completely a reader can answer the questions raised above, the

---

[207] For a broad example, consider the way many Jews in Jesus' time had rightly turned the Old Testament prophecies of <u>national</u> glory into a promise of <u>individual</u> salvation, which would be realised, not on earth (as the prophets had taught), but in heaven.

[208] One simple example: up until hardly more than 200 years ago, everybody read aloud, and would have found it nearly impossible to read silently. Now, of course, the reverse is true. Today you would be surprised if you came into a room and found someone reading aloud to himself. How much, I wonder, does this alter both the nature of the books we read, and the way they impact our lives? And what about the Bible? Is there a difference in the effect it has upon a person who *speaks* the words through his mouth instead of only in his mind?

more likely he or she is to gain the best possible sense and value from the book – including the Bible – that is under perusal.

WHAT ARE WORDS?

A problem arises also from the very nature of words. Each word is a *symbol*, it stands for something else, yet is different from the thing it represents. Each person who uses or hears a word is also different, and therefore likely to view the symbol in changing ways. Seldom do words mean exactly the same thing to every user. Also, since words *are* only symbols people may choose to refer them to different things, or to represent those things by different words. For example, the Bible uses the common word *"tree"* to refer to the manner of Jesus' death: *"he was hung upon a tree"* (Ac 5:30; 10:39; Ga 3:13; etc). What does that mean? If other information were not available it could be understood in several ways – and indeed, apart from the fact that scripture elsewhere tells us that Jesus was crucified, we do not know the exact fashion of his death. The shape of the cross, just how he was fixed to it, and other details, remain unsolved. [209]

This symbolic nature of words tends to complicate their meaning, especially when people are widely separated from each other historically, socially, culturally, or in some other way – just as we are from the culture of Bible days. Here then is a book that was written a long time ago by people who lived in a world vastly different from ours, and who used language in a way that is often puzzling to us. This creates between them and us an inescapable ***linguistic*** gap, which takes various shapes –

---

[209] The first three gospels simply say that he was "crucified", which in those days could mean several different ways of execution – including merely tying the victim to a stake, and leaving him (or her) to die of exposure, starvation, and from the beaks and claws of vultures (cp. Pr 30:17). Up until about 200 years ago the British had a similar punishment, in which a felon was "hung in chains", or sometimes a cage, and left to die miserably. Only *John*, written some 60 years after the event, and in a very different style to the other gospels, refers to "nails" or "spikes" (20:24-26). The evidence (because of John's witness) does suggest that Jesus was nailed, not merely tied, to the cross. But the alternative view has some validity. It is certainly true that people, drawing on church tradition, often assume more than the Bible actually says.

HYPERBOLE

Notice their ready use of hyperbole, such as in the lurid curse formulae that pepper the writings of the psalmists and prophets. [210] We of course have the advantage of sitting at Jesus' feet, and learning both a higher moral impulse and more temperate emotions. [211] So we do not use the kind of extravagant language that occupies so much of the Old Testament. We have been taught to speak with restraint and to express ourselves with sobriety. Our culture has been shaped by sentiments like those expressed by Lord Bacon –

> The speaking in a perpetual hyperbole is comely in nothing but love. [212]

But early Hebrew writers laboured under no such restraint. Their culture allowed, indeed required them to say much more than they actually meant. A careful reader will be aware of this usage and not put more meaning into biblical expressions than their authors intended. [213]

Notice for example the claims made for King Solomon, who is said to have *"excelled all the kings of the earth in his riches and wisdom, so that the whole earth desired to come into his presence"* (1 Kg 10:23-24). There were many kings in the world during the time of Solomon (in Africa, Asia, the Americas, etc), who lived and died without so much as hearing his name, let alone anything of his wealth and wisdom. Some of them, too, were probably richer than Solomon and ruled greater empires. Likewise, it is a piece of pious exaggeration to say that *"the whole earth"* yearned to be instructed by him. Hardly more than a small portion of north Africa (including Egypt), along with the lands of the eastern Mediterranean, and those linked with the Euphrates and Tigris rivers, knew anything at all about Solomon. The same calming influence should be put

---

[210] See Ps 35:4-6; 58:6-10; 59:12-13; 69:22-28; 132:3-5; 137:7-9; Is 13:19-22; Je 18:21-23; etc.

[211] He was not impressed when James and John, emulating Elijah, wanted to call down vengeful fire from heaven (Lu 9:54). He said they had a wrong spirit, and should realise that he had come to save people, not destroy them. Note also other places where he expressed opposition to vehement language (e.g. Mt 5:22, 34).

[212] Francis Bacon, Viscount St Albans (1561-1626); Essays (1625), "Of Love."

[213] Apart from love, the main exception in our culture to Bacon's rule can be found in the outrageous claims made for various products in TV commercials and their ilk. Every kind of health, happiness, prosperity, peace, and plenty are associated with things that cannot conceivably bring such splendid benefits. We remain untroubled, however, for, without even thinking about it, we heavily discount the advertisers' claims, and bring their flowery speech down to more prudent levels. The difference between us and the ancient Hebrews is that they carried extravagance into ordinary conversation.

also on the claim that God would keep his name on Solomon's temple *"for ever"*, and that *"his eyes and his heart would be there for all time"* (1 Kg 9:3). Hardly more than 500 years after those words were written, the temple was a pile of smoking ruins.

But if those biblical sayings are too lavish, then perhaps the same kind of hyperbole exists in the description of Noah's Flood? We are told that *"all the high mountains under the whole heaven were covered by the waters"*. [214] Why should anyone read one statement literally, but not the other? If one universal saying must be understood in a limited sense, perhaps others should also be given a more restricted meaning? If so, then at once we have a solution to the puzzling problems raised by the story of the Flood, such as –

- how could the whole earth be literally covered with water, so that no land was anywhere visible?
- how could the thousands of varieties of animals, insects, and birds, find refuge in the small Ark?
- how could the ark contain enough food in enough variety for every creature?
- how could plant life survive a universal inundation?
- how could salt-water and fresh-water fish survive the mingling of seas, lakes, rivers, ponds, and indeed the total destruction of their normal environment?
- what happened to all the water?
  - and there are other difficulties.

Those questions vanish if in fact the Flood was confined to the "world" of the ancient historian – that is, to the Mesopotamian plain and its adjacent lands.

Nor is such hyperbole absent from the New Testament –

- *Acts 21:30-31*. Was *"the whole city"* truly aroused and *"all Jerusalem in an uproar"*, or in fact only a part of the total population? (See also Mk 1:5.)

- *Romans 1:5,8*. Only in some sort of secondary sense can Paul be said to have *"brought people of all nations to faith in his name"*; nor was it literally true that the story of the Corinthian church was being

---

[214] Ge 6:17; 7:19. And for similar universal statements, which nonetheless have an obviously limited geographic range, see De 2:25; 1 Kg 18:10; Je 25:31-32; Ez 20:48; etc. Notice also the obvious exaggeration in Jg 7:12; 2 Sa 1:23; Ps 6:6; Jn 21:25; and many other similar places.

told *"over all the world"* – indeed, the statement was hardly true even of the more limited Roman "world".

- *Romans 10:18.* Even in Paul's day the passage he quotes (Ps 19:18) was true only if the meaning of "world" is limited to a handful of nations; it is still not wholly true even today. The same must be said about his claim in *Romans 16:26* that God's Word had been *"made known to all nations"*. [215]

- *1 Corinthians 8:13.* Did Paul really mean that *"he would never eat meat again"*? Or was this just a piece of hyperbole, which in fact meant only that he would refrain from eating certain meats in the presence of someone who might be offended by his action? In other company he would presumably obey his own injunction, and receive with thanksgiving whatever food was set before him (1 Ti 4:3-4).

- *Colossians 1:6, 23.* Surely *"the whole world"* must be understood as nothing more than the Roman empire; and *"every creature under heaven"* cannot be taken literally, for hardly more than a few thousand people had actually heard the gospel when Paul wrote *Colossians.*

- *James 5:12.* Is this truly the most important command in the Bible, the nne that must be set above all others? [216]

- *1 John 3:9; 5:18.* Is it strictly true that we do not and cannot sin? If so, I have yet to meet a true Christian, including myself!

Similar statements occur in other places in the New Testament. Found in a *modern* piece of formal writing we would call them irresponsibly exaggerated, or at best careless. But that is because we use words more circumspectly than the

---

[215] Was it really true, in a sober sense, that the penetration of the gospel had been so extensive within Paul's lifetime? No, as late as the year 100 there were still millions of people in the Roman Empire who had not so much as heard the name of Jesus, let alone knew anything about the Christian church in Rome (Paul died around the year 65). So even when Paul's words are reduced from *"the whole world"* to *"the Roman Empire"*, they are still an overstatement!

[216] Commentators differ on how to understand the phrase *"above all things"* – all the way from simple hyperbole (Augustine), to a true superlative (Matthew Henry), to a caution against always beginning a sentence with an oath ("stop putting an oath in front of everything you say"), plus a variety of other views.

ancients felt any need to do. [217] The problem is ours, not theirs. The people who used those colourful expressions, and also their hearers, fully understood what was meant. We too can avoid being misled by them if we have some sense of the linguistic gap that exists between their culture and ours. Failing to capture such a sense, modern readers all too often make the Bible say more than it actually means.

THE PSALMS

You can find a noteworthy example of this linguistic principle in *Psalm 109:6-19*, where David curses an *"enemy"*, who was probably Saul. We know that in real life David often forgave Saul and refused to do him any harm, [218] so why does he now use such savage and disturbing language? He probably wanted to provide a counter-curse strong enough to repel the black-magic curses of his enemy. [219] However, David did understand that his maledictions could have no effect apart from the intervention of God; he refused to follow his enemy's descent into the witchery of seeking to work havoc by the power of words alone. So he added to his curse a prayer of humble petition, [220] asking God to *"deal well"* with him and to *"deliver"* him from his foe.

If that is a proper reading of the *Psalm*, then we find the poet deliberately using *words* that went far beyond his actual *deeds*, or even his real *desire*. This should at once make us cautious, for it suggests that there are other passages in the Bible that must be read with similar restraint.

Our problem is that both the environment in which such verbal transactions occurred, and the intemperate language used, are foreign to us. We do not talk so fiercely unless we actually mean it. We are prone to think that language, if it

---

[217] In an earlier footnote I mentioned the extravagant claims made by advertisers. I will add here another example of modern usage akin to that of the ancients: in non-formal, or informal, speech, we can indeed be as wild as they were. Thus: "absolutely everyone was there . . . the whole world knows about it . . . it's ages since I last saw you . . . this pastor is an apostle to the nations . . . he has a truly international ministry . . . I nearly died laughing . . . I wish he would drop dead." Or perhaps the worst offender, the publisher of this book, *Vision Christian College*, whose motto is "The Whole Word to the Whole World"! The point once again is this: the Hebrews did not use such over-heated language only in special settings, as we do, but everywhere.

[218] Cp. vs. 3-5.

[219] Note vs. 2,17-18; and cp. 58:3-6.

[220] Vs. 20-31.

cannot be taken at face value, must be false. The ancients laboured under no such burden. [221] So before carrying into our world the passionate ideas frequently expressed in scripture we need to be sure that we are handling the word rightly; that is, among other things, we must anchor its soaring language down to a more practical reality. This is part of what it means to *"rightly divide the word of truth"* (2 Ti 2:15, KJV).

A good hermeneutic recognises these literary and linguistic gaps and takes them into account in its interpretation of scripture. **More importantly**, a good hermeneutic will apply the gap not only to biblical *execrations,* but also to biblical *affirmations.* That is, the embellishments added by biblical writers to their curses were just as readily used when they recorded a *promise*. Do the curses mean less than they actually say? Then so do many of the promises! Here is one example of a promise that is far from literally true: *"No harm can come upon the righteous, but the wicked know nothing but trouble"* (Pr 12:21). The only way that proverb can be given its full meaning is either *(a)* to spiritualise it right off the planet; or *(b)* to understand "harm" and "trouble" in a moral rather than a physical and material sense. But neither of those is what Solomon had in mind. When he composed his aphorism he used its words in their ordinary earthly meaning; in which case the promise (like many others in scripture) expresses in absolute terms what is actually only a general truth. We may be uncomfortable with such usage, but the Hebrews employed it constantly.

> The Bible is the truest utterance that ever came by alphabetic letters from the soul of man, through which, as through a window divinely opened, all men can look into the stillness of eternity, and discern in glimpses their far distant, long forgotten home. (Thomas Carlyle)

---

[221] Nor is this restricted to the past. Travellers in the Middle East still observe that people in those lands are prone to discuss quite ordinary matters in a furious manner, with angry gesticulations and violent language, that seems (to us) astonishingly disproportionate to the issue.

CHAPTER TWENTY-TWO

IRONIC – ISN'T IT?

PART FIVE – 2. THE LINGUISTIC GAP (cont.)

The Hebrews were neither reprehensible liars nor irresponsible exaggerators; rather, they lived under a cultural imperative of overstatement – that is, they were *expected* to say more than they meant. Their hearers, of course, were aware of this, and instinctively made the necessary adjustments. But *we* have to make that correction deliberately. But what happens when modern readers fail to do so? They become guilty of loading the promises with an excessive weight. The result? The promises, carrying a burden too heavy for them, fail to behave as expected, and so become a source of bitter disappointment.

There are plenty of instances in scripture of prodigal language that must be tempered by cool reason. Notice, for example, the contrasts, even seeming contradictions, in *Joshua*. The writer boldly asserts the complete fulfilment of God's promise – Israel had gained possession of Canaan and its inhabitants had been destroyed. [222] Yet the record clearly shows that the land was only partially conquered. [223] So was it fully conquered, or not? The problem in fact is not

---

[222] See De 7:1-2; 20:16-18; Js 21:43-45; 23:14-15; and cp. 11:23 with 13:13; and see also 15:63; 16:10; etc. According to Js 10:28-42 (esp. vs. 40, *"destroyed all that breathed"*), the whole of the south was conquered, including Adoni-Bezek and his capital Jerusalem (10:1), and the Negeb, Hebron, Debir, etc, were all obliterated. Yet in Jg 1:1-15, <u>after</u> Joshua's death, they all still remain unconquered.

[223] See 11:22; 13:13; 15:63; 16:10; 17:11-12; 13:1; 18:3; etc. See also Jg 1:1,19,21,27,29-34 (note the repeated statement *". . . (they) did not drive out the inhabitants . . . "*); 2:3-4, 21,23; 3:1-6; etc.

historical but cultural. The style of Hebrew writing requires simply that enthusiastic claims must be cooled by the record of what actually happened.

Note how Midian was apparently completely annihilated (Nu 31:7-17), yet later was still a formidable foe (Jg 6:1-5; etc). Likewise, scripture says that Saul, in obedience to Samuel's horrific command, destroyed every Amalekite man, woman, and child (1 Sa 15:3,8-9,20). Yet shortly after, Amalek was still numerous and powerful (27:8; 30:1-2; 2 Sa 1:1). [224]

Was Jerusalem conquered in the time of Joshua (Jg 1:8) or not (Js 15:63; Jg 1:21; 19:10-12)? In fact, the city was not taken until the time of David (2 Sa 5:6-9).

The writer of *Judges* (1:18) claims that Gaza, Ashkelon, and Ekron were captured early in Israel's history. In fact, they were Philistine cities that were not taken until the time of David. Even *Judges* acknowledges that Ashkelon was still a Philistine city in the time of Samson (14:19).

How can we account for such apparent discrepancies, which would be intolerable in a modern historian? Read on –

EMBELLISHMENTS

Embellishing a story was typical of ancient Hebrew descriptive writing. It demonstrates how much the Hebrews differed from us in their use of language. However, there may also have been elements – perhaps unconscious, yet intended by the Holy Spirit – such as these:

(1) *a faith-statement*, in which something is declared true in the spiritual realm that is not yet fully realised on earth; or

(2) *a prophecy*, using the standard "prophetic present-past tense", in which something that is still future is described as if it has already happened; or

---

[224] You may notice, too, that they were more merciful to their captives than David had been (1 Sa 30:2). Who then was the more civilised nation? Was it really *God's* will that Saul and David should be so pitilessly cruel to boys and girls, and even toddlers and babies? Even allowing for exaggeration in the claims of Israelite genocide, there must still have been many children and infants killed by the ruthless swords of Saul and David.

(3) *a faith-dichotomy*, in which there may be elements of the kind of tension we ourselves experience between a *claim* that God's promise is perfect while our *experience* of it remains imperfect.

Each of those ideas has been posited by various commentators as a way out of both the moral dilemma of genocide and the seeming contradictions in the record. I cannot deny the truth that may lie in all three suggestions, and in others like them. Nonetheless, the plainest answer is simply to accept that the Hebrews had no interest in writing history as we like it written. They used language, and told stories, in their own way, and it is foolish for us to reach across thirty centuries and try to impose our literary prejudices upon them.

PHILISTINES

Another example of biblical hyperbole can be seen in the story of Israel's wars with the Philistines. In one place we are told that Israel had crushed the enemy (1 Sa 7:13-14), but in another that they were far from being annihilated (9:16). Still later, the same writer talks about the *"governor"*, or perhaps *"garrison"* [225] (10:5; 13:3), which shows that Israel was still subservient to the Philistines. Note also *1 Kings 11:16*, which again is typical of many such theatrical claims in the Old Testament.

Someone may respond: "Surely evangelical scholars can offer solutions to all these apparent discrepancies?" They certainly do. But two awkward things still stand –

- the very fact that explanations must be invented demonstrates that these riddles exist in the sacred text; and
- it is impossible to know which, if any, of the different clarifications offered by scholars are correct.

So the problems remain. Does this mean that the pages of the Bible are peppered with falsehood? Of course not. We are not facing deception, but simply a different way of speaking. Bible readers who fail to recognise that difference force the biblical writers into saying more than they intended to say, and certainly more than their original readers would have read into their words.

---

[225] The Hebrew word can be rendered either way.

A SAFEGUARD

Perhaps the best safeguard can be found in allowing scripture to modify itself. For example –

- Solomon's promise in one place that a *"skilful man will stand before kings"* (Pr 22:29) must be balanced against his observation in another that *"time and chance"* determine the fate even of *"the swift, the strong, the wise, the intelligent, and the skilful"*! (Ec 9:11-12)

- Similarly, his assertion that a child raised in a godly home will grow into a godly adult (Pr 22:6) must be diminished by his numerous warnings about children who mock God. He tells parents to prepare themselves for the heartbreak that wayward offspring may bring (17:25; and note also 10:1,5; 13:1; 15:20; 28:7; etc; and see also Is 1:2; Ez 18:15-17).

Do you know parents who are trying to turn Solomon's promise into a guarantee that their children will one day become fine Christians? Follow the king's example; tell them also about his warnings, for they too must be given due weight. In fact, those warnings remove all possibility that the promise was ever intended to provide a *guarantee* of salvation for anyone.

- Likewise, the story of *Job* must modify the bold promise to the upright, of freedom from all adversity (Pr 12:21).

- Is it always true that a man who finds a wife *"finds a good thing"*? (Pr 18:22). Not even the king believed that, even though his hand wrote the promise! (21:9)

- And how shall we reconcile the promise that no one in Israel would be poor (De 15:4), with the command to be generous toward the poor? (vs. 7).

- And what about the claim that the people had been supernaturally sustained throughout their entire journey (De 29:5-6), when in fact there were times when they lay exhausted and helpless before their foes? (25:17-18).

IRONY

Sensible readers will recognise then that many bold biblical statements are affirmations of a general rule rather than of an absolute promise. Sometimes also there is an element of *irony*, which a careless reader may miss. Consider this piece of wisdom –

> *When a king makes a decision his lips are inspired; no one can fault the judgment his mouth pronounces* (Pr 16:10).

If that is intended to be a statement of invariable fact, then it is manifestly wrong; for even Israel's most godly kings could be and were sometimes false in their pronouncements. The proverb becomes universally true only if one gives it a sarcastic meaning: that is, whether or not the king's words are inspired, unless you want your head chopped off you had better believe that they are! Even then the proverb works only in a setting of absolute monarchy, where the king has unfettered power of life and death over all his subjects. In that environment, anyone who values his skin will gladly call every word the most wicked sovereign pronounces a veritable oracle from heaven!

Likewise, is it always or only sometimes true that a wise slave will gain authority over a foolish son (Pr 17:2), or that diligence and careful planning bring prosperity (21:5)? Even a casual look at life is enough to show that often fools rule the wise; and the lazy may gain riches [226] while a hard-working person struggles to survive. Irony is embedded in all those claims.

Perhaps too we can solve the problem of *Proverbs 18:22* by treating it as irony, or maybe sarcasm. It becomes more true to life if it is read like this (which the Hebrew allows) –

> *If you actually find a good thing when you find a wife, then you must be one of God's particular favourites!*

Nor is such irony lacking from the New Testament, for Paul in particular employs it in several places (e.g. 2 Co 11:19 & 20-21; 12:13; Ga 5:12; etc.)

---

[226] Think about people who win millions of dollars in a lottery that they have done absolutely nothing to deserve.

AMBIGUITY

If the passages I have mentioned must be read in a general rather than an absolute sense, then perhaps the same rule applies to other bold statements that are not so obviously softened by our observation of life? Western Bible readers must accept that the Hebrews were inclined to speak more emphatically than suits our taste. We prefer moderate talk; we dislike extreme language. We expect words to mean neither more nor less than they say. But that is *our* problem; such niceties did not bother the Hebrews. They spoke brazenly, dramatically, colourfully, turning (as it seems to us) a general observation into an absolute rule, or a frequent outcome into a fixed promise. This difference in language style must be taken into account before a decision is made about how much weight to give a biblical statement.

Ambiguity, then, is an inescapable part of scripture. But if the Book is to reflect real life, how could it be otherwise? Can anyone deny the contradictions that surround us every day? The Hebrews were well aware of life's crazy twists. They understood that a good rule in one place may become false in another; hence they did not hesitate to enunciate contradictory principles. A fine example can be found in *Proverbs 26:4,5*. We are helped in this case, because the opposites stand side by side; so we have no choice but to allow the first statement to qualify or modify the second. Elsewhere, however, contradictory sayings are separated, sometimes by many chapters, or even books, which leads ill-informed readers to take as an absolute promise a statement that is quite denied by another passage (I have given several examples above). Each statement is true in its appropriate setting; but the question we have to answer is which of them (if any) fits our present circumstance.

In the maelstrom of life, if we claim a biblical promise that truly belongs to us, then we may expect our claim to be backed by all the authority of heaven. But if we wrongly apply or misinterpret scripture, if on the strength of one verse we try to make the Bible say what it does not say, then our hope of divine support will probably be dashed. We may find ourselves alone, helpless, and abandoned to the ruinous fate of fools. [227]

---

[227] Those *Proverbs* I cited earlier (about the rod looking for the back of a *"fool"*) gain significance here. While they no longer allow us to whip *"fools"*, they certainly show God's indignation against wilful or careless stupidity!

LOST MEANINGS

Another aspect of the linguistic problem is this: the full meaning of many Old Testament words remains either uncertain or unknown, and translators must make an informed guess about how to put them into English. Likewise, the Hebrew text of many verses is garbled, and there are many gaps in the extant manuscripts. [228] These deficiencies in all the copies that we possess of the original documents lead to the preparation of different master-texts, and are one reason for the striking variations among our English translations. The safe course is to compare as many different versions as possible, which will bring the reader as close to what the biblical authors wrote as it is possible for a person unfamiliar with the original languages to come.

> The Bible is no mere book, but a Living Creature, with a power that conquers all who oppose it. (Napoleon Bonaparte)

---

[228] If you have a Bible with textual footnotes, or marginal notes, a quick glance will show you a score of places where the Hebrew text of the Old Testament is deficient in one way or the other. Here is a set of examples of just *one* of the problems mentioned above, namely, places in the Psalms where the meaning of the Hebrew text is uncertain. I have drawn this list from the *New Revised Standard Version* of the Bible. In each of the following texts either some part or all of the verse has been marked by the translators thus: "The meaning of the Hebrew is uncertain." *Psalm 2:11,12; 10:18; 16:2,4; 22:16; 32:4; 37:35; 40:7; 42:4; 49:15; 51:6; 58:7; 68:30; 74:5; 88:15; 92:10; 103:5; 118:27; 119:128; 139:20; 141:5-7.* A different translation might give a different list, with either fewer or more references.

CHAPTER TWENTY-THREE

BURN THE WITCH!

PART FIVE – 3. THE CULTURAL GAP

The terrible cruelty of the witchhunts in England between 1542 and 1684 resulted in thousands of witches being executed. In Scotland the number killed was even higher, and death was by burning. In Europe from the 15th to the 18th century over two hundred thousand witches died at the stake. [229]

What an appalling record. A hideous death imposed upon scores of thousands of women, most of whom were guilty of no crime except being in some way different from their neighbours. Even if they were guilty as charged (of practising witchcraft), still their execution by burning was an act of unspeakable atrocity. Yet the church was in the thick of it, never doubting that scripture sanctioned the screams of those tortured and writhing women. And they were right – but only if Old Testament law is valid for the church; if it is not, then they were tragically wrong.

How did such terrible crimes against God and humanity gain acceptance?

They began when Moses told Israel, *"You shall not permit a witch to live"* (Ex 22:18) – a law that was more honoured by Israel in breaching than observing it (apparently the laws against witchcraft were only spasmodically observed, and it was not difficult to find a practising witch; cp 1 Sa 28:3; 2 Ch 33:6; Is 8:19).

---

[229] Barbara Cartland, A Witch's Spell, Magna Print Books, Long Preston U.K., 1985; pg.241.

But soon after the publication of the English Bible [230] preachers throughout the land discovered the Mosaic laws and began to thunder against witchcraft. Even King James, that devout *Defender of the Faith*, [231] wrote a furious blast against all witches and their devilish practices. In one year (1660) in Scotland alone 120 women were condemned as witches and burnt to death. Each of those cruel executions was attended by a Bible-quoting clergyman who could find nothing better to do than to urge the terrified and sobbing women to repent and to thank God for the kindness of the church – for could they not hope to escape the eternal flames of hell by the fiery torment they were about to suffer on earth? Thus the church showed them its mercy and love. [232]

Yet prior to the Protestant Reformation and the sudden widespread availability of the Bible, there had been little fear of witches in Christendom. Renaissance writers in the 14th and 15th centuries were generally enlightened and humane in their understanding of the ancient biblical laws. Even St Augustine (5th century) thought that witchcraft depended mostly upon trickery and illusion, and scarcely gave it serious consideration. [233] Indeed, the practice of witchcraft is seldom mentioned in the writings of the Church Fathers across more than five centuries, nor did it figure much in church history for another thousand years. But suddenly there arose a phalanx of literalists, holding new Bible translations in their hands, and determined to enforce even the most savage Old Testament precepts. Across Europe horror entered the lives of thousands of harmless people.

VOICES OF PROTEST

Throughout the Reformation period and beyond there were always a few thoughtful teachers who decried the superstition, the fundamentalist frenzy, the misreading of scripture that motivated the persecution and burning of witches –

> Here it should be stated, to the honour of the Church of England, that several of her divines showed great courage in opposing the dominant doctrine. Such men as

---

[230] Several English translations of the Bible were produced during the 15 and 16th centuries, culminating in the renowned *King James Version*, which was published in 1611.

[231] A title that still appears on British coins.

[232] Some of the information in the next few paragraphs on witches comes from, A History of the Warfare of Science with Theology in Christendom, by Andrew Dickson White, 1896 Version; Sage Digital Library, Albany, Oregon, 1996. Other sources used were various encyclopedias, both secular and sacred, and the writings of Augustine.

[233] Confessions Book IV, Ch. 1.

Harsnet, Archbishop of York, and Morton, Bishop of Lichfield, who threw all their influence against witch-finding cruelties even early in the seventeenth century, deserve lasting gratitude. But especially should honour be paid to the younger men in the Church, who wrote at length against the whole system: such men as Wagstaffe and Webster and Hutchinson, who in the humbler ranks of the clergy stood manfully for truth, with the certainty that by so doing they were making their own promotion impossible. [234]

But until the end of the 18th century those sane voices remained a minority. Even the great John Wesley (1703-1791) stood with the majority –

> In 1768, we find in Protestant England John Wesley standing firmly for witchcraft, and uttering his famous declaration, "The giving up of witchcraft is in effect the giving up of the Bible." The latest notable demonstration in Scotland was made as late as 1773, when "the divines of the Associated Presbytery" passed a resolution declaring their belief in witchcraft, and deploring the general scepticism regarding it. [235]

One cannot help but feel that Moses, [236] with his brutal command to kill witches, has much to answer for. The story of the hideous torments – the racking, scraping, tearing, lacerating, scream-wrenching tortures – that so many thousands of girls and women were made to suffer, is the stuff of nightmares. So unimaginable were their agonies that they were driven to admit every possible foul offence against God and man, all of which were solemnly recorded by the authorities and implicitly believed. To scape those awful torture chambers – made more horrible by the presence of priests and pastors, both Catholic and Protestant – the women rushed to embrace even death by fire at the stake. And again and again, across pulpits and judicial benches, the harsh edicts of the Old Testament rang out.

Gradually, however, the fundamentalists began to lose ground, until those who held more moderate views far outnumbered them. Only then was it possible for the state to break loose from the grip of the hoary laws of Moses and to institute more enlightened policies. How did this radical change happen?

---

[234] White, op. cit. pg. 346.

[235] Ibid. pg. 347

[236] Perhaps, to be fair to the great law-giver, I should rather blame those mad "Christian" priests and clergymen who took Moses so literally, and developed a refinement of torture (it has been said) that far exceeded even what the ancient pagan Romans had practised.

THE LAWS REPEALED

In England, a rising humanistic scepticism gradually undermined the biblical literalism of the 16th and 17th centuries. This process was enhanced by the strong reaction of the nation against the cruelties of the English Civil War (when witches were hunted down remorselessly). Sickened by the harshness and inhumanity of the fundamentalists, the people turned away from them and sought a better way. The last witchcraft trial was held in Britain in 1717, and all witchcraft laws were repealed in 1736. Legal violence against witches in England then terminated, although for another 100 years, in some backward and superstitious areas, covert persecution continued, often incited by the clergy.

I do not mean that the hunting of witches across those awful three centuries arose solely out of a particular reading of scripture. There were other legal, social, and cultural factors involved. But biblical literalism cannot escape a large share of the blame for the terrors of the torture chamber and the stake. Without biblical support, or if moderate voices had then been prevalent, as they are now, the frightful shrieks of the tormented victims would never have rent the air, nor would the awful smell of burning human flesh have spread its sickening odour across the land.

But there is a deeper problem: why did Moses command such a cruel law (and others like it) in the first place? Here we meet again the depth of the *cultural gap* that lies between our world and his –

A HARSH SOCIETY

By our standards, the ancient Hebrews lived in a harsh society, often barbarous, frequently pitiless, in which women, children, slaves, and foreigners, because they had scant legal protection, were easily exploited –

- Joshua was told by Moses (who plainly believed he spoke the mind of God) to destroy all his enemies – to kill man, woman, and child, without mercy or pity. (De 7:2)

- A thousand years later Ezekiel was still able to echo the same savagery: *"Kill them without showing any pity or compassion. Slaughter old men, young men, maidens, women, children – kill them all!"* (9:5-6)

- Even David, the sweet singer of Israel, cried vehemently, *"You know how much I hate those who hate you, O Lord. Do I not loathe*

> *those who rise up against you? Are they not my enemies? I hold for them nothing but hatred!"* (Ps 139:21-22)

- Likewise Jeremiah: *"Let a curse fall upon anyone who holds back the sword from shedding blood!"* (48:10).

Would anyone dare to preach such vicious sentiments across a pulpit today? That kind of bloodthirsty language is far removed from a Christian ethic. But during the English Civil War (for example) the combatants never hesitated to cite such passages as their authority for the merciless slaughter they visited upon each other.[237] Even the glorious John Milton, in his work *Of Christian Doctrine*, sternly used those texts to enforce his opinion that "we are commanded to curse, in public prayer, the enemies of God and the church."[238]

If those rabid writers had been better informed, if they had been guided by a wiser hermeneutic, they could never have so foully abused the Word of God. Yet in one sense they were logical. Since they believed in a literal approach to the whole Bible they saw no reason why they should not give as much weight to one passage as to another.

The same rationale was cited by the early colonists in the Americas, Africa, and elsewhere. For if the Israelites were justified in attacking Canaan and slaughtering everyone who refused to embrace the religion of Yahweh, then none could oppose the right of the Christian invaders to do the same. Thus Christopher Hill writes –

> Colonial conquest was justified, among other things, by a desire to spread the truth of Christianity and the rule of the chosen people of God. God's commandment to the Jews was clear: there was to be no false pity. Wars of extermination, or for domination and enslavement, were justified by God's command. Columbus, we are told, got from the Bible his attitude towards the Indians whom he met in America. The consequences could hardly have been worse, or more lasting.[239]

I cannot refrain from asking how modern literalists manage to wriggle away from this dilemma? How can they justify the arbitrary manner in which they apply some passages of scripture exactly as written, but with wondrous dexterity strip others of all their sting? If there is anything beyond a tame surrender to cultural pressure in such capricious meddling with the Word of God, I have yet to

---

[237] Christopher Hill, op. cit. pg. 91.
[238] Ibid. pg. 384.
[239] Ibid. pg. 397-398.

discover it. Such picking and choosing among the sacred texts seems to have no valid *hermeneutical* thrust behind it. How else can it be seen except as a vagary motivated by social convenience?

PRIMITIVE AND CRUEL

Returning again to the Bible world: it was an age dependent upon a crude and often ill-informed medical practice, more akin to folklore herbalism than to modern science. There was little medical research; disease was thought to come either from demons or from God (cp. De 32:39), so why bother to investigate its natural causes and cure? If sickness has a mainly spiritual origin then it must need a mainly spiritual remedy. So prayer, superstition, magic, and primitive medicine were all mixed up in the treatment of illness.

The legal system too was harsh and inadequate, often depending upon bizarre and unreliable practices, such as trial by ordeal. Those who were found guilty faced an array of harsh penalties, such as –

Banishment....... 2 Sa 14:13; Ezr 7:26; Re 1:9
Beating............... Ac 16:22-23; 2 Co 11:25
Beheading......... Ge 40:19; Mk 6:16,27
Blinding............. Jg 16:21; 1 Sa 11:2
Burning.............. Ge 38:24; Le 20:14; Da 3:6
Caning............... Ps 89:32; Pr 10:13; 13:24; 22:15; 23:13,14; 26:3; 29:15
Casting............... 2 Ch 25:12
Chaining........... Ps 105:18
Confinement..... Je 38:6; Zc 9:11
Confiscation...... Ezr 7:26; Mt 18:25
Crucifying......... Mt 20:19; 27:35
Crushing........... Pr 27:22
Drowning.......... Mt 18:6
Enslavement...... Mt 18:25
Exposure........... Pr 30:17; Da 6:16,24; Mt 25:20; 1 Co 15:32
Fines................... Ex 21:22; De 22:19
Hanging............. Nu 25:4; De 21:22,23; Js 8:29; 2 Sa 21:12; Es 7:9,10
Hard Labour..... Ex 1:11-14; Js 9:27; Jg 16:21
Imprisonment.... Ezr 7:26; Mt 5:25
Mutilation.......... Jg 1:5-7; 16:21; 2 Sa 4:12; Ne 13:25; Is 50:6; Ez 23:25; Da 2:5; Mt 24:51
Restitution......... Ex 21:36; 22:1-4; Le 6:4,5; 24:18
Sawing............... He 11:37
Retaliation......... Ex 21:24; De 19:21
Scourging.......... De 25:2,3 Mt 27:26 Ac 22:25 2 Co 11:24
Shooting............ Ex 19:13
Stocks................ Je 20:2; Ac 16:24

Stabbing	1 Sa 15:33; Ac 12:2	*Torture*	22:21; Ac 7:59 Mt 18:34; He 11:37
Stoning	Le 24:14; De 13:10; 21:18-21;		

Notice those references above that come from the gospels. Jesus mentions various harsh punishments without any comment on their grisly cruelty. He seems to have accepted the penalties imposed in his day as a proper exercise of justice. How could he have done otherwise? In the flesh he was a man of his times, and probably never thought to question many aspects of the contemporary culture. He could not possibly have foreseen the shape our society would take, any more than we can imagine what the world might be like twenty centuries from now.

Hence when Jesus wanted to describe divine punishments he did so by using retributions that were familiar to him, such as –

Beating, Stoning, and ***Killing***	Mt 21:35; Lu 19:27	***Flogging***	Lu 12:46-48
Torture	Mt 18:34-35	***Enslavement*** and ***Confiscation***	Mt 18:25 (notice how barbarously the debtor's wife and children are included in the penalty, which Jesus may or may not have approved, but nonetheless mentions without comment); and cp. also Lu 12:58-59.
Mutilations	Mt 24:51		
Burning	Lu 16:23; Mk 9:48; Mt 25:41		
Exposure	Mt 8:12; 22:13; 25:30		

A MAN OF HIS TIME

Many Bible readers, failing to recognise that in such references Jesus is simply speaking in terms of contemporary practice, are offended by them. The gentle readers cannot construe how a merciful God can behave so viciously. But if the details are left where they belong, back in an ancient and long-dead world, the problem is removed. We need see in the words of Jesus nothing more than an affirmation that sin will be punished; his sayings do not oblige God to descend to the pitiless savagery of the ancients. [240]

---

[240] Note also the acceptance by the thief, and presumably also by the apostles, of crucifixion as a proper punishment for crime (Lu 23:41, *"in our case it is plain justice, we are paying the price for our misdeeds"* [REB]); yet to our minds the punishment is hideously disproportionate to the offence.

If we fail to make such an adjustment we will be driven to embrace the very arguments that our forefathers depended on to endorse their atrocities –

> Torture was used (in Scotland) far more freely than in England, both in detecting witches and in punishing them. The natural argument developed in hundreds of pulpits was this: If the Allwise God punishes his creatures with tortures infinite in cruelty and duration, why should not his ministers, as far as they can, imitate him? [241]

But if we banish from our minds any thought that divine penalties are a heavenly counterpart to a medieval torture-chamber, then such specious arguments will be at once rejected. The Holy Spirit may be bound to *speak* to us in human categories, but he is certainly not obliged to *emulate* them!

We may assume too that in the coming Judgment whatever punishments are imposed will be recognised by all as suited both to the crime and to divine justice. Divine wrath will match divine mercy, and will be in accord with the practice, not of Greek, Roman, Jewish (or even our own) jurisprudence, but of heaven's love. However, since we cannot possibly know in this life the actual nature of events in the life to come, those future judgments had to be revealed to the biblical writers (and hence to us) in terms that belonged to contemporary society.

But what happens when that cultural gap is ignored, and the words of Jesus are taken as a sanction for the actual punishments he mentions? The result is ethical dementia! Thus, despite the abolition of torture and the stake in England, law-makers of the last century were still citing *Luke 12:59* (and other similar texts) as a ground for the incarceration of entire families. The Fleet Prison in London was notorious for the horrors suffered by debtors, along with their wives and children, who were together jailed there. Many, unable to pay their debts, were confined for life, and perished in misery.

Charles Dickens (whose own parents and siblings were once jailed for debt) provides a graphic picture of the wretchedness of those impoverished victims. His novel *The Pickwick Papers* [242] describes a debtor who because of the foul conditions became consumptive, and after six months of illness died. Mr Pickwick, who later pronounced the death an act of judicial murder, visited the sick man in his squalid cell –

---

[241] White op. cit. pg. 345.
[242] Chapter XLIV.

... he lay stretched (on his cot), the shadow of a man: wan, pale, and ghastly. His breathing was hard and thick, and he moaned painfully as it came and went. ...

"I hope," he gasped after a while: so faintly that they bent their ears close over the bed to catch the half-formed sounds his pale lips gave vent to: "I hope my merciful Judge will bear in mind my heavy punishment on earth. Twenty years, my friend, twenty years in this hideous grave! My heart broke when my child died, and I could not even kiss him in his little coffin. My loneliness since then, in all this noise and riot, has been very dreadful. May God forgive me! He has seen my solitary, lingering death."

... They whispered together for a little time, and the turnkey, stooping over the pillow, drew hastily back. "He has got his discharge, by God!" said the man.

He had. But he had grown so like death in life, that they knew not when he had died.

If such rabid injustice is no longer allowed in our land, it is not because of adherence to but rather in defiance of a literal reading of scripture. Literalists who would today oppose the idea of people being incarcerated for life for debts they could not avoid, do so not under biblical but under cultural pressure.

A BLEAK WORLD

The world of the ancient Hebrews was a world without books, magazines, or newspapers, possessing few of the amenities that provide us with so much entertainment and pleasure. Such writings as existed had to be inscribed on parchment or papyrus, which were expensive, scarce, and beyond the purchase of most people. Simple messages were scratched on potsherds. [243] The abundance and cheapness of writing materials that we take for granted would have been inconceivable to them.

Hence their knowledge of the larger world, and their ability to share with each other even what they did know, was extremely limited. Who can tell how much our attitudes have been shaped by our well-informed familiarity with the affairs of many nations? How much is our worldview affected by the things that even poorly educated people in our society know about science, history, geography, art, and many other matters? We must at least acknowledge that we can no more fully enter into the world-view of the ancients than they could have imagined ours.

---

[243] Pieces of broken pots, or other clay vessels.

They enjoyed music, but lacked the technology to produce the finely honed and perfectly tuned instruments that are common to us; nor did they possess our many-toned scale. No one today would enjoy listening to the discordant, thin, and monotonous music that was the best they could produce. In the opinion of one authority, "it is very probable that if we could hear a piece of ancient Greek music accurately performed, we should regard it as bizarre, uncouth, and possibly barbaric." [244] Hebrew music was certainly no better, and may indeed have been worse!

How different is our society! Music shapes us in many ways today that were unknown to them, and, along with a multitude of other cultural factors, it inescapably alters our approach to God, and the way we look at life.

Their understanding of hygiene too was primitive, so that disease was constantly rampant, with blindness a distressingly frequent affliction. [245] Indeed, it was a world laden with threats that came upon the people from many directions, so that they were driven into a deep fatalism. Knowing that they had scant control over the shape their lives would take, what else could they do but accept without complaint whatever each day produced? [246] We are not so submissive to fate, nor so accepting of the inevitable, but expect to exert a large influence over our daily affairs. Plainly, we and our world have only a limited kinship with Old Testament times, and care must be taken to carry into modern times only those things that truly belong to both worlds. And the further back one goes in biblical history the more true that observation becomes.

---

[244] The Oxford Classical Dictionary, article "Music"; Oxford University Press, 1979.

[245] The gospels show how many sick, blind, and infirm people there were in the time of Jesus.

[246] See Pr 19:21; Ec 7:14; 8:6-7; 9:11-12; 1 Co 16:7; He 6:3; Ja 4:13-15; 5:13; etc.

CHAPTER TWENTY-FOUR

BRIBES AND LOTTERIES

PART FIVE – 3. THE CULTURAL GAP (cont.)

> I have carefully and regularly perused these Holy Scriptures, and am of the opinion that the volume, independently of its divine origin, contains more true sublimity, more exquisite beauty, purer morality, more important history, and finer strains of poetry and eloquence, than could be collected within the same compass from all other books, in whatever age or language they may have been written. (Sir William Jones)

There is, of course, much truth in Sir William's fulsome praise of scripture. Indeed, viewed from its divine perspective as the inspired Word of the living God, no encomium could soar too high! Yet such exalted adulation may lead people to spread a mystic aura around the Bible that prevents them from reading it soberly. They thread the Book with an esoteric spirituality that causes them to abandon common sense when they open its pages. Accordingly, thousands of Bible readers, deeply imbued with a godly awe of scripture, refuse to take properly into account the cultural hiatus that lies between us and old Israel.

All Christians, of course, should bountifully reverence the Word of God, and deem it their most precious possession. But we are still required to read it intelligently, and to work with it responsibly, searching for the true message the Spirit wants to speak to us each day. Dogmatic superstition will hardly open the doors to correct understanding. So let me ask this question of those who still cling to the idea that most (if not all) biblical precepts can be carried into the modern world without modification: will you obey the following injunctions?

(1) **_Beatings._** *"If you want to purge away evil, then strike hard enough to wound, for a severe beating scours even a sinner's inward parts!"* (Pr 20:30). Try to employ that rule today, whether on a child or an adult, and you will go to prison on a charge of violent assault! [247]

Hardly more than 100 years ago, though, keen floggers did quote such passages to justify whipping a man until his flesh hung from his bones in shredded ribbons and the ground at his feet was puddled with blood. Even women and children were sometimes treated with the same horrific brutality, while pious clergymen quoted sundry biblical texts.

(2) **_Bribery._** See *Proverbs 6:35; 17:8; 18:16; !9:6; 21:14; etc.* Those passages (especially in the Hebrew text) advocate bribery as a means of solving certain problems, or of smoothing one's path through life. There are other passages which argue against bribery (Ex 23:8; De 16:18-19; Ps 15:5; Pr 15:27; 17:23; 33:15; Mi 3:11; and a dozen other references).

How shall we reconcile this apparent contradiction? Perhaps the Hebrews saw a distinction between a gift used to secure some desirable end, and a gift used to pervert justice or to encourage crime (cp. 2 Ch 19:7, where bribery is forbidden in just such a context; similarly, see Is 1:23). To us, however, both gifts are bribes, and anyone engaged in such practices today would be scorned as morally corrupt.

(3) **_Lotteries._** Would anyone today place any serious dependence upon casting lots? Yet the Hebrews frequently did so (Le 16:8; Nu 26:55; Js 18:10; 1 Sa 14:41; Es 3:7; Pr 16:33; 18:18; Jo 1:7; Mt 27:35; Ac 1:26). Notice the claim (Pr 16:33) that every cast of the lot is determined by God.

Unless we narrow the application of the verse down to certain "religious" or pious settings (and the text itself gives no reason to do so), we are faced with a severe ethical problem. If God *does* intervene in every lottery, how can we account (say) for the seeming indifference of divine providence toward the winners in a modern lottery, who are seldom numbered among the righteous? Apart from the dubious ethics of gambling, think what good could be done with the millions of dollars that are disbursed each year through lotteries – millions that many Christians no doubt think are falling into the "wrong" hands.

---

[247] While I was in the act of writing these very pages I received a phone call from a pastor seeking advice in relation to one of his parishioners. The man had been charged with child abuse after chastising his small son with a stick. He wanted the pastor to back him in court by quoting that very scripture (Pr 20:30), as a sanction for the wounds he had inflicted on the boy! The pastor asked if he could use the text for that purpose. You know already what I told him!

Someone might say that gambling for money is not the same as casting a lot to discover the will of God. True, there is a difference in aim; but there is no difference in process. And in our day, whether the dice are thrown to learn the will of God or to make money, there is no evidence that heaven normally interferes with chance. Plainly the ancient writers either saw something that we don't in casting a lot, or, which is more probable, they were more fatalistic about life.

In her classic novel *Silas Marner* (published in 1861), [248] George Eliot included a scene in which Silas has been falsely accused of stealing some money from a church. Unwilling to go to court, the church elders decide to test the matter by drawing lots, basing their action upon the relevant texts in the Bible (such as Pr 16:33). The draw pronounces Silas guilty, and he leaves the church embittered both against the congregation and against God –

> On their return to the vestry there was further deliberation. Any resort to legal measures for ascertaining the culprit was contrary to the principles of the Church: prosecution was held by them to be forbidden to Christians, even if it had been a case in which there was no scandal to the community. But they were bound to take other measures for finding out the truth, and they resolved on praying and drawing lots. ...
>
> Silas knelt with his brethren, relying on his own innocence being certified by immediate divine interference, but feeling that there was sorrow and mourning behind for him even then – that his trust in man had been cruelly bruised. [249] *The lots declared that Silas Marner was guilty.* He was solemnly suspended from church membership, and called upon to render up the stolen money: only on confession, as the sign of repentance, could he be received once more within the folds of the church. Marner listened in silence. At last, when every one rose to depart, he went towards (the real thief) and said, in a voice shaken by agitation –
>
> ... "*You* stole the money, and you have woven a plot to lay the sin at my door. But you may prosper, for all that: there is no just God that governs the earth righteously, but a God of lies, that bears witness against the innocent."
>
> There was a general shudder at this blasphemy. ... (But) poor Marner went out with that despair in his soul – that shaken trust in God and man, which is little short of madness to a loving nature.

While it is only a piece of fiction, the story echoes well enough similar tragedies that have been repeated across the centuries in countless churches. Many people

---

[248] Book One, Chapter One, George Eliot's emphasis.
[249] By the false accusations that had been spoken against him.

who have been unjustly penalised have blamed God, as Silas Marner did, for his non-intervention. Yet the Lord seldom interferes in human actions, and he is not obliged to rescue us from our follies. If people insist upon following silly superstition [250] instead of good sense, then it is hardly God's fault if they reap pain and misery. Not even the sufferings of the innocent can place God under any obligation to change the normal course of events. It is *our* responsibility to deal with scripture soberly, wisely, intelligently, and if failure to do so harms us, or even others, then we have none to blame but ourselves, or our leaders.

Surely we can learn from these things at least one lesson: it is perilous to transport biblical practices unchanged into modern times. Does that mean we should banish as worthless all the scriptures that talk about casting lots? Of course not. We may learn much from them, which any good commentary will show you. But I will say this: it is madness to pluck out of those verses a credulous belief in the efficacy of an omen for determining the mind of God. The experience of a multitude of victims shows the truth of what George Eliot made her fictional hero suffer. Those who throw a pebble, randomly poke a finger at their Bible, or the like, in dependence upon divine intervention, will probably find, not a pathway to divine wisdom, but to great confusion.

(4) *__Mutilations__*. Jesus was adamant: *"If your hand causes you to stumble, cut it off; it is better for you to reach heaven maimed than to keep both hands and be sent to hell"* (Mk 9:43-48). How is it that those who insist on taking literally other declarations made by Christ do not treat this one in the same way? I do not see many one-hand, one-eye, one-foot persons in the church! Do their limbs never offend them? Have they never put a foot wrong, nor touched any evil, nor gazed upon any iniquity? Why then are they not maimed? Do they not wish to enter heaven? Or is it rather because they take literally only those verses that either suit their convenience or conform to modern culture? There is nothing in the words of Jesus to suggest that they should be read differently from any of his other statements.

What then should we do? Certainly not arbitrarily pick and choose which parts of scripture we will obey and which we will ignore. Rather, let us find a uniform, reliable, and workable way to read the entire Bible. That is why I still have two hands, eyes, and feet, despite Jesus' words, and despite the many times those members have caused me to stumble! I have learned how to leave in the past

---

[250] Such as casting lots, drawing straws, looking for omens, plucking isolated verses out of the Bible, putting out "fleeces", asking for a "sign", and the like.

what belongs there, and to obey only what belongs in the present. In other words, I search scripture for *principles* that remain valid for all time. [251]

TRIAL BY ORDEAL

If you need further proof of how little we understand the Hebrew world-view, then meditate on the peculiar test of conjugal fidelity imposed by Moses upon women (and only upon women, not men) – see *Numbers 5:22-24*. Citing just such biblical passages as their authority, church and civil authorities across many centuries subjected thousands of helpless women to bestial torments by fire, water, and other barbarous means. "Trial by ordeal," as it was called, became a standard test for conjugal fidelity, witchcraft, and other supposed crimes. The clergy argued that God could be trusted to ensure a just outcome of the trial, that divine intervention would cause wickedness to be revealed and right to triumph.

So the victims were made to pass through flames, to grasp red-hot iron, to thrust their hands into burning coals, or were chained and dropped into water. If the fire burned them, or if they did not drown, they were adjudged guilty, and suffered even more terrible punishments. If their flesh remained unsinged, or if they drowned, [252] they were pronounced innocent. There were other tests, equally horrible, which trembling and terrified prisoners were compelled to undergo – all in the name of Christ, all sanctioned (as the church ignorantly thought) by the Bible. But those dignitaries could never have found any such sanction if they had adopted a better hermeneutic; that is, if they had de-mystified the Bible and understood that the outdated precepts of Moses cannot not be imported unchanged into the church.

One has to admit, though, that those murderous priests were at least more consistent in their reading of scripture than many modern readers are. Deeming that the whole Bible speaks with literal authority to every generation on every matter, they not only whipped their children brutally (while quoting scripture), but just as enthusiastically (still quoting scripture) flogged, burned, mutilated, crushed, drowned, and tortured countless other wrongdoers, young and old, male and female. But what happens today? Vast numbers of modern readers with a literal bent, not daring to flaunt the humane standards of our time, obey only such

---

[251] The same hermeneutical rule must be used to modify the seemingly impossible demands made in other difficult passages, such as Matthew 5:21-42.

[252] It was argued that the sanctified water would not receive the body of a sinner, and would cause it to float, despite being bound hand and foot and weighted.

Old Testament passages as they can utilise without risking a criminal charge. That seems to me at best capricious and at worst dishonest. I prefer to look for a way to deal fairly and consistently with every part of the Bible.

> Blessed Lord, who hast caused all holy Scriptures to be written for our learning; Grant that we may in such wise hear them, read, mark, learn, and inwardly digest them, that by patience, and comfort of thy holy Word, we may embrace, and ever hold fast the blessed hope of everlasting life. [253]

---

[253] The old Book of Common Prayer, "The Collects – The Second Sunday in Advent."

CHAPTER TWENTY-FIVE

HOW BIZARRE!

PART FIVE – 3. THE CULTURAL GAP (cont.)

Perhaps the meaning of the "cultural gap" we have been talking about will become clearer if I abandon the past and look at some examples of the extraordinary cultural divides that exist in *our own* world. It is immensely difficult for us to enter sympathetically into some *modern* cultures, let alone those of the *past*. While I was gathering illustrations for this book, I came across a report on the use of human urine in various African and Asian societies. In some cases the liquid is drunk; in others it is massaged over the entire body, working from the ankles to the thighs, and then from the neck to the thighs; and in others it is used both internally and externally. The urine of pre-pubescent boys is favoured, voided early in the morning, and preferably still warm. If fluid from a boy is not available, then a girl's may be used, or failing that, one's own urine. I also came across this conversation among some British soldiers during the Peninsula War in Spain, outside of Talavera in 1809 – [254]

> Unconsciously Sharpe felt the leather bag around his neck. It was heavier by six gold pieces thanks to the dead on the (battle) field. He drank some wine.
> "It's filthy!"
> "There's a rumour," Leroy said drily. "I hear that when they tread the grapes they don't bother to get out of the wine-press to relieve themselves."
> There was a moment's silence and then a chorus of disgusted voices. Forrest looked dubiously into his cup. "I don't believe it."

---

[254] From the novel <u>Sharpe's Eagle</u>, by Bernard Cornwell; Harper Collins, London, 1996; Chapter Eleven, pg. 125.

> "In India," Sharpe said, "some natives believe it very healthy to drink their own urine."
> Forrest looked owlishly at him. "That cannot be true."
> Leroy intervened. "Perfectly true, Major. I've seen them do it. A cupful a day. Cheers!"

Do you find that offensive? Do you think such things have no place in a book like this? I don't like it either; but surely that just proves the point: *we find it almost impossible to empathise with customs that are utterly foreign to our own way of life.* If that is true even of modern cultures, how much more difficult must it be to reach across the gulf of many centuries! Think also about this: there are things in the Bible that are far more unpleasant than the bizarre (to us) practice of drinking urine!

The point is, in their own time, and in their own culture, practices that are abhorrent to us were valid. But they have no place in our world. Good hermeneutics recognises this, makes no attempt to re-locate the past in the present, but looks instead for the unchanging principles that lie behind every biblical practice or idea.

GIVE YOUR GUEST A BATH!

Anyone who has some familiarity with medieval society will be aware that for several centuries it was the custom in England for all ladies of noble birth to offer personal care to any person who visited their homes. This care included undressing the weary and soiled travellers and bathing them in a hot tub. Despite the nakedness of the visitors, and the fact that their gentle hostesses soaped and washed them all over (which often produced a natural phallic response in male guests), neither embarrassment nor immorality was attached to this practice. I have read about it in several places, including a passage by Elizabeth Chadwick, in which she describes such a scene in the early 12th century. The Lady Eleanor is called upon to fulfil her duty to a young knight who has arrived at the castle, and in this instance, because of an emotional attachment between them, there is some awkwardness –

> It was the customary duty of the wives and daughters of a great household to see to the well-being of all new arrivals to the keep, be they visitors, friends, or family. The offer of a bath-tub and comfortable clothing was always the first hospitality. Eleanor had performed the function of hostess so many times now that this particular occasion should have come as

second nature. The fact that it hadn't and that she was intensely aware of him, naked and in a volatile mood, was extremely unsettling. [255]

Nonetheless, they both behaved properly, for to have taken immoral advantage of the situation would have plunged them into an abyss of reproach.

Today of course, if I were to ask my wife or my daughter to body-wash every male visitor to our home I would be rejected with scandalised horror, by wife, daughter, guest, and everyone else! That does not make us either more or less moral than they were; but it does make us different! [256]

SURGERY WITHOUT ANAESTHETIC

Consider also how difficult it is for us to understand the terrors that must have beset people less than 200 years ago who had to undergo surgery with no anaesthetic. Here is an account from a novel by Thomas Armstrong, set in the early 19th century. Elizabeth Rochefort, the wife of a wealthy banker, has a cancer in her breast, which has to be removed. The surgery takes place in the breakfast room of the lady's home, while she is sitting in a chair, with a maid holding her hands. The surgeon murmurs a few words of encouragement, and then, "before the words were out of his mouth, he had begun." –

> As the sharp scalpel burnt deep, a tremor passed through the emaciated body; Mrs Rochefort's head lolled, her eyes closed, and outwardly it seemed that she had fainted, though all the while Martha Teddiman could feel the ever-tightening grasp of a deathly cold hand.
>
> With incredible speed the surgeon worked . . . until his purpose was done. Then followed the dressing and final bandaging.
>
> Mr Nussey stood off. "I have finished, madam," he said, for the first time the strain showing in him.
>
> Henry Rochefort's wife raised a face which appeared to consist of nothing more than a pair of agonised eyes.
>
> "You . . . have . . . finished . . . sir?" she asked wearily.

---

[255] The Leopard Unleashed; pub. By Michael Joseph Ltd, London, 1992; pg. 104.

[256] For another lively description of this ancient custom of the wives and daughters of noble households personally unclothing, bathing, and dressing an honoured guest, see also the novel Once a Knight, by Christina Dodd; Harper Paperbacks, New York, 1996; pg. 65, 84-91.

"'Tis over, ma'am," he replied compassionately. And never, ma'am, in my experience have I encountered such courage and – "

Elizabeth Rochefort's senses at last left her. [257]

We shiver at the thought of such horror, but people two hundred years ago had to accept many similar agonies as part of ordinary life. Each new day was shadowed by the threat of being seized by some ailment – perhaps appendicitis, a tumour, an ulcer, a dead baby in the womb – that would require surgery or amputation, without any way to alleviate the torment of the physician's knife. Can you imagine how much that threat gave a shape to their worldview very different from ours? At the very least they had to develop qualities of stoicism and fatalism almost unknown in our culture.

Consider too this account of the sufferings of Queen Caroline (1768-1821, the wife of George IV). She contracted a rupture, which led to a series of eventually fatal operations. A courtier and politician of the time, Lord John Hervey, who was fond of the queen, has left us this report of her courage –

> Every day once at least, and sometimes oftener, (she had to endure) some new incision; and before every operation of this kind which she underwent, she always used to ask the king if he approved what the surgeons proposed to do; and when he said they had told him it was necessary, and that he hoped she would consent to anything they thought so, she always submitted immediately, and suffered them to cut and probe as deep and as long as they thought fit, with the utmost patience, resignation, and resolution. . . . (If) any involuntary groans or complainings broke from her during the operations, she used immediately after to bid the surgeons not to mind her, and would make them apologies for interrupting them with her silly complaints, when she knew they were doing all they could to help her. [258]

Few people in our culture will ever have to endure so helplessly such brutal, raw pain. We expect to live each day, in the main, with comfort, good health, pleasure, peace and abundance. We cannot hope to understand fully the minds of our forefathers, whose lives were daily assailed by many perils from which even people who possessed limitless wealth could not escape.

---

[257] Dover Harbour, Harper Collins, London, 1942; pg. 108, 109. The lady died. Indeed, few people survived the shock of such operations. Perhaps the best that can be said is that the brief time of severe pain relieved them from a more prolonged period of ever-sharper suffering – and there was always a chance that they might actually recover.

[258] T. H. White, op. cit. pg. 78.

AN ABUSED BOOK

We have seen that within only the last 200 years, and in some cases during our own lifetime, the Bible has been used to justify many wicked things: slavery; child labour; torture; burning and hanging of witches; branding and stoning of adulteresses; genocide; and other horrors.

Those practices are now rightly forbidden in Australia (and in other western lands). Biblical literalists agree with this prohibition. But why? Literally understood, the Bible, far from opposing such conduct, approves it. I can only repeat my earlier observation: the true reason why literalists accept the prohibition is because they dare not flout the culture. They choose to blind their eyes to an inconsistent application of scripture, and, yielding to social pressure, quietly shelve practices that the Bible seems to endorse.

Does the Bible sanction those practices?

By now the answer should be clear: of course not!

How do we reach that conclusion?

Simply by using a proper hermeneutic. My point is that biblical literalists are trapped in ambivalence. They insist on obeying literally commands that are *socially* acceptable; but when they are confronted with *impermissible* commands, they relegate them to antiquity. Yet the ancient laws, kind and cruel alike, stand unequivocally together on the sacred page. Literalists who allow cultural pressure to determine which ones they heed seem to me to show a culpable inconsistency. A "pick and choose" [259] hermeneutic is hardly admirable.

A LOVE ETHIC

Perhaps someone will say, "But surely the compassionate advances we enjoy today are themselves a product of the Bible's influence?"

---

[259] The phrase derives from an old expression that conveys the idea of a fussy, and somewhat arbitrary, choice. "Pick" has the sense of "clearing away unwanted matter", of separating out only what is desirable, as one does when using a garden pick. The term has a more distant origin in the old Germanic name for a woodpecker's beak, which was "pek" – thus to "pick", as the bird does, when, in order to get a grub, it digs away the unwanted wood.

Undoubtedly that is true. The high and noble ethic of love that is taught in scripture (even in the Old Testament but especially in the New) has been a major source of the gradual abandonment of harsh penalties, of the growing compassion of our society, and of many other improvements, such as

- equality of the sexes
- rejection of racism
- denunciation of slavery
- abandonment of child labour
- care of the aged and infirm
- and the like.

But we have taken nearly twenty centuries even to get this far! Sadly, one of the reasons for that long delay has been the church itself, which has often been the most merciless advocate of flogging, hanging, burning, and other barbarities, all in the name of Christ and scripture. The repulsive scene of a clergyman with a whip in one hand and a Bible in the other has been repeated countless times. [260] Scripture has been used to justify the most despicable cruelties, all because of a blind refusal to deal wisely and sensibly with the Word of God.

There is little doubt, if power should fall again into the hands of biblical literalists like those who have ruled in the past, that many of those horrific practices would be resurrected. [261] I think it is by the mercy of God that we are

---

[260] One of the books on my shelves contains an old engraving of a scene from a medieval torture chamber, in which a poor naked woman, accused of some religious "crime", is being subjected to merciless torture at the behest of the church. Two priests stand piously by, prayer books in hand, urging the victim to confession and repentance, while the torturer fulfils his vile task. Citing Moses, David, and other biblical authorities, the priests no doubt sincerely believed, amid the shrieks, sobs, and groans of their tormented captive, that they were simply doing God's will

[261] I have mentioned in an earlier footnote what is happening in countries where Muslim fundamentalism is resurgent, and the *Shari'a* (the rule of the Qur'an) is being imposed. For example, at the time of writing these lines, in Sudan a woman caught wearing trousers can be sentenced to a savage whipping of 40 lashes. The *Shari'a*, with its *"eye for eye"* theme, and its barbaric penalties (mutilations, stonings, floggings, and the like), is closely akin to the laws of Moses, and indeed is based on them.

Church history gives us no reason to believe that a dominant Christian fundamentalism (wedded to literalism) would behave any better. In fact, it would probably be worse. As one historian has said:

"Under paganism, the rule regarding torture had been that it should not be carried beyond human endurance; and we therefore find Cicero ridiculing it as a means of detecting crime, because a stalwart criminal of strong nerves might resist it and go free, while a physically delicate man, though innocent, would be forced to confess.

Footnotes continued on the next page

governed today by enlightened secularists rather than the kind of narrow Christian bigots who have seized authority in the past and in their mad zeal produced measureless grief and rivers of blood.

VEILS AND FOOTWASHING

The manner in which even the most ardent fundamentalists modify their reading of scripture to meet cultural imperatives is shown by the near-universal abandonment of Paul's injunctions about women wearing a veil in church (1 Co 11:6-7). [262]

Likewise, notice the heavy modification of the eucharist into a brief symbolic meal; the general abandonment of foot-washing; and the like. The conclusion is obvious: when it suits us better, we don't hesitate to forsake ancient decrees, or at least to modify them for modern convenience.

I have no objection to that; I do it myself with aplomb. What I object to is the inconsistency that allows literalists to make free with some scriptures while they insist that others of the same sort must be obeyed to the letter. Yet they have no better reason for doing so than cultural expedience. Their choices in those cases are certainly not theologically driven.

"Hence it was that under paganism a limit was imposed to the torture which could be administered; but, when Christianity had become predominant throughout Europe, ***torture was developed with a cruelty never before known***. There had been evolved a doctrine of 'excepted cases' — these 'excepted cases' being especially heresy and witchcraft; for by a very simple and logical process of theological reasoning it was held that Satan would give supernatural strength to his special devotees — that is, to heretics and witches — and therefore that, in dealing with them, there should be no limit to the torture.

"The result was in . . . tens of thousands (of cases), that the accused confessed everything which could be suggested to them, and often in the delirium of their agony confessed far more than all that the zeal of the prosecutors could suggest. . . . (Great numbers) of worthy people were sentenced to the most cruel death which could be invented. The records of their trials and deaths are frightful.

"The treatise which in recent years has first brought to light in connected form an authentic account of the proceedings in (these affairs), and which gives at the end engravings of the accused subjected to horrible tortures on their way to the stake and at the place of execution itself, is one of the most fearful monuments of theological reasoning and human folly." (White, op. cit. pg. 453)

[262] The dainty confections that hatted women wear in church today bear scant resemblance to the coverings Paul had in mind.

But if the Bible is the true Word of God (and I fervently believe that it is), then we have only one duty: find out what it says, *all* that it says, and do it, whether or not secular society approves. Yet I must add that in practice a sound hermeneutic will seldom if ever find it necessary to interpret scripture in a way that opposes the best impulses of the secular world.

JESUS AND THE JEWS

The gospels show Jesus pitting his own sweetly enlightened reading of scripture against the harsh dogmatism of the Jewish leaders. Watch him enraging a synagogue ruler by healing a crippled woman on the Sabbath day (Lu 13:13-15). Watch him supporting his disciples when they pick and eat some ears of corn on the Sabbath (Mt 12:1-8). Watch him on many other occasions violating the narrow legalism, the hard casuistry, of the scribes and pharisees. Jesus called his opponents *"hypocrites"*, and lashed them with scorn.

But what was the source of that hypocrisy? Simply an insistence upon reading the ancient commands too literally, which obliged them to be inconsistent in their application. To leave their animals hungry and thirsty on the Sabbath day was culturally (and commercially) unacceptable, so they broke the Mosaic law without scruple. But when they met a sick woman, whose healing they could safely postpone, they suddenly insisted upon a strict observance of the Sabbath rule.

Their hypocrisy arose from an unviable reading of scripture, which forced them to be arbitrary in their application of the commands of God. Jesus was arguing for, and demonstrating, a more consistent application of scripture, based not upon an impossible literalism, but upon a grasp of the inner spirit of the sacred word, a comprehension of the unchanging principles that undergird every page of the Bible. Any kind of casuism or sophistry was abhorred by the Master.

JESUS AND USURY

Did you know that the Old Testament strictly forbids usury (adding interest to a loan)? [263] Yet Jesus told two parables in which he mentions without criticism an

---

[263] Ex 22:25; Le 25:37; De 23:19-20; Ps 15:5; Pr 28:8; Ez 18:8; etc. The prohibition initially did not include non-Israelites, although it seems later to have done so, for the prophets forbade usury altogether.

exaction of interest (Mt 25:27; Lu 19:23). Apparently he thought that Moses had something more than commercial profit in mind when he laid down his usury laws. So long as that deeper ethical principle was observed, the use, or non-use, of interest in monetary transactions was unimportant.

We too, nowadays, cheerfully ignore the ancient strictures, and without hesitation give and take interest on various monies. [264] But for over a thousand years [265] the church *did* strictly observe the Mosaic rule, and imposed heavy penalties on any Christian who violated it. That is what allowed the Jews (who had by then learned how to read the scriptures more flexibly, or at least more realistically) to become the financiers of the world.

But then the scene changed again. Under the impact of the burgeoning mercantile states that began to grow in prosperity and power some 600 years ago, immense pressure came upon the church to revise its interpretation of the rules against usury. Theologians finally came to the conclusion that the ban on interest was intended only to show that rich people must treat the poor with generosity, and not exploit them. The ban had nothing to do with commercial loans, nor with extracting a reasonable profit from business activities.

So once again, scripture was re-interpreted to match a cultural imperative. Yet I wonder why those critics who take umbrage at the ideas I am presenting here, and who insist that every possible scripture must be read literally, are so flexible on the matter of usury? The injunctions Moses gave are plain enough. Why do they feel free to ignore those commands while demanding that other similar rules be observed to the letter? It puzzles me.

JESUS AND THE APOSTLES

Jesus refused to adopt a strict reading of scripture when he dealt with the woman caught in adultery. Yet the law clearly demanded that she should be stoned to death. How then could he refuse to join in her execution? Simply because he insisted on reading the law in a way that looked, not for *rigid rules* that had to be

---

[264] Sometimes a distinction is made between "interest" (which is deemed lawful) and "usury" or excessive interest (which is deemed unlawful). But no one has yet managed to define when interest becomes usury, and, in any case, the distinction does not exist in scripture. All taking of interest by one Israelite from another was forbidden by Moses.

[265] As late as the Third Lateran Council in 1179 the exacting of interest was still being condemned by the Church.

rigidly obeyed, but for *eternal principles* of God's justice, mercy, grace, and love.

Notice the apparent tension created between Christ and scripture when he said to the woman, *"I do not condemn you!"* But it could not be denied that the law of Moses *did* condemn her. And did not Jesus himself say that heaven and earth could pass away more easily than even the tiniest swirl on the end of one letter of the law? (Lu 16:17) How can the law be at once irrevocable and yet susceptible to change?

The problem is not in the law, but in the way people have chosen to read it. God's law is immutable. But that law comes to us through human channels, and therefore inevitably carries the cultural baggage of those channels. Jesus recognised this, and looked past the mere grammar of the sacred text to its larger purpose. Thus the Master saw something more in scripture than a seemingly relentless demand for punishment. He saw the life and love of God threaded through every line, and that is what he looked for. Not dogma, but revelation. Not law, but grace. Not stern rules, but dynamic principles. Not legislation, but guidelines. Not unyielding strictures, but steps to paradise.

This same flexibility, this humaneness in applying the ancient scriptures, this search for an undying principle sheltered within an inevitably changing mode, is often reflected in the way that Jesus and the apostles quoted the Old Testament. Christ, as we have seen, did not hesitate even to countermand Moses when he thought that the great Lawgiver's rules had become obsolete (cp. Mk 7:14-19; Mt 5:38-39). Paul too was brave enough to *re-write* Moses! He called the *Ten Commandments* a *"ministry of death"* (2 Co 3:7); and he turned *Exodus* on its head, by insisting that when Moses veiled his face, it was *not* to hide the "glory", but rather to hide the *loss* of the glory! (cp. 2 Co 3:13 with Ex 34:30-35). Similarly, Philip preferred the Jewish tradition that an angel, not *Yahweh*, had communicated the *Decalogue* to Moses (Ac 7:38,53).

How then *did* the apostles view scripture? Plainly, they looked for the *divine sense* of each passage, and were not much troubled by its *exact wording*, unless that sense (as it sometimes did) happened to rest upon a particular expression (cp. Mt 22:31-32; Ga 3:16). Notice too their familiarity with the Greek version (the *LXX*) [266] of the Old Testament, which they did not hesitate to cite, instead of the

---

[266] The Greek version of the OT is known as the "LXX" because of a tradition that it was translated from the Hebrew by a group of "seventy" scholars. It is cited in the NT in the following places, which sometimes differ significantly from the Hebrew/Aramaic text: Mt 1:23; 3:3; 12:21; 13:14-15; 15:8-9; 21:16; Mk 1:3; 4:12; 7:6-7; Lu 3:4-6; 4:18-19; 8:10; Jn 1:23; 12:38,40; Ac 2:17-21,25-28; 4:25-26; 7:42-43; 8:32-33; 13:34,35,41; 28:26-27; Ro 2:24;
Footnotes continued on the next page

Hebrew/Aramaic text, when it suited their purpose better. Since the *LXX* contains the writings that we now call the Old Testament *Apocrypha*, Jesus and the apostles must have often read those additional books, and quite possibly treated at least some of them as scripture. Whether or not that was so, they were certainly influenced by the *Apocrypha*, and their own writings often reflect that influence. [267] Many allusions to the *Apocrypha*, and at least one direct quote (Jude 14-15 quoting Enoch 1:9), are scattered through the New Testament. [268] Several pagan writers are cited also. [269] This freedom and flexibility, so often demonstrated in the New Testament, argues against the kind of rigid verbalism that many literalists try to adopt, with such disastrous results. The Bible is a living book, not a dead letter. It should be read with the sparkle of life, not crushed by the heavy hand of stifling dogma, nor turned into the bitter lash of legalism.

> This Bible is for the government of the People, by the People, and for the People. (John Wycliffe, c. 1320-1384. Abraham Lincoln modified Wycliffe's words into his own famous saying about democracy.)

3:4,13,14; 9:17,27-29,33; 10:11,16,18,20,21; 11:9,10,26,27,34; 12:20; 14:11; 15:12,21; plus at least another 20 places.

[267] The number of books included in the *Apocrypha* varies. In the NRSV they are as follows: Tobit; Judith; Additions to Esther; Wisdom of Solomon; Wisdom of Sirach; Baruch; Letter of Jeremiah; Prayer of Azariah; Song of the Three; Susanna; Bel and the Dragon; 1 Maccabees; 2 Maccabees; 1 Esdras; Prayer of Manasseh; 2 Esdras; 3 Maccabees; 4 Maccabees; Psalm 151.

[268] In the New testament there are more than one hundred allusions or verbal parallels to various passages from the Apocrypha.

[269] Aratus (Ac 17:28); Epimenides (Tit 1:12); Menander (1 Co 15:33); and perhaps others.

CHAPTER TWENTY-SIX

GOD AND A STORM

PART FIVE – 4. THE PHILOSOPHICAL GAP

How different from ours was the *world-view* of the ancient Hebrews! In particular, they saw God in everything, and attributed every event to the immediate action of God. Habakkuk watched while a majestic thunderstorm came out of the desert and rumbled with terrifying splendour across the Holy Land. But to him it was no mere natural phenomenon. Instead he saw *"God coming from Teman, and the Holy One from Mt Paran"* (Hb 3:3; Jg 5:4-5). Similarly, *Psalm 29* is a poetic celebration of nothing more heavenly than a thunderstorm – at least, that is how *we* would interpret the sights and sounds all around us. But to the *psalmist* the Lord was inextricably part of the storm, covering the land with terror, shattering the earth with his awful voice. Hence at the end of the poem the frightened people are gathered in the temple (vs. 9), pleading with God to return quietly to his heavenly abode and to leave them in peace! (vs. 11)

This means that a thoughtful modern reader cannot advance far into the Bible before discovering that between us and the Hebrews there exists a ***philosophical gap***, [270] which we might also call the barrier of

---

[270] Just a reminder that we have so far looked at three other "gaps": *historical; linguistic;* and *cultural.*

A DIFFERENT WORLDVIEW

Consider, for example, the assertions in *1 Samuel 2:6-8* and many parallel passages. [271] These all express an immediacy of divine involvement in every aspect of human life, and a quality of fatalism, that would be uncommon in our day even among very pious Christians. *Our* worldview, which is shaped partly by the New Testament and partly by the culture, does not encourage a passive acceptance of whatever happens, as if we were helpless to do anything to change our fate or to influence our destiny. [272] The early Hebrews looked at life differently. They were not wholly fatalistic, but they were substantially so. Nor is that surprising when one remembers that they attributed each drought, locust plague, natural disaster, illness or recovery, and all poverty and prosperity to the direct action of God. Hence the author of *Samuel* did not hesitate to explain the obduracy of the sons of Eli by saying, *"It was the will of God to kill them"* (1 Sa 2:25). He also sings,

> *Who but the Lord chooses to kill or to bring to life? Who but the Lord can cast into Sheol or raise up again whomever he pleases? He alone creates wealth or brings poverty; he abases some and exalts others.* (1 Sa 2:6-7)

Did a foreign people invade the land, inflicting slaughter, rape, and ruin? Then it must have happened by the specific command of God! [273] Imagine someone today trying to say about Adolf Hitler what Isaiah had no hesitation in affirming about the equally brutal Cyrus (45:1; 46:8-11). For two hundred years Persia imposed its despotism upon Israel; yet despite this ruthless tyranny the prophets never doubted that the emperor ruled by the will of God (Je 50:41-42; Is 41:2-3,25). They even went so far as to say that the bitter cruelty of the enemy was a proper outworking of divine anger (Is 13:3,9,15-18). Anyone who made such a

---

[271] Ru 1:21; 1 Sa 14:14-23; 18:10; Ec 7:13-14; Is 10:5-6; 45:7; Je 51:20-23; Ez 14:15-21; Am 3:6; etc.

[272] There is, of course, a necessity laid upon all of us to accept what we <u>cannot</u> change – cp. *Philippians 4:11-13*. Nonetheless, the New Testament presents a vista of freedom of action, and of a potential to reshape one's personal world that was quite startling to its first readers. Consider the world-shaping ramifications of Jesus' words about *"moving mountains"* (Mk 11:22-24), drowning *"mulberry trees"* (Lu 17:6), doing the *"impossible"* by faith (Mt 17:20; 21:21-22), and many other similar statements. They all imply a nearly limitless capacity to alter the shape of things by prayer, and to carve out a new pathway through life. Such concepts are utterly antagonistic to any kind of fatalism. No Hebrew prophet could have spoken them. In his own time the words of Jesus were breathtaking in their promise of spiritual authority and of personal determinism.

[273] See the references just above, and in the relevant footnote, and also Jl 1:16-17; 2:1-2,11; etc.

claim today about the torture chambers of the Inquisition and the Nazis, or about the callous Stalin and his slaughter of millions, would be reckoned insane.

Even worse than the Persians was the pitiless ferocity of the Assyrians, who raped, murdered, enslaved, tortured, flayed, and inflicted countless other barbarities upon their hapless victims. Yet Isaiah does not hesitate to say that God sent Sennacherib to *"make fortified cities crash into heaps of ruins"* – with all the accompanying killing, pillage, horror, and the measureless grief suffered by ordinary men, women, and children (37:21,26-27; etc). They may have been sinners – who is not? – but did they deserve such unspeakable anguish? Such miseries can be endured as an act of mindless history; but how could any sensitive person today accept them as direct acts of God, done by his immediate will and in full harmony with his purpose?

Likewise, Jeremiah calls the merciless Nebuchadnezzar the servant of Yahweh, and believes that the terrible inhumanity of the Babylonians was in the main an outworking of the anger of the Almighty (21:7; 25:9; 27:6,8; 28:14; 39:6-8).

FATALISM REJECTED

No modern preacher could safely attribute such vile behaviour either to the direct purpose or the deliberate action of God. Any person who tried to speak such oracles would be scornfully rejected by the church. Indeed, even by the time of the apostles the shocks of history had largely driven that level of fatalistic thinking out of Israel. It is almost entirely absent from the New Testament, whose worldview is much nearer to our own.

This change of philosophy must be taken into account when one reads the Old Testament and endeavours to discover its message for our time. Failure to do so, and an insistence upon giving full authority to the literal meaning of Old Testament passages, has been the cause of too many horrors already. What foul cruelties Christians have perpetrated in the name of God over the centuries! If those blood-hungry people had read the scriptures more sensibly they would never have been able to find pious excuses for their barbarities.

VICTORY IN WAR

> *An army may make itself ready for war, but the winner will be determined by the Lord* (Pr 21:31).

Anyone today who tries to give that proverb the same meaning it had for its author will be quickly tangled in an awkward moral dilemma. How can we say that every victory won by the ungodly has been, or will be, achieved by a decree of God? How repulsive that idea is to us! Yet the ancient writer was happy to accept it! Why do we *reject* it? For two reasons –

First, our wider knowledge of history (of which the Old Testament writers knew almost nothing) has taught us that loathsome tyrants often win battles and crush nations in bloodbaths of rape, murder, robbery, and frenzied cruelty. Eventually the people of Israel came to realise the same. A few centuries after Solomon wrote his proverb – having in the meantime been ravaged by the Assyrians, the Babylonians, the Persians, the Egyptians, the Greeks, and the Romans – the Jews themselves abandoned the king's optimistic view of history.

Second, the New Testament reveals a philosophy that strongly modifies the older worldview. So much so that Luke was able to say (which the ancient author could never have written) that all the nations of this world, with their glory, power, and riches belong to the devil, and he can give them to anyone he pleases! (Lu 4:5-7; Mt 4:8-9).

Accordingly, modern commentators soften the plain meaning of Solomon's dictum; usually by arguing like this –

- God is certainly free to exercise his sovereign power and to determine the outcome of any battle or any war; and if he decides that victory will go to the enemy, then no effort of ours can upset his decree

- however, since God seldom interferes in the ordinary outworking of human affairs, whether on a personal or national level, success or failure mostly depend upon natural rather than supernatural factors

- or else, they turn the proverb into a command, which says that the righteous should align their lives with God's purpose so that he may prosper their endeavours. [274]

No doubt those ideas convey the best message we can glean from the text today, but they were not in Solomon's mind. He simply took it for granted that winning or losing were entirely in God's hands, and one had no choice but to submit to the divine edict.

---

[274] The Hebrew text might allow this translation: *"Arm yourself to fight God's battles, and victory will surely be yours!"*

Other Old testament passages, of course, do modify the king's fatalism by adding the idea that righteousness will exalt a nation, and that a godly people can expect the Lord to heap prosperity upon them. Yet even that notion posed an ethical puzzle, and indeed was one of the things that finally drove Israel away from its old philosophy. All too often the people had watched the *ungodly* flourishing, while the *righteous* nation was crushed. Even after the Jews returned from exile, utterly purged of idolatry, and had rebuilt their temple, God did not favour them with freedom. They strove to obey the law, and to worship Yahweh faithfully, yet they remained under continuous foreign oppression. Five hundred years later, when Jesus began his ministry, their miseries were unabated, and a foreign tyrant still held them in galling bondage. [275]

No doubt the nation bore a measure of guilt because of its sins; nonetheless, compared with the iniquities rampant among the pagans Israel's crimes were small. Why then did she suffer so bitterly and for so long? Such questions forced righteous people to look less for justice to be found on earth, and more toward a heavenly recompense, which became essentially the Christian position. Israel moved away from a strongly fatalistic view to one in which life was seen to happen according to natural law, sometimes with divine intervention, but mostly without.

CASTING A LOT

This change of philosophy is nowhere more obvious than in the matter of casting lots. Earlier Israelites had no doubt that they could throw some pebbles and discover the mind of God; they believed implicitly that the outcome of every lot is determined by God (Pr 16:33; 18:18; etc). I have mentioned this already in a different connection, but it applies here also. Over the centuries, because of the many times when the cast obviously gave a false result, the use of lots began to die out. The pebbles or straws were still trusted occasionally, even in apostolic times (Ac 1:26), but the apostles soon found (as the *Acts* story shows) that they were an unreliable way of discerning God's will, and the practice was soon abandoned.

Yet since then, foolishly quoting *Proverbs* and other Old Testament passages, many Christians have tried to resurrect the lot in one form or another. They have found no more success than their forefathers. Surely only the naive, the ignorant,

---

[275] Even during the brief Maccabean interlude, the Jewish nation enjoyed only semi-autonomy; for it remained within the boundaries of the Seleucid empire, and paid tribute to the emperors.

or the superstitious would now pin any trust to such a flawed device. We are expected to operate at a much higher level; our tools are the wise use of scripture and believing prayer (Ja 1:5-8); we are called to possess the mind of Christ (Ro 12:2), and to live under the direction of the Holy Spirit (8:14). By such resources as those – not by magical customs that are more pagan than Christian – we should both discover and do the will of God.

DAVID AND RIZPAH

David apparently mistook the purpose of God in the case of Rizpah (2 Sa 21:1-14). At the king's command, and supposedly in response to a divine directive, her two sons were impaled (a ghastly, ugly, and lingering death), along with five other young men, all of whom were guiltless of any crime against the king. It was an act of insensate revenge, and of pitiless murder. Yet still the ravaging famine was not eased. Indeed, heaven remained hard until David had repented, prayed, and done all he could to rectify his inexcusable killing of his victims. Only then did the rain begin to fall.

So did God really tell David to stain his hands with blood? Probably not. When the story says that the king enquired of the Lord it likely means only that he (or a priest) had cast a lot. The falling pebbles gave David an answer that he interpreted in a certain way, but his reading of the stones proved to be wrong. Indeed, it seems impossible that God *could* have told David to kill those young men. Why? Because the king's judicial murder broke God's own law, which said that *"children shall not be put to death for the sins of their parents"* (De 24:16). Can the Giver of a law justly command its violation? David also broke another law, which said that the corpse of an executed person must not remain on a stake overnight (De 21:22-23).

Some commentators excuse David's violation of the law by arguing that the executions were a special case of blood atonement, designed to rescue Israel from divine wrath. There was therefore nothing unjust in the summary killing of seven innocent victims. Such writers seem to accept without shrinking that this was all done by God's express will – which to me is a moral abomination. It is also just the kind of thoughtless reading of scripture that countless Christian torturers and executioners across the centuries have used to justify their atrocities. I can only be grateful that in our time such wild and unreasonable men, unlike their barbaric forbears, no longer have the power to misuse scripture so wickedly – at least, not at the level of civil law and government. Yet one can hardly doubt that many of them would if they could – and, what is worse, remain piously convinced that they were doing the will of God amid the cries of their `gonised victims.

Much later in Israel's history, the prophet Ezekiel showed by the higher ethic he had come to embrace that David's actions were morally repugnant (18:1-32). Ezekiel, echoing Moses, but more vigorously, insisted that the genuine justice of God could not tolerate one person being made to suffer for the crimes of another.

GOD BRINGS GOOD AND EVIL?

> *Who can make anything happen unless the Lord approves it? Good and evil alike come in response to his command* (La 3:37-38).

There is a fatalism in those words that no one today could express so absolutely and be accepted. Yet that was the view of the Hebrews. Was a man put to death by hanging? Moses insisted that he could not have so died unless in some way God had cursed him. [276] Was knowledge withheld from the people? Then for this human ignorance the Lord must be responsible. [277] Moses gave solemn and extended directions on how to cure a *house* of leprosy [278] – a matter of baffling irrelevance to us. Yet the same lawgiver had no scruples about advocating the truly outrageous crime of genocide! (Nu 31:7,15-17; 1 Sa 15:3). Those passages, along with others, have been madly used by both Catholics and Protestants to justify murdering each other in the name of a holy war! But at least they had a more consistent hermeneutic than many modern readers do. People who insist upon taking one Old Testament injunction literally, and <u>without question</u> applying it to our time, should do the same with them all! But that would be absurd. Rather, let us develop a sound hermeneutic that will enable us to deal responsibly, fairly, and consistently with the whole Bible – by which I mean a hermeneutic that fully takes into account the hiatus that exists between the ancient world and ours.

This wide gulf surely means that no Old Testament saying can be applied unchanged to our world. The entire book must be read *first* through the eyeglass of an ancient philosophy, and *then* interpreted in the light of the New Testament. Only then can we understand what the Old Testament teaches, promises, or commands us. The fact that sometimes at the end of that process a statement will reach us unchanged does not cancel the validity of the rule.

---

[276] De 21:23; and cp. Is 53:4b.

[277] De 29:4.

[278] Le 14:33 ff.

GENOCIDE

Let me come back to the crime of genocide, which must have been as morally repugnant to God in ancient times as it is now. [279] In the name of a holy war, or sacred "ban", genocide was a frequent practice of the ancients. For example, King Mesha of Moab (circa 830 B.C.), boasted that his god Chemosh had told him, "Go, take Nebo from Israel!" So he attacked the Israelites, conquered them, and

> "slaughtered all the people (of Ataroth) so that Chemosh and Moab were drunk on their blood . . . and (in Nebo I slew) seven thousand men, boys, women, girls, and maid-servants, for I had devoted them to destruction for the glory of Chemosh." [280]

As the Israelites had dealt with their neighbours, so was it dealt to them. And if the genocide practised by Moab upon Israel was ethically abominable, it was no less so when practised by Israel upon Moab, unless the reader wishes to place Yahweh on the same level as Chemosh.

The rationale behind the "ban" (devoting a whole people to destruction in the name of a god) was the idea that each nation was "holy" to its god, and belonged to that god. All wars were therefore fought in the name of the national deity, and were deemed to be waged by one god against another (cp. 1 Sa 17:45-47). It followed that upon the defeat of that god everything belonging to him or her, must be reckoned unholy by the victorious deity, and had to be destroyed.

Happily, because of its moral and practical difficulties, the "ban" was seldom fulfilled absolutely. [281] King Mesha's boast was probably no more accurate than similar claims by Israel's warriors. He no doubt captured the towns he had attacked, but the number "7,000" (which was symbolic of perfection) sounds

---

[279] *He is the Lord, he does not change, he is the same yesterday, today, and for ever!* (Ma 3:6; He 13:8) In order to preserve the autonomy and dignity of his people God must continually accommodate himself both to their ignorance and to their inadequate moral development. He must therefore seem from time to time to endorse behaviour that later generations will find repugnant. But we cannot suppose that God's own moral character has improved or changed over the centuries. He is immutable, the source and expression of every perfection from the very beginning.

[280] Part of the inscription on the "Moabite Stone". See The Ancient Near East Vol. One; ed. by James B. Pritchard; Princeton University Press, 1958; pg. 210.

[281] Notice, for example, the refusal of the army to kill Jonathan, despite the sanction of a divine oracle. Their moral compunction against such an act of judicial murder was greater than their fear of the king's oath or even of divine retribution (1 Sa 14:36-46).

suspiciously like an *ideal* rather than an *actual* number. Notice also *1 Kings 11:14-16*. If *"every male"* had in fact been killed, then how could Hadad have raised a successful rebellion so soon? Yet apparently he was able to do so without difficulty. The writer plainly saw no contradiction nor any problem, which shows that *"every man"* was a kind of synonym, or shorthand, for a *"massive defeat"*. It is usually foolish to read it literally. People in Bible days gave a factual meaning to such sayings only if something in the context showed that they were not idioms.

We are now faced with a problem –

- did God actually command genocide;
- or were his words given a softer meaning by the people;
- or was the saying no more than a human misreading of the divine will;
- or does it simply reflect the philosophy and language-style of the ancient world?

The evidence suggests that at least some of Israel's believed that Yahweh did indeed want Israel to slaughter all their foes. See for example the actions of

SAMUEL AND SAUL

At the behest of those monarchs the Israelite army sometimes did kill every person, and later had cause to regret their brutality. For example, the seed of savagery sown by Samuel in his grim demand that Saul slaughter every living thing, human and animal, resulted in a bitter harvest. Doeg the Edomite, deeming that Nob had been placed under the "ban" by Saul, went far beyond the king's actual wish, and slew not only the priests, but every inhabitant of the town, and all its livestock (1 Sa 22:19). He was not condemned for the act by Saul. How could the king accuse him? Had not Saul done the same to other cities? And what about David's implacable murder of helpless civilians? (1 Sa 27:9-11). If what Doeg did at Nob was a foul crime, then so were the actions of David, no matter what religious justifications may have been (or are) offered to excuse them.

DID THEY DESERVE TO DIE?

Some commentators justify the genocide recorded in scripture because of the wickedness of the victims. They commit two grievous errors –

- they deem an entire community unspeakably foul, when in reality its citizens would have been no worse and no better than most people are today in pagan lands, or, for that matter, in our own; and

- they use the same de-humanising rationalisations as, say, the slave owners in the USA did last century, or, in our time, the Nazis in their concentration camps – they see people as mere objects, no better than cattle.

But the gospel forbids us to treat human beings as "things", to devalue their dignity and personal worth, to strip them of ordinary emotions and feelings, to reduce them to exploitable chattels, to lump them with animals, to deny that they contain anything of the likeness of God.

It seems to me, then, if genocide is morally odious in the 20th century *after* Christ, then it must be reckoned equally despicable in the 20th century *before* Christ (cp. He 13:8). Was it then truly *God* who commanded Moses, Joshua, and others, to *"slaughter every inhabitant"*? The question is painful to answer, for to say either "yes" or "no" raises serious problems. But perhaps a solution lies in the suggestion given above, that the mere fact that something *happened*, or was even *attempted*, was enough for an ancient Hebrew to say that God had decreed it.

What else could they do? They had to speak in terms that were familiar and acceptable to them just as we do. This means, for example, that just as *we* are incapable of saying that Stalin was obeying God when he murdered more than ten million people, so *they* would have been incapable of describing the event in any other way. The difference is not one of divine action but of human interpretation of each happening. *They* could not help but say, "It is the will of God!" *We* cannot help but deny that God commands such horrors. We see the world one way; they saw it another. It is a disparity, not of biblical reliability, but of philosophy and of worldview

JESUS AND MOSES

By the time of the New Testament world events had forced the Jews to modify their attitudes toward divine providence and also toward life in general. There are hints of that changed outlook in the way Jesus spoke. Notice these contrasts –

- Christ refrains in *Matthew 5:33* and *38* from attributing certain Mosaic commands to God; yet in *Leviticus 19:12* and *24:19-20* they are clearly said to be spoken by Yahweh.

- Likewise in *Mark 1:44* and *12:19* he uses the expression *"Moses commanded"* rather than *"God commanded"*. In *Mark 7:9-10* he places the two expressions side by side.

Do these changes suggest that the ethical **principles** underlying the commands came from God, but the **way** in which the commands were expressed was in the hands of Moses, and therefore conditioned by the surrounding culture?

Notice also in the context of the above passages how freely Jesus modified Moses, how easily he reached behind the outer *form* of the ancient laws to the unchanging *principles* they were intended to reflect. He did not hesitate to discard the brutal aspects of the old laws, and to give them a universal and compassionate shape. As soon as we hear him, we instantly recognise his ruling as far more in harmony with the character of God.

What have we learned? Simply that many Old Testament statements embody a concept that was central in ancient Hebrew life: absolutely nothing can happen except by the immediate command, and with the direct involvement, of the Almighty. We do not view our world, nor the ordinary events of each day, through such a prism of divine imminence. We are hesitant about ascribing any event – especially tragedies – to the deliberate will and action of God. [282] The worldview of the Hebrews is not transportable into the 20th century. It must be diligently filtered through the teaching of Christ and the apostles before it can speak to us in our time. [283]

---

[282] We are, however, not so reluctant to attribute *good things* to divine intervention. Yet there is no valid reason to call nice things more than nasty ones always an act of God. Mostly we must suppose that God lets life follow its own course, whether for good or ill. He sometimes intervenes (especially in answer to prayer) in a manner that is obvious to all. But on other occasions his actions cannot be easily recognised. And sometimes it is impossible to tell whether or not the Lord's hand is directly ionvolved in some event. The ancient Hebrews, of course, faced no such difficulty; they just called *everything* an act of God!

[283] On the matter of divine involvement see also Jb 2:10; 12:7-25; 16:11-14; Am 3:6; La 3:38; Sir 11:4-6,14; 33:7-13; etc. However, cp. the overthrow of Sodom & Gomorrah, the drowning of the Egyptians, the destruction of Jericho, the slaughter of the Assyrian army, etc, which do seem to have been acts of God. The difference is that none of those deaths were the result of human violence, but rather of indifferent natural forces. How much God was the direct cause of those upheavals, or merely used them, or how much they simply reflect the language-style of the Hebrews, is impossible for us to say. But surely there are few writers today who would be willing to say that God was the direct cause of the deaths of thousands of men, women, and children by flood, fire, famine, earthquake, or similar disaster? Anyone who did so would be deservedly ridiculed, at least by the secular world, and also by many Christian authorities.

> After all, no book, teaching, or word is able to comfort in troubles, fear, misery, death, yea, in the midst of devils and in hell, except this book, which teaches us God's Word and in which God himself speaks with us as a man speaks with his friend. [284]

---

[284] Part of an autograph that Martin Luther (1483-1546) once wrote on the fly leaf of a friend's book. The autograph included the words of Psalm 119:99, "I have more insight than all my teachers, for your words are my chief delight."

CHAPTER TWENTY-SEVEN

READING THE PROPHETS

PART FIVE – 5. THE COGNITIVE GAP

Our age insists that knowledge must be precise, formal, sequential, comprehensive, and consistent. There is no room in our epistemology [285] for contradictory notions, vagueness, mutually exclusive concepts, or fiction mixed with fact. The Hebrews carried no such cultural burden. They were able to intermingle fact and metaphor, poetry and prose, history and fiction, with what sometimes seems to us a cavalier abandon.

Nowhere is that flexibility better demonstrated than in the oracles of the prophets. They frequently surround a kernel of reality with a husk of imagery – albeit a husk that is often vividly dramatic, or delightfully charming. It is perilous to press too much out of an Old Testament prophecy until one has done enough study to recognise what the prophet truly meant to say – that is, to separate his *actual prediction* from the *colourful surrounds* in which it usually reposes. Here then are some examples of

THE INTERPRETATION OF PROPHECY

> We now understand the prophets so little because we do not understand their language; apart from this, they have spoken clearly enough. Therefore understanding them is not difficult for those who know their languagd and have

---

[285] The theory of knowledge, including its *nature* (just what is "knowledge"?), its *limits* (how much can we truly "know"?), and how it is *gained* (what constitutes valid "evidence"?), and the like.

> the Spirit of God, whom all believers have . . . But if one does not understand their language and does not have the Spirit . . . the prophets appear to be intoxicated and full of wine.
>
> Yet if we are to lack one of the two, the Spirit without a knowledge of the language would be better than a knowledge of the language without the Spirit. . .[286]

Any attempt to be consistently *literal* in the interpretation of Bible prophecy requires an unwarranted and arbitrary selection of "proof texts" – that is, the interpreter places too much emphasis on prophecies that fit the scheme, while ignoring passages that cannot be made to fit. I have often observed this fault and can see no just excuse for it.

How then *should* the reader handle Bible prophecy?

I cannot take space here to give a full answer to that question, but let me say at least this: the correct interpretation of Bible prophecy depends upon recognising that *the general thrust of an oracle, rather than its detail, is the important thing.* For example, see **Isaiah 10:27-32**. The predicted invasion did occur, but not in the direction nor in the sequence described by Isaiah.[287] Was the prophet wrong? Of course not. The *intention* of his oracle was fulfilled in the mere *fact* of the invasion, which adequately satisfied the threatened divine judgment. The rest was simply dramatic fill-in.

The same is true of the *parables* that are scattered through the Bible, including those told by Jesus. Each story usually has just one main point (or central lesson), which is normally set into a fictitious framework. The details exist only to give structure, drama, and life to the moral of the story. I do not mean that the details can be ignored, for sometimes they do bear on the over-all meaning of a parable. But care must be taken not to read into the particulars of a story more than is warranted.

Many examples of this principle (of a primary lesson surrounded by imaginary detail) lie scattered among the prophetic oracles. I have compiled a longish list of them, which some readers may find tedious, so I have placed it in an *Addendum* at the end of this chapter. Nonetheless, if what I am suggesting is new to you,

---

[286] What Luther Says Vol III; compiled by Edward M. Plass; Concordia Pub. House, Saint Louis, Missouri, 1959; selection # 3665.

[287] I cannot take space here to prove the various assertions made above, or in the examples given in the *Addendum* at the end of this chapter. Any good commentary should be able to provide you with the necessary details.

then you should peruse the list and so gain a better sense of how to interpret the colourful words of the prophets.

Did you notice that there is little that is obviously symbolic in Isaiah's invasion oracle? On the contrary, his entire prophecy (like those in the *Addendum*) appears to be factual. Yet despite this semblance of reality, the prophets did not expect every detail of their words to be taken literally. They received their oracles by visions, dreams, revelations, and sometimes in a state of ecstasy, and then retold them in a style that, despite appearances, is highly figurative and symbolic (Ho 12:10). It is misleading, or true only in a very restricted sense, to say (as some have) that prophecy is "history written beforehand". Those who make that claim commit two faults –

- they fail to recognise the peculiar nature of Hebrew prophetic writing; and
- they cause endless confusion.

Readers who try to force every soberly expressed oracle (I mean those that are not obviously figurative or symbolic) into a piece of factual prediction, usually end up with a mass of irresponsible theories and absurd claims. What wild promises are made! What silly controversies and vagaries are spawned by these fervent wielders of the Bible in one hand and a newspaper (or a history book) in the other!

But the prophets of Israel were not soothsayers. They dealt with morality and righteousness, with justice and judgment, not with curious predictions. They used their dramatic oracles primarily to display the holiness of God. They assumed that their readers were familiar with the prophetic style, and that those readers, ignoring the poetic detail, would extract from the oracles the major thrust each one contained.

So much were those things true, that in one special instance – the shattering overthrow of Jerusalem by Nebuchadnezzar – when the oracles *were* fulfilled in hideous detail, the Jews were stricken with horror (see Jeremiah's *Lamentations*; and note also Daniel's lament: *"What has been done against Jerusalem has never before been done under the whole heaven"* [Da 9:12, NRSV]). That is, the level of destruction wreaked upon Jerusalem by the Babylonians went far beyond the normal practice of the time. The city and temple were reduced to piles of smoking rubble; the slaughter was merciless, and havoc, ruin, devastation, misery engulfed the entire nation. It was a calamity unparalleled in the annals of the ancient world (La 1:12).

Jeremiah's complaint seems to have been shared by God himself, who pronounced doom upon Assyria and Babylon because they brutally exceeded his mandate when they so utterly crushed Israel. (See Is 10:5-12; 37:21-22,28-29; 47:5-6; and note the remarkable sentiment in Je 42:10c. Now *there* is a nice problem in theodicy, not to mention hermeneutics!)

ADDENDUM

Here are some further examples of prophetic oracles that on the face of it are sober predictions, yet whose details are imaginary –

♦ ***Babylon (Is 13:17-22; 14:22-23; Je 50:39,40; etc)***. As the book of *Daniel* shows, the Medes entered Babylon with ease; there was little bloodshed, and the city continued on as one of the greatest in the Persian empire. It was later conquered by Alexander the Great, and later still became part of the Parthian Empire. In the time of Jesus it was a populous commercial centre.

Did Babylon's continuing existence embarrass the Master? No; despite Isaiah's passionate dooms, neither Jesus nor the apostles ever thought that the prophet's words had failed. They were apparently satisfied that the city's ongoing prosperity in no way diminished the truth of the ancient judgments – which shows that they did not read the oracles in the literal way that many moderns favour!

Soon after the time of Christ, Babylon began to decline (mainly because of changing trade routes). It was visited by the emperor Trajan in 115, who found it already partly ruined, and 84 years later was reported by the emperor Septimius Severus as being deserted. But that was 800 years after Isaiah had pronounced its collapse!

Once again, must we say that the was prophet wrong? Of course not. His oracle, bared of its dramatic colouring, meant only that God would judge the proud city, which happened sufficiently when Babylon's pomp and power were stripped away by Cyrus the Great (539 B.C.). The provincial town that finally vanished at the end of the second century of the Christian era no longer had any connection politically, morally, or spiritually, with the arrogant imperial city of Isaiah's time.

♦ ***Moab (Is 15:5-9; 16:4-5, 13-14)***. This oracle describes either an invasion by Assyria or a series of attacks by desert tribes; but there is no historical record of either event. In any case, 200 years after Isaiah's time Moab still existed as a distinct nation, and the land remained occupied well into the Christian era. The prophet's savage indictment applied only to contemporary Moab, and it had a sufficient (though not a detailed or literal) fulfilment when Nebuchadnezzar conquered the land.

Note in particular the oracle in 16:4b-5, which assures Moab in highly idealistic (but not very realistic) language that her only hope lay in accepting once again the sovereignty of the King of Judah (Moab had earlier thrown off the Jewish yoke). Predictably, the Moabites refused to submit to Jewish hegemony, and despite numerous invasions by various powers, continued for another thousand years, when the ravages of time finally erased the last remnants of its ancient identity.

♦ ***Damascus (Is 17:1-2)***. Although Syria was invaded and crushed by the Assyrians, Damascus was never destroyed. It was later conquered again by the Babylonians, then by the Persians, Greeks, and Romans, but was still a thriving city in the time of Paul (who was led there after he was blinded on *"the road to Damascus"*). It still continues to the present day, and is possibly (despite the dooms of other prophets, e.g. Am 1:3-5) the oldest continuously inhabited city in the world.

♦ ***Egypt (Is 19:2-10, 17-25)***. The historical fulfilment of this oracle remains uncertain. It may refer to one of the later Assyrian invasions of Egypt (perhaps by Sargon or Esarhaddon), or to an 8th century Ethiopian invasion.

Verse 18, using normal prophetic hyperbole, probably means only that there will be substantial Jewish colonies in five cities. The "City of the Sun" was probably Heliopolis, which may have had Jewish inhabitants but was certainly never converted to Yahwism, for it was and remained the main centre of Sun worship in ancient Egypt.

In ***verse 19*** the *"altar"* and the *"pillar"*[288] are synonyms for a temple; however, no actual temple to Yahweh was ever built in Egypt, although large and influential colonies of Jews were later established in Alexandria and Aswan, with other groups of Jews scattered throughout the land, who remained faithful to Yahweh. Some Egyptians were no doubt converted to Yahwism, but never to the extent implied by ***verse 21***. Any attempt to apply the oracle to a date still future is precluded by the mention of *"Assyria"*, which was crushed and obliterated by the ancient Babylonians.

Ignoring then the lively detail, the oracle basically declares three things:

- God's judgment on ancient Egypt through civil war, drought, and invasion;

---

[288] I reject as nonsense the idea that Isaiah was referring to the Pyramids.

- God's control over the entire earth, every nation, and all the activities of mankind; and
- Yahwism would be carried to Egypt and to other lands by his scattered people.

Within those terms, the prophecy was satisfactorily accomplished.

♦ ***Arabia (Is 21:16-17)***. It is not possible to identify which historical invasion is referred to here; and in any case, more than 100 years later Jeremiah describes the same people as still prosperous and doomed to be conquered by Nebuchadnezzar (49:28-33). Subsequently the tribe of Kedar dwindled in its influence and was eventually assimilated into other tribes; but by that time, for those people, Isaiah's oracles had long lost any relevance. Whatever event the judgment referred to, it was well gone by the time the tribe finally vanished. Or, to put it differently, even if the tribe were still in existence today, the oracle would not be invalidated, for its adequate fulfilment did not depend upon every detail being literally accomplished.

♦ ***Tyre (Is 23:15-17)***. Tyre and Sidon were ruinously involved in a series of savage clashes between Egypt and Assyria in the middle 7th cent. B.C., and later suffered again when Nebuchadnezzar invaded the region (vs. 13). Tyre fell before the Babylonians in 572, after a gruelling 13-year siege. Two centuries later the city angered the Persians and was conquered once more; then again by Alexander in 332; and eventually it became part of the Roman Empire. It was still a flourishing town in the time of Jesus, and has remained continuously occupied until today (despite Ez 26:13-14). The "70 years" mentioned in *Isaiah 23:15* probably refers to the *total* period of Babylonian hegemony; in fact, Tyre was under immediate Babylonian dominion for only about half that period. (See also below.)

♦ ***Edom (Is 34:5-17)***. Although Edom suffered various invasinns (mixed with periods of restored prosperity) during the centuries after Isaiah's death, at least some of her cities (e.g. Petra) were still thriving commercial centres as late as the 2nd century A.D. The ultimate decay and disappearance of the nation was a result of altered commercial, political, and environmental factors, and could have had no reasonable connection with Isaiah's long-forgotten curse. Certainly, the extravagant details [289] of his oracles were never fulfilled. [290] (See also just below, under *Jeremiah 49:13,18*.)

♦ ***Jewish Refugees** (Je 42:17-18)*. Despite an oracle of total annihilation, the refugees overcame sundry hardships and invasions, eventually flourished in Egypt, and developed into several prosperous communities (especially in Alexandria) that were still there in the time of Jesus (notice the amelioration tacked onto the end of *Jeremiah 44:14*, and enhanced in *vs. 28*).

♦ ***Egypt** (Je 43:10-13)*. Although Nebuchadnezzar did defeat Pharaoh Amasis in battle, in 566 B.C., Egypt remained independent, and apparently entered into a friendly alliance with Babylon. There was never any literal fulfilment of the ravages predicted by Jeremiah.

♦ ***Edom** (Je 49:13, 18)*. These oracles were not fulfilled literally. **Bozrah** was a powerful fortress and royal city, well-situated to control the King's Highway (a major trade route). Its modern name is Buseirah. Far from being turned into a *"perpetual waste"* it has remained more or less continually occupied until the present time. **Teman** (vs. 20) also still survives today as the modern town of Tawilan, about 5km east of Petra. **Edom** escaped depredation at the hands of Nebuchadnezzar by becoming allies of the Babylonians. However, Jeremiah's oracles were sufficiently fulfilled by the fact that Edom later fell completely under the domination of the Nabataean Arabs. After that the original Edomites never regained their independence.

♦ ***Hazor** (Je 49:33)*. The territory mentioned was never bereft of all inhabitants. Jeremiah seems rather to be using conventional terminology, a kind of apocalyptic idiom, or shorthand, that was never intended to be taken literally (cp. *"haunt of jackals"* 9:10; 10:22; 51:37; and *"desolation"* 4:27; 6:8; 9:11; 10:22; 12:10,11; 32:43; etc; and *"no one shall dwell there"* 4:7,29; 9:11; 26:9; 33:10; 44:22; etc).

♦ ***Babylon** (Je 50:39-40; 51:20-26)*. As mentioned above, the description of Babylon's destruction by Cyrus was not literally fulfilled.

---

[289] Streams turning into pitch, soil into sulphur, smoke rising for ever and ever, lying waste for many generations, no one ever again to pass through it, the land soaked with blood, inhabited only by goat-demons, Lilith, wild creatures, and the like.

[290] The hyperbolic nature of oracles that decree a complete removal from the land of both humans and animals is suggested by Jeremiah's words about Judah and Jerusalem (26:9; 36:29). Of course, as the account in Jeremiah itself makes plain, a significant number of people and flocks remained in the land after the Babylonians withdrew from Palestine.

See also other oracles in Jeremiah 4:25-29; 9:10-11; 31:40; 32:37-41; 33:17; 46:19. [291] *And for an illustration of how the fulfilment of an oracle could be considerably less draconian than the oracle itself, cp. Jeremiah 33:10 with 39:10, 14; 40:6-12. Note that Gedaliah was a member of the Jewish nobility, and that other commanders and nobles were left in the land after the departure of the Babylonian army (note also the considerable number of people, leaders, and commanders, mentioned in 41:1-16).*

♦ ***Ammon & Edom (Ez 25:1-7, 10, 12-14)***. If these oracles are taken literally, then Ezekiel contradicts Jeremiah (49:6). As it happens, even today Ammon is still inhabited and prosperous. Likewise, the dooms of Ezekiel against Edom never had a literal fulfilment, and many of its ancient communities remain inhabited to this day. The same can be said of his later oracles about Edom ("Mt Seir"): *"I will make Mount Seir a waste and a desolation; and I will cut off from it all who come and go. ... I will turn you into a wasteland for ever; never again will anyone dwell in your cities"* (35:7-9).

Notice, too, how Daniel, in an oracle that reached forward to the time of Antiochus IV Epiphanes (circa 170 B.C.), was able to describe Edom, Moab, and Ammon as still flourishing long after their utter ruin had been foretold by other prophets. Did he blush when he read their predictions? No, for he knew that within its actual intention each prophecy had been adequately fulfilled.

♦ ***Tyre (Ez 26:1ff.)***. Nebuchadnezzar (vs. 7) and his army laid siege to Tyre for 13 years (circa B.C. 567-554), but the city was not overthrown and the siege ended with a negotiated settlement (as Ezekiel himself intimates in 29:18). Tyre in fact did not fall until some 220 years later, when it was conquered by Alexander the Great in 332 B.C. So the city was not destroyed by Nebuchadnezzar, he did not pull down its houses (26:12), nor did he turn it into a bare rock (vs. 4, 14), nor did he make any attempt to ensure that the city was *"never rebuilt"* (vs. 14). Neither did Alexander do so. Since the city still stands today, then *Ezekiel 27:36*, [292] if it were intended to be read *literally*, would be a piece of irresponsible mendacity. The truth is that in their main thrust of divine punishment upon a godless city, Ezekiel's oracles were quite fulfilled; but the ferocious details were not, and were never intended to be, fully realised.

---

[291] However, by contrast, some prophecies did (and do) have a closely literal fulfilment, as, for example, Jeremiah's prediction that the Jewish captivity in Babylon would last 70 years (Je 29:10, plus other references); and note also the fulfilment of his oracle about the kings (22:10-19).

[292] *"You have come to a dreadful end, and shall be no more forever"* (NRSV).

- ***Egypt (Ez 29:10-12; 30:6-19; 32:2ff)*** [293] What I have just said about Tyre applies equally to these oracles. They never were, and plainly never will be done literally in all their particulars.

- ***Jesus (Jn 7:27)***. The misunderstanding among even the devout of that time about the manner of the Messiah's first appearance should make us cautious of dogmatism about his second coming! *(Note also the difficulties inherent in Matthew 10:23; 16:28. See also Matthew 11:14, which shows that Jesus was quite willing to accept the fulfilment in principle of an oracle rather than a literal fulfilment.)*

> The words of the Bible do not lose in value, but they grow in wealth with the increase of years. Every new perplexity only brings out that they are capable of new applications, and meant more than they were imagined to do. When you give to a people the Bible, you give it a whole literature, and a literature far the most elevating and educating which the world possesses; you enrich it with incalculable treasures of poetry, of eloquence, of history, of moral instruction, of social and political principle, of spiritual truth; but above all, you enrich it with the knowledge of the revelation of God in Christ, the knowledge whence springs eternal life, eternal blessedness. (Robert Flint (1838-1910), Scottish philosopher and theologian.)

---

[293] Note especially 32:7-8, in which the details are manifestly figurative. This passage marks the need to be careful about taking literally similar oracles, such as *Joel 2:30-31* and *Matthew 24:29*, etc.

CHAPTER TWENTY-EIGHT

ARE WE ANY BETTER?

PART FIVE – 6. THE SPIRITUAL GAP

Twenty centuries of Christian history and theology, the staggering industrial and technological revolutions of the past two hundred years, the universal literacy our culture enjoys, and a thousand other influences, may not have made us any *better* than the Hebrews, but they have certainly made us *different*! Nor should you imagine (as one reader has said) that I seem to "pity the biblical authors for their simplistic approach to nature, and for their tendency to see God in everything." If I were to do so it would be nonsense. Instead, I fully recognise that we are all just as much prisoners of the culture in which we live as they were of their culture.

So then, who is correct? The ancients who believed that although God was transcendent he was nonetheless everywhere and in everything active and present? Or 20th-century western man, who is inclined to take a far more naturalistic view of life and of its bewildering vicissitudes? I cannot say. The question is not so much about *hermeneutics* as it is about the sovereignty, providence, and imminence of God, all of which lie outside the scope of this book. Then again, even in *our* culture people hold different opinions about how much God is involved in, or controls, the details of each person's life. [294]

So, once again, I do not mean to say that we are *better* than the ancient Hebrews, nor that our culture is in every way superior to theirs. In some areas we may indeed be *inferior* to them. But no one can sensibly deny that we *are* different! Nor can anyone rightly understand scripture, or apply it to modern life, who does

---

[294] I discuss this issue in much more detail in my book *Discovery*, which ostensibly deals with divine guidance, but might more accurately be called a treatise on theodicy.

not take that difference into account. So I have tried, in the previous chapters, both to define that gap and to show how it may be bridged. My aim has been to preserve the integrity and authority of the Bible for our modern world.

If the solutions I have offered are not the right ones, then let someone show me a better way. In any case, if scripture is not to be reduced to a shambles of contradictory notions and impossible demands, some such attempt must be made. I must now leave you to judge whether I have built a good bridge or a bad one. But I will say this: my own feet find the footing firm enough, and by walking over the span I have been able to reconcile scripture with scripture and find a consistent way to read and apply the Spirit-breathed counsels of the Almighty.

CONCLUSION

The six-fold hiatus we have explored in the previous several chapters lead me to two principles –

(1) We must recognise that the Bible was not written initially for citizens of the 20th century A.D. but for an ancient people far removed from us in culture, attitude, and understanding.[295] The Holy Spirit necessarily had to permit scripture to be written in terms that would be meaningful and acceptable to those people, which means that we need to be cautious about how we transfer its words to our day. There is an eternal *message* in every part of scripture, which is true for every generation; but that message is couched in an exotic linguistic form, and within a rudimentary social structure that is far removed from our everyday world. That outer fabric must often be deeply penetrated before the Bible can yield to us its true riches.

(2) This "bridging the gap" rule applies to the whole Bible, not just to those parts that are difficult or obviously obsolete – like, for example, Moses' *"bitter water of jealousy"*, or the bloodcurdling curses, or the savage punishments. One cannot remove the plainly objectionable parts, and then read the remainder as though it were written last week. The *entire* book must be read as an ancient document, and the question then asked: what is the message of this

---

[295] This is especially true, of course, of the Old Testament; but it is also true in a number of ways of the New Testament. <u>Note also</u>: I do not necessarily mean that our culture is superior to theirs. Indeed, there may well be areas in which their social structures were better than anything that now exists. I mean only that there is a great disparity between their world and ours, and any valid reading of scripture must take that disparity into account.

book for today? If these pages have helped you to grasp that process better, then I am content.

POSTLUDE

I cannot help but feel that this is not the best place to leave you. As one correspondent put it, "this book tends to leave the reader aghast at the prospect of reading the Bible, rather than determined to get it right and encouraged to believe that the task of rightly dividing the Word is achievable."

Not everyone will react so negatively, of course; but if you *are* feeling bewildered, then the problem will be mostly solved if you remember the middle sections of the book, where I do give some basic and simple rules for reading the Bible wisely, and for reaping from it the treasures of heaven. I might also refer you to my many other books, in which the Bible is everywhere quoted and depended upon as the utterly reliable word of God.

You could also turn to several books that are companions to this one in the courses that are offered by V*ision Christian College* (for whom this book was written), such as –

Creative Bible Study Methods
by Harvest International

Research Writing Made Easy
by Dr Stan DeKoven

The College also has other papers and guidelines available on how to vrite a thesis, how to prepare a word study, and some practical advice on setting up regular study times. Similar materials can be obtained from many other Bible colleges or from Christian book shops.

CHRIST, PRE-EMINENT IN ALL

Now let me close with two passages that emphasise something we must never forget: *the purpose of scripture is not to provide a source of scholarly debate, but to bring us closer to God in worship*. If Bible study does not in the end serve that purpose, then we have read it in vain! To put it more bluntly, the issues raised in this book won't save anybody, so don't preach them next Sunday! ***Preach Christ.***

He alone is *Alpha* and *Omega*; he alone must have pre-eminence in all things; in him alone is eternal life. Now here are the two passages –

- from Dean Eaton – [296]

The question of God's disclosure of himself to humanity via the medium of his *written* Word, the Bible, is complex, and discussion of it can do harm unless special pastoral effort is made to keep the attention of the people focussed upon the *living* Word, Christ. Carl. F. H. Henry has written: "the God of the Bible is wholly determinative in respect to revelation" [297] This means that God's purpose in revelation is that we may know him personally, as he is, and may avail ourselves of his gracious forgiveness and his offer of new life. The end of all Bible study should be an escape from the coming catastrophic judgment and a discovery, both now and for ever of personal fellowship with the Father through the Lord Jesus Christ. *"I will . . . be your God, and you shall be my people"* (Le 26:12).

The complex issues of *hermeneutics* can become hard going for ordinary Christians unless they have fully come to grips with the Incarnation. Jesus challenged the Pharisees about *"searching the scriptures"*, hoping that in them they would find salvation, when the real intention of scripture is to act as a "cradle for Christ" (John Calvin). As a pastor, I find that any theological debate that ultimately fails to point me back to Christ has failed. If it is not *"useful for edification"*, then it is probably good for nothing. "Good theology" is surely relational by nature, rather than merely Platonic – that is, a thing of intellectual debate alone, intriguing perhaps, but ultimately sterile.

- and from David Swing – [298]

When the modern critics, in the church and out of it, are enlarging upon the "Mistakes of Moses" and upon the historical childishness of the Bible, they should not forget to tell us that there ran through the whole Bible period a something that was no mistake, a something whose history rises up before us as real as the earth itself and as beautiful as its four seasons, as magnificent as its June. That something was worship! Theology came and went; the laws of Moses were passed and obeyed and repealed; fables were told and forgotten; Paul and Apollos differed; James and John were unlike – but in worship all seemed to meet, and the Jacob who saw angels on the night-ladder is beautifully akin to St. John and Paul. All are wonderfully akin to our age, which sings the one hymn of the whole race, "Nearer, My God, to Thee."

---

[296] Australian Assembly of God pastor, in a letter to the author of this book, September 1996.

[297] God, Revelation, and Authority, Vol. 2, pg. 19.

[298] (1830-1894) American Presbyterian pastor and preacher of renown and deep spirituality.

www.ingramcontent.com/pod-product-compliance
Lightning Source LLC
Chambersburg PA
CBHW031948080426
42735CB00007B/306